Vijay Mukhi's

The 'C' Odyssey

C++ & GRAPHICS

– The Future Of C

Meeta Gandhi
Tilak Shetty
Rajiv Shah

TECH PUBLICATIONS PTE LTD
10, Jalan Besar, #B1-39 Sim Lim Tower, Singapore 0820

First Edition 1992

© **TECH PUBLICATION PTE LTD**

ISBN 981-3005-93-9

Printed at Continental Press Pte Ltd, Singapore

Foreword

If you took a leisurely walk down the choked arteries that line computer paths, there's one horn you'll hear blaring incessantly. C. Loud and sonorous, the booms have dominoed into echoes that have transcended space and time boundaries.

In this absolutely crammed world, where men who know C are the men who matter, there are four C connoisseurs that I rate as the best there ever were. My mom, my dad, my dear aunt and my sister-in-law. All of whose knowledge of computers rests languidly at the fact that it is what their youngest born tinkers around with, teaches and writes books about. It is from these denizens of C that I drew the inspiration to imbibe the true spirit of C.

For C is not merely a programming tool, a super-efficient road roller that smoothens all the bumps that ever arose. Rather, it is a philosophy and a way of life. Like a benevolent parent, it allows a long rope within a loosely woven web of rules and principles, encouraging bouts of exploration on one's own.

C is an attitude.

It is this feeling that I wanted to share most with others. The excitement of having glanced beneath diaphanous veils and seen what lay there. It was a revelation that opened even more gates for me. Most books that I have read so far - and I have as. unreasonable a passion for collecting books on C as philatelists have for stamps, have been "how to" books on C. They left me incomplete though, because they had not captured the soul behind those nuts and bolts.

Hence, this book.

Here was an honest language, humble and straightforward, that admitted its weakness without a qualm - it could not do everything. And that perhaps was the secret of its strength. It was nurtured by people whose goal was not to please ruling committees, but to design an apparatus that catalyzed efficiency. Like the proverbial knives for slicing butter, C was the finely honed one which could cut your hand while cutting through the butter neatly. It is this ability to produce clean and unjagged slabs, and the macho drops of blood, that has brought the world to heel. Today, evolution theorists would go one step further from Darwin and admit that survival of the C-fit is what propagation of species is all about.

C had to be separated from its relegated place in the herd and its character unveiled.

Hence this book.

And the best way I could treat something so honest would be with total honesty. It was quite some time ago that I admitted, rather ruefully, that I wasn't the greatest writer around. And this was one book that I wasn't going to sacrifice at the altar of my ego. So I garnered a team of professional writers to work with my team of professional computerists and baked this mammoth pie.

As we embarked on a task we knew would be awesome, there were more realities we woke up to along the way. The philosophy which could very well have sat comfortably in 20 pages grew into seven volumes, aggregating roughly 3500 pages.

We've tried to move away from the serious and unbending tone that most texts on all things technical take. And we're not sorry for having fun. Fun, it has been all the way. But that's what C is all about. How to mix business with pleasure. We've littered the search with blasphemously unserious comments, lightened the most complicated and poker faced concepts with a few laughs. And our happy faces could brighten a dark and moonless night.

What was most appropriate was the colorful group of people we were. Like the band of Clipper players, who breathed music but were famous for the Clipper 5.0 and P.J Plauger, who cut his teeth on science fiction and dirtied his fingers in software, we were a varied bunch of people. We had psychology students, archaeology graduates, commerce collegians, engineers, hoteliers and bankers, all scrubbing joyously at unraveling the mystery of C.

And I think our versatile personality has seeped through in our Odyssey.

You can join this seven sea Odyssey from anywhere - the beginning, the end or the middle. Each one is an individual trip by itself, unserialized and distinct. But you'd definitely be a better C-farer if you found your feet in the first, the C-Primer. Once you've imbibed the philosophy that I've been harping about, perhaps the rest of the volumes - C under UNIX, C under OS/2 and PM, C under Windows, C with Networks and RDBMS' ... will appear in a slightly different light? That's what I divined.

My teaching background shouts through a loudspeaker out of this Odyssey. I like to teach, although I've tried to refrain from preaching. We've resisted the temptation of writing "textbook" programs sandpapered with error checks, we've restrained ourselves from writing small code fragments that you have to fit together like a jigsaw puzzle. Our aim has not been to fish for you so you could eat fish today, but rather it has been to teach you to fish so that you can eat fish for the rest of your life.

We've worked towards a certain crescendo that rises steadily as we move on. From simple two line programs that do or do not work to programs spreading over reams that definitely do work. We have about 1800 programs, some original, some borrowed. We've siphoned from Dr. Dobbs and other treasure houses of programs, sometimes word for word. We've not attempted to change a single comma at times, because we didn't know how to. They were the best we could have laid our hands on and we grabbed them with both hands. And we'd be happiest if you grabbed a few of ours too. That's again the spirit of C. No dark secrets and no locked doors.

I must also warn you of the errors that may have slipped into some corner of our 3500 page tryst. We looked very hard but sometimes the sandman just couldn't wait and exhaustion and sometimes the sandman just couldn't wait and exhaustion and sleep drove the pins into our eyes. Before we embarked on book writing, we never could understand how prestigious books could harbor errors, silly errors that were carelessly allowed to reside. Now we know. Only too well.

But nobody, not even Microsoft, IBM and God are perfect.

Our aim was to motivate you to don your starched thinking caps. And stoke the fire in your belly and the light in your eye. The flame that burns within a true C programmer is like a beacon that kindles the darkest skies. So, this book.

And there's also the quiet large-heartedness of C that I wanted to drag out of the closet. C opens the coffers that lie under powder-coated steel plates hammered together to make the computer, lays it bare and gives you the freedom to meander, to carry the wealth in the direction you choose. Like my parents. They opened the doors wide for me, armed me with priceless heirlooms and set me free ... to buy the hundreds of C books that fortify my library shelves.

There's still the debt I owe my mom, dad, my aunt and my dear sister-in-law, Vaidehi Mukhi for teaching me C. The rest of the people who made this a success

Hence this book.

Vijay Mukhi

Table of Contents

Section 2 : Graphics And C

Index

Introduction

If you're one of those people who read the newspapers everyday to keep abreast of the events in the world, and if you're one of those people who never likes to be left out of what's happening around you, if you're one of those people who believe in moving with and ahead of the times, and if you're one of those who revel in abstractions, this volume is definitely for you.

The volume has been sectioned into two parts. C++ and Graphics. The two do not share a similar platform, but both belong to the realm of the abstract. And that has been our justification for merging them under one umbrella. This is basically a volume that deals with abstract ideas and concepts.

The first section, C++, is about today. The only degree that you need to possess is a graduation in C. We've gone about the business of giving you this latest gig in computer languages, assuming that you are a regular and comfortable C programmer. If you're still unsure and apprehensive about C, we suggest you retract to our C volume before you dip your hands here.

For those of you equipped to travel this leg, all we can say is "Welcome Aboard". As we'll keep repeating again and again, C++ is littered with bombastic jargon. We've tried to smooth the path as best as we can. The structure we've given the volume exhibits a steady progression from C to the enhanced topics of C++.

Chapter 1 - From C to C++. Naturally, the beginning. Smoothening the movement from C to C++. Small additions that tie up the loose ends that C harbored. So that even if you're still a C programmer, you can take hints from this chapter to improve your programming. It teaches you the importance of prototyping, default parameters and function overloading among other concepts.

Chapter 2 - Object Oriented Programming. The core of C++. The ethos of this book. The reason this volume is here. We've attempted to initiate you into this difficult concept systematically. One step at a time is the rule we followed, filling the narration with examples and instances to break the ground gently. The building of objects and classes, and the encapsulation and abstraction of data have been covered in great depth.

Chapter 3 - The Laws Of Inheritances. This is the most crucial chapter in the C++ saga. The fundamentals of OOPs, inheritances - linear and multiple, polymorphisms, virtual functions and late binding are the areas visited.

Chapter 4 - Streams. Examining the built-in classes in C++ is the focus here. Input streams, output streams, their operations, insertors, extractors, and manipulators are some of the topics discussed. Another important aspect we've studied is file handling.

Chapter 5 - Building Classes - The Window Class. A culmination of all the fundamentals that we imbibed so far. A steady progression has been envisaged, from a small *Point* class to a full-fledged *Window* class. The reason for this chapter is to give you an idea of how a class is built.

Chapter 6 - Building Classes - The String Class. The building of another important class, a utilitarian class. Again we build it from scratch, carefully and systematically. Along the way pick up knowledge on writing *const* methods and overloaded *int*s.

Chapter 7 - Advanced C++. The last chapter with nuggets that you might never actively use, but that you might need at some distant future. For that one in a million chance keep this chapter handy.

We've attempted to deal with Graphics similarly. Graphics requires from you not only a comfortable association with C, but strong roots in Mathematics. For Graphics is not merely pretty pictures and images, but a very logical and mathematically conceived set of equations.

The formula we've followed throughout was not an impulsive idea, but a systematic translation of the feelings that we experienced when we studied Graphics.

We've taken the laborious route. From teaching you to untie the knots of the package to letting you loose in the fascinating meadows that comprise Graphics.

Chapter 1 - Getting Started. The tools of the trade, the software required, the actual switching onto the Graphics mode, experimenting, and learning to break out of the repressions of agonising overheads. These are the areas we'll begin with. Getting started is starting at the grassroot level.

Chapter 2 - About Color. Absorbing the concept of palettes. Mixing colors, changing them, fooling around with foreground and background colors, getting comfortable with the palette, easel and the brush. That's the lesson this one imparts.

Chapter 3 - Lines And More. Lines is the issue here. Drawing single lines, adding color to them, examining myriad styles and patterns of lines, stretching them and merging them, inculcating the gist of lines.

Chapter 4 - The Turning Point(Curves And Related Objects). After simple lines, its a logical step towards curves. Arcs, circles and ellipses. From curved bodies to angular pictures, rectangles, bars - two dimensional and three dimensional. The rear of the chapter is brought by an application, using bar graphs. The figures dealt with are still raw and unformed, in the sense that they're merely outlines of structures.

Chapter 5 - Drawing And Filling Images. The chapter veers on applications. A convergence of the preceding chapters. Pie graph applications form the gist of the chapter. Stuffing outlines and completing figures is the story told.

Chapter 6 - Text etc. Text in the Graphics mode. The lessons are full of controls and fonts. The myriad fonts available, and the ways and means of manipulating them, working on sizes of the fonts, the characters, applications and of course, how to reduce irritating overheads. Additionally, the chapter holds the secrets to building an important tool - tiding the deficit of functions for receiving inputs. And finally, fun programs after some hard work.

Chapter 7 - Of Pixels And Dots And Lots. Zeroing in on the tiniest grain of the screen is the purpose of this chapter. Applications rule. The concept of bit-mapped graphics has been introduced here. The major attraction of this show is probably the scripting of the Devanagari script with the regular English scoreboard. And that's not all. There's animation, crude and primitive, there's a lesson on the building of your own video games, and some more about adding finesse to clipping images and the rest.

Chapter 8 - A Little More On Animation. The technical aspects. The ASPECT ratio, video pages, and windows. Animation, animation, and more animation. And some more animation.

Chapter 9 - An Encounter With The Third Dimension. 3-D bar graphs. That's the focal point. We've tried to coagulate the basics to arrive at an extremely application of Graphics.

Chapter 10 - MATHing Away... The core of Mathematics. Sine, Cosine, Tan waveforms, plotting of parabolas, circles and other of the old stuff, only this time plotting them with their equations. The rest of the chapter deals with saving graphic images on the disk and restoring them from there.

Chapter 11 - Hello Fractals. This is one of the most powerful absorption of mathematics in Graphics. We've simplified the grouchiest concepts of Math, and generated the most amazing images with that knowledge. Plotting of Malthus curves and other important mathematical equations.

The crafting of this volume has given us immense satisfaction. To begin with the climb was laborious. It was, after all, a total shift of attitudes. But once we moved into it, we just took off. And by the end of it, we were still charged with the same level of excitement that we started with.

We hope the picture we tried to draw will take you on exciting flights of fancy too.

C++. Extensions to C

From C To C++

That's the logical second step. C++, an augmentation to C, finds the loopholes, the quick sands in C, and trovels those shut. C++ is a lot tighter, not in terms of rigidity, but rather in terms of channelizing directions. C allowed you to meander so much and so far, that your direction often tended to go haywire. It allowed you so many trials and errors, the temptation to deviate was irresistible. The glitches were many. And the concentration and caution required of you as a conscientious programmer were phenomenal. C++ introduces small rules to the malleable masterplan of C. They are simple and convenient rules that don't take anything away from the sweet taste of freedom you relished in C.

A program to initiate us into the modified realm:

```
PROGRAM 1
main( )
{
    printf("Hello World\n");
}
```

As a seasoned C programmer, you'd figure you'd get by without a hitch. But what did the C++ compiler throw back at you? An error? Before we check in to find out why, we'd like to say "Welcome to C++".

Now why was the error flagged?

The undemanding C structure would function unerringly to give you Hello World. C++, on the other hand, asks for very strong and conspicuous prototype checking.

C was primarily unconcerned with the logistics of passing variables to a function. But C++, in keeping with its role of the meticulous guide, demands clean and unambiguous definitions. It calls for, what are called, function prototypes.

Function Prototypes

A function prototype is a declaration that defines both, the parameters of the function and its return type. The prototype is checked against, each time the function is called, to ensure stability and unambiguity in code. The arguments passed in the called function are examined to determine whether these arguments correspond to the data types in the prototype checklist.

The C++ compiler, thus, would understand the same program if you included the standard header file, STDIO.H, which contains the prototype of the function *printf( )*, in the following manner:

```
PROGRAM 2
#include <stdio.h>

main( )
{
    printf("Hello World\n");
}
```

Consider this program. Do you think it will work?

```
PROGRAM 3
#include <stdio.h>

fumbler(int foo, int beep)
{
    printf("%d ... %d\n", foo, beep);
}

main( )
{
    int boo = 10, bap = 20;
    fumbler(boo, bap);
}
```

No, it won't. Because the function definition must include the return value as well. C took the unspecified return value as an *int* by default. C++ asks for the return value to be spelt out in so many words.

Parameter Lists And Return Values

Let's start with an example:

```
PROGRAM 4
#include <stdio.h>

void fumbler(int foo, int beep)
{
    printf("%d ... %d\n",foo, beep);
}

main( )
{
    int boo = 10, bap = 20;
    fumbler(boo, bap);
}
```

The prototypes have been affirmed, the return values have been specified, and your program will run without a flicker of doubt. The *printf( )* outputted will be 10 and 20.

Now, take this program:

```
PROGRAM 5
#include <stdio.h>

main( )
{
    int boo = 10, hoo = 20;
    fumbler(boo, hoo);
}

void fumbler(int foo, int beep)
{
    printf("%d ... %d\n",foo, beep);
```

```
}
```

This program will again not work. That's because the prototype hasn't been specified initially. So, *fumbler( )*, when the prototype is not there to be checked against, does not mean anything to the C++ compiler. Hence, the error.

Which means if the definitions are enumerated later, the prototype should be defined initially.

Now let's get the program to work:

```
PROGRAM 6
#include <stdio.h>

void fumbler(int, int);

main( )
{
    int boo = 10, bap = 20;
    fumbler(boo, bap);
}

void fumbler(int foo, int beep)
{
    printf("%d ... %d\n",foo, beep);
}
```

It will work perfectly. Because the prototype has been specified before the definition. The result outputted will be 10 ... 20.

Let's go ahead with another program:

```
PROGRAM 7
#include <stdio.h>

void fumbler(int, int);

main( )
{
    int boo = 10, bap = 20;
    fumbler(boo);
```

```
}

void fumbler(int foo, int beep)
{
    printf("%d ... %d\n",foo, beep);
}
```

Error! While defining the prototype, you've explicitly mentioned that it will accept two *int*s. And then you go and pass it one parameter. C would have compiled this program and run it merrily. But C++ demands strong prototype checking. So, if you say you're passing it two parameters, you better stick to your word. C++ makes no excuses for shoddy programming.

Default Values

Here's a program that will work:

```
PROGRAM 8
#include <stdio.h>

void fumbler(int foo = 0, int beep = 0)
{
    printf("%d ... %d\n",foo, beep);
}

main( )
{
    int boo = 10, bap = 20;

    fumbler(boo,bap);
    fumbler(boo);
    fumbler( );
}
```

While defining the function prototype, we've also defined a default value for each parameter. Unlike C which takes any random value, C++ permits arrangements to be made for function parameters to take default values. Now, we can call the function with two or one or no parameters.

The output of the above program will be:

10 ... 20
10 ... 0
0 ... 0

C++, in other words, builds a bridge between the user and the programmer. It functions in the middle ground between two extremes - on the one hand, C with its complete indifference to what variables you pass and how many, and on the other, the extreme prototyping tendency of C++ itself.

This middle ground provides a stand-by value, the default parameter. Allowing the user to state his parameters, in which case the default parameters are overwritten. But on those occasions when the user fails to define his own parameters, the default parameters bail him out. The program runs anyway, providing the freedom to choose one's own values, and if that choice is not taken, making the relevant provision.

Taking that further, when one parameter is passed, the default of the first parameter is overwritten, while the second default retains its value.

Now run this program:

```
PROGRAM 9
#include <stdio.h>

void fumbler(int, int);

main( )
{
    int boo = 10, bap = 20;
    fumbler(boo);
}

void fumbler(int foo = 0, int beep = 0)
{
    printf("%d ... %d\n",foo, beep);
}
```

Error ahoy! That's because when the function is called and the prototype checked, the default values are not found. Since the compiler first looks at the prototype, the default values also have to be passed in the function prototype definition itself.

So, to a workable program:

PROGRAM 10

```
#include <stdio.h>

void fumbler(int = 0, int = 0);

main( )
{
    int boo = 10, bap = 20;
    fumbler(boo);
}

void fumbler(int foo, int beep)
{
    printf("%d ... %d\n",foo, beep);
}
```

Because the default values have been notified in the function prototype definition, there will be no hurdles to this program. The point we are making is, the definition of the specific function can come later, although its default parameters must be included in the prototype checklist.

Do you think this one will run?

PROGRAM 11

```
#include <stdio.h>

void fumbler(int = 0, int);

main( )
{
    int boo = 10, bap = 20;
    fumbler(boo);
}
```

```
void fumbler(int foo, int beep)
{
    printf("%d ... %d\n",foo, beep);
}
```

It won't. The error given will be the same as when you didn't pass a single default value. Default value missing and Too few parameters in call to 'fumbler(int,int)' in function 'main( )'. Specifically, that is the error message that you will receive when you attempt to compile the program.

One would expect the C++ compiler to accept the single parameter passed to it and use the single default value in its prototype to account for the other parameter. But that's not what happens. The default values are overwritten from left to right. Therefore, the default value of *foo*, which is 0 would be overwritten by the value of *boo* - 10, but since the other default value has not been specified and the second parameter not passed to the function, the error will be generated.

What you can do is:

PROGRAM 12

```
#include <stdio.h>

void fumbler(int, int = 0);

main( )
{
    int boo = 10;
    fumbler(boo);
}

void fumbler(int foo, int beep)
{
    printf("%d ... %d\n",foo, beep);
}
```

In this program, you're on the right track. You've passed the first parameter to the function, and you've specified a default value for the second. This time, the value of *boo*, 10, which you have so correctly passed will be taken by *int foo* and even if you haven't passed the second parameter, the default value in the prototype will have no problems being accepted. *foo* will thus be printed as 10 and *beep* as 0.

Let's keep on at our zigzag routine - interspersing erroneous programs with workable ones. We'll understand better. So, it's time for an erroneous program:

PROGRAM 13

```
#include <stdio.h>

void fumbler(int, int = 0, int);

main( )
{
    int boo = 10, bap = 20, zap = 30;
    fumbler(boo);
}

void fumbler(int foo, int beep, int pop)
{
    printf("%d ... %d\n",foo, beep);
}
```

The error messages at compilation will be the same: Default value missing and Too few parameters in call to 'fumbler(int,int,int)' in function 'main( )'. What we've got to understand simply, is that the prototype is checked from right to left. Therefore, the default values should also be passed from right to left. You commit a grave error if you pass a default value bang in the middle of a three-parameter function prototype. Consistency and sequential logic is what C++ aims for.

Let's make that program work:

PROGRAM 14

```
#include <stdio.h>

void fumbler(int, int = 0, int = 0);
```

```
main( )
{
   int boo = 10;
   fumbler(boo);
}

void fumbler(int foo, int beep, int pop)
{
   printf("%d ... %d ... %d\n",foo, beep, pop);
}
```

The output you'll get will be: 10 ... 0 ... 0

The default values will be checked from right to left. The compiler will find everything above board and perform flawlessly. The single parameter passed in the function definition will output its prescribed worth. The second parameter will get its value by default, and so will the third parameter.

That is the controlled flexibility of C++. A notch above C, keeping the virility of C intact while adding more structure to that kind of thinking. We'll move on to another aspect of C++. Global scoping. Taking the concept of global variables and extending their reach, or more properly, making them pliable to your wishes. So, jump into the driver's seat and meet the new concept head-on.

Global Scoping

Let's leap into this program straightaway:

```
PROGRAM 15
#include <stdio.h>

int i = 100;

main( )
{
   int i;
   i = 10;
   printf("%d ... %d\n", i, ::i);
```

```
    ::i = 20;
    printf("%d ... %d\n", i, ::i);
}
```

Let's look at the output before we get into the explanations proper:

```
10 ... 100
10 ... 20
```

Unlike C which makes a global variable inaccessible when a local variable of the same name is available in the block, C++ allows you the flexibility of accessing the global variable despite a local presence. With a simple symbol like :: prefixing the variable.

As the above example would have proved, not only can you access a global variable and print its existing value, you can also re-initialize it to another value. Hence, the latter output: 10 ... 20.

Here's another program with a global scope:

```
PROGRAM 16
#include <stdio.h>

int i;

main( )
{
    int i;
    i = 10;
    printf("%d ... %d\n",i, ::i);
    {
        int i = 20;
        printf("%d ... %d\n",i, ::i);
    }
    printf("%d ... %d\n",i, ::i);
}
```

That's right, this is an extremely interesting example. The first *printf( )* shouldn't give you any trying moments nor for that matter should the other two. But we think we should explain the point we're trying to make. Take the next block and before you peek into the output, try and solve it.

What should the second *printf( )* output? *i* will, of course, be equal to 20 and *::i* will be equal to ... what? 10 or 0? 0, of course. That's because *::* refers to global scoping. It is not an operator that gives access to variables above the concerned block. When you say, *::i*, therefore, you are referring to the global *i* and not the local *i* one block above.

The output obtained will be:

```
10 ... 0
20 ... 0
10 ... 0
```

Referencing

After that short stop at a tiny concept, let's take on another fundamental concept. Referencing. A reference is like a pointer. But, let's tune in to a program before we focus on the concept.

```
PROGRAM 17
#include <stdio.h>

main( )
{
    int i = 17;
    int &p = i;
    printf("p = %d ... i = %d\n",p,i);
    p = 55;
    printf("p = %d ... i = %d\n",p,i);
}
```

If you look at the output that this gives you, 17 ... 17 and *55 ... 55*, you'll realize that *&p* is like a pointer. That is exactly what it is. A pointer and more.

A reference, as the name suggests, is like an alias. Call it by this name or that, it "refers" to the same entity. What is the advantage of referencing, then? Where does C++ score over C when it comes to a concept like referencing.

Referencing goes a long way in erasing untidiness in code, making it more sophisticated and readable. A reference dulls a pointer to a clumsy operator with its stars and spangles. You'd write that part of the program in C, like this:

```
int i = 17;
int *p;
p = &i;
```

The distracting elements are not all that make a reference more pleasant to the eye, but the fact is, that a pointer has to be de-referenced before it is dealt with, while a reference need not be. It works more directly in that sense.

Let's take another program and get the essence of references really clear:

```
PROGRAM 18
#include <stdio.h>

main( )
{
    int i = 17;

    int &p = i;
    printf("p = %d ... i = %d\n",p,i);

    p = 55;
    printf("p = %d ... i = %d\n",p,i);

    i = 90;
    printf("p = %d ... i = %d\n",p,i);
}
```

The theme of this program is that a variable and its reference are so tightly inter-locked, that a change in one necessarily results in a change in the other. So, whether you change the value of *i* or *p*, both the values will change concurrently. Cross check that with the output:

```
17 ... 17
55 ... 55
90 ... 90
```

Operators too work on reference variables similarly. For example:

```
PROGRAM 19
#include <stdio.h>

main( )
{
    int i = 17;

    int &p = i;
    printf("p = %d ... i = %d\n",p,i);

    p++;
    printf("p = %d ... i = %d\n",p,i);

    i++;
    printf("p = %d ... i = %d\n",p,i);
}
```

Whether you augment the value of *i* or you augment the value of its reference *p*, both the values will augment similarly. So, look at the output:

```
17 ... 17
18 ... 18
19 ... 19
```

To reiterate that bond further, let's ask for the addresses of the two, the variable *i* and its reference *p*.

```
PROGRAM 20
#include <stdio.h>

main( )
{
```

```
    int i = 17;
    int &p = i;

    printf("%u ... %u\n",&i,&p);
}
```

If your output resembles this, do we need anything more to prove the point?

65524 ... 65524

Having established the fact that a variable and its reference speak about the same body, let's get ahead with the concept.

Take this program:

PROGRAM 21

```
#include <stdio.h>

main( )
{
    int i;
    int &p = i;

    p = 17;
    printf("add of i = %u ... add of p = %u\n",&i,&p);
    printf("value of i = %d ... p = %d\n",i,p);

    int j = 55;

    p = j;
    printf("add of j = %u ... add of p = %u\n",&j,&p);
    printf("value of i = %d ... j = %d ... p = %d\n",i,j,p);
}
```

Without beating about the bush, this program goes on to say that once a reference variable has been defined to refer to a particular variable, it cannot refer to any other variable.

In the program above, therefore, by initializing *j* to the variable *p*, we are, in no way changing the reference of *p*. *p* will continue to refer to *i* and will not shift to *j*. Take the *printf( )*s to give you the true picture:

```
add of i = 64435 ... add of p = 64435
value of i = 17 ... p = 17
add of j = 64565 ... add of p = 64435
value of i = 55 ... j = 55 ... p = 55
```

The 'const' Keyword

First, a program:

```
PROGRAM 22
#include <stdio.h>

main( )
{
    const int i = 17;

    int &p = i;
    printf("p = %d ... i = %d\n",p,i);

    p = 55;
    printf("p = %d ... i = %d\n",p,i);
}
```

Do you think the value of *i* can be changed through its reference now? The term *const* prefaced to *i* renders the reference powerless to change the value of the variable referred to. Check the output and make the thought crystal clear:

```
17 ... 17
55 ... 17
```

Check one more program out:

```
PROGRAM 23
#include <stdio.h>

main( )
{
```

```
    int const i = 17;

    int &p = i;
    printf("p = %d ... i = %d\n",p,i);

    p = 55;
    printf("p = %d ... i = %d\n",p,i);
}
```

All we're trying to say is that prefixing or suffixing the *int* is not the issue. Either way, a *const* is a *const* is a constant. It rephrases the variable in such a way as to close it to change through a reference.

The outputs:

```
17 ... 17
55 ... 17
```

Now let's tie the reference down by defining it as a *const*.

PROGRAM 24

```
#include <stdio.h>

main( )
{
    int i = 17;
    const int &p = i;

    p = 55;
    printf("p = %d ... i = %d\n",p,i);
}
```

This program won't even compile. The error flagged will be: cannot modify a const object in function 'main( )'. You cannot, but cannot make a *const* out of a reference, and expect to use it to change anything, leave alone the variable it refers to.

Try writing it the other way around: *int const* instead of *const int*.

PROGRAM 25
```
#include <stdio.h>

main( )
{
    int i = 17;
    int const &p = i;

    p = 55;
    printf("p = %d ... i = %d\n",p,i);
}
```

The same error will be generated. A *const* object cannot be modified. That is the moral of the story.

Let's get deeper into the groove of constant objects. Run this program:

PROGRAM 26
```
#include <stdio.h>

main( )
{
    int i;
    const int j;

    printf("%u ... %u\n",&i,&j);
}
```

An error again! A *const* object has to be initialized. That would, of course, be very obvious. If you do not initialize a constant object, what would it be constant at?

Let's initialize it and see what happens.

PROGRAM 27
```
#include <stdio.h>

main( )
{
    int i;
```

```
    const int j = 0;

    printf("%u ... %u\n",&i,&j);
}
```

There'll be no compilation errors for this one. But the output is especially noteworthy.

Our output was:

65524 ... 168

Which means a normal variable and a constant variable occupy locations in memory blocks completely removed from each other.

Let's linger some more in constant objects and references. Let's do some more homework:

PROGRAM 28

```
#include <stdio.h>

main()
{
    int i = 17;
    int const &p = i;

    i = 55;
    printf("p = %d ... i = %d\n",p,i);
}
```

The output you'll receive:

p = 55 ... i = 55

What does that imply? The reference is dependent upon the variable it refers to. So, change the value of the variable, and you change the value of the reference automatically, constant or otherwise.

Here's another program in the same vein:

PROGRAM 29
```
#include <stdio.h>

main( )
{
    int i = 17;
    const int &p = i;

    i = 55;
    printf("p = %d ... i = %d\n",p,i);
}
```

int const or *const int*, the value of the reference changes when you change the value of the variable it refers to.

Referencing Of Strings

From referencing of single integers, let's get down to referencing of strings. Take a program before we really get down to the logistics:

PROGRAM 30
```
#include <stdio.h>

main( )
{
    char *p = "Hello World";
    char * &s = p;

    printf("%s.....%s\n",s,p);
}
```

p is a pointer to the string *Hello World*. *char * &s = p* indicates a reference to a pointer that points to the string *Hello World*. Thus, both *p* and *s* point to the same string. In other words, a reference to a string doesn't work differently from a reference to an integer.

Just as we were able to manipulate integers through references, it is possible to manipulate strings as well.

```
PROGRAM 31
#include <stdio.h>

main( )
{
    char *p = "Hello World";
    char * &s = p;

    s[0]='M';
    printf("%s.....%s\n",s,p);
}
```

Run this program and you'll see your Hello World change to a Mello World. *s* works exactly like a pointer to a string and so it is possible to manipulate every element in the string.

Constant Pointers

Constant pointers behave in the same way as constant variables. You cannot modify a constant pointer, just as you couldn't touch a constant variable. Take a program to confirm that:

```
PROGRAM 32
#include <stdio.h>

main( )
{
    char* const ptr = "Its a mad mad world";

    printf("%s\n",ptr);

    ptr = "Its a bad bad world";

    printf("%s\n",ptr);
}
```

The program won't even clear the compilation hurdle. It will stop right there because the simple truth is, you cannot modify a *const* pointer.

Thus, you cannot change the pointer to point to another string, but you can change the elements of the string. Like this:

PROGRAM 33

```
#include <stdio.h>

main( )
{
    char* const ptr = "Its a mad mad world";

    printf("%s\n",ptr);

    *ptr = 'A';

    printf("%s\n",ptr);
}
```

The output you'll get is: Ats a mad mad world. The pointer cannot be shifted to another string, but the existing string can be changed.

Let's keep the string constant and unshackle the pointer:

PROGRAM 34

```
#include <stdio.h>

main( )
{
    const char* ptr = "Its a mad mad world";

    printf("%s\n",ptr);

    ptr = "Its a bad bad world";

    printf("%s\n",ptr);
}
```

Now we cannot change the string, but we can get the pointer to point to a different string. In the program above, thus, you can get *ptr* which was pointing to Its a mad mad world to point to Its a bad bad world.

Let's try another variation:

```
PROGRAM 35
#include <stdio.h>

main( )
{
    const char* ptr = "Its a mad mad world";

    printf("%s\n",ptr);

    *ptr = 'A';

    printf("%s\n",ptr);
}
```

Since your string is constant, you cannot change it with anything. The program will result in an error without fail.

Reference Puzzles

Let's trot through these teasers as quickly as we can:

```
PROGRAM 36
#include <stdio.h>

void setval(int &i) { i = 17; }

main( )
{
    int z = 25;

    setval(z);
    printf("%d\n", z);
}
```

This program is basically a reiteration of all that we've studied about pointers and references. We're merely substituting pointer notation with references. Simply because it is a cleaner user interface.

printf( ), in the above program will output the value of *z* as 17.

Another plaything puzzle:

```
PROGRAM 37
#include <stdio.h>

void chval(int& p)
{
    p += 20;
    printf("In func chval( ) p = %d\n", p);
}

main( )
{
    int x = 50;

    chval(x);

    printf("In main( ) x = %d\n", x);
}
```

The parameter passed to *chval( )* will be taken as a reference. *p* is thus unmistakably bound to *x*. Therefore, the value of *x* after the call to *chval( )* will be 50 + 20 = 70.

Here's another interesting program:

```
PROGRAM 38
#include <stdio.h>

void chval(int& p)
{
    p += 20;
    printf("In func chval( ) p = %d\n", p);
}

main( )
{
    int y = 100;
    int x = 50;
```

```
    chval(x+y);

    printf("In main( ) x = %d\n", x);
    printf("In main( ) y = %d\n", y);
}
```

Although the role of the reference is to change the values of the variables it refers to, it cannot change the values of x and y. x and y are distinct from x+y and p refers to the sum of x and y. What the compiler will do is, create a temporary variable to store the sum of x and y and pass it to chval( ). So, the values of x and y will remain as 50 and 100, resply.

And another in the same tradition:

PROGRAM 39

```
#include <stdio.h>

void chval(int& p)
{
    p += 20;
    printf("In func chval( ) p = %d\n", p);
}

main( )
{
    float r = 5.0;

    chval(r);
    printf("In main( ) r = %f\n",r);
}
```

All datatypes are taken by the compiler and adjusted, promoted or demoted as required. chars, ints, longs, floats, all belong to the same category, and within them they can be adjusted. Take the program above and subject it to that logic. The function has been defined as a reference to an int, but we are passing it a float. The compiler will take the value of r and adjust it into a temporary variable which will be an int. Thus, what will be passed to chval( ) will be the temporary variable with the value 5.

The value of r in function *main( )* will, thus, remain unchanged. The output generated will be:

```
In func chval( ) p = 25
In main( ) r = 5.000000
```

Swaps

Let's see some real comparative examples of pointers and references. We'll use the *swap* function to understand the differences:

PROGRAM 40

```
#include <stdio.h>

void swap(int a, int b)
{
    int t;
    t = a;
    a = b;
    b = t;
    printf("%d ... %d\n",a,b);
}

main( )
{
    int i,j;
    i = 10;
    j = 20;
    printf("%d ... %d\n",i,j);
    swap(i,j);
    printf("%d ... %d\n",i,j);
}
```

This was the first swap program that we handled in C. If you remember it did not work, because there were no pointers to the variables. We modified that with a program like this:

PROGRAM 41

```
#include <stdio.h>
```

```
void swap(int *a, int *b)
{
    int t;
    t = *a;
    *a = *b;
    *b = t;
    printf("%d ... %d\n",a,b);
}

main( )
{
    int i,j;
    i = 10;
    j = 20;
    printf("%d ... %d\n",i,j);
    swap(&i,&j);
    printf("%d ... %d\n",i,j);
}
```

We used pointers and their tedious notations to get the swap going. Let's replace those pointers with references, easier on the eye and easier on the mind.

PROGRAM 42

```
#include <stdio.h>

void swap(int& a, int& b)
{
    int t;
    t = a;
    a = b;
    b = t;
    printf("%d ... %d\n",a,b);
}

main( )
{
    int i,j;
    i = 10;
    j = 20;
    printf("%d ... %d\n",i,j);
    swap(i,j);
```

```
    printf("%d ... %d\n",i,j);
}
```

Take a long look at that. Isn't it so much more simple and so much more economical? All you had to do was declare that your function was going to accept a reference. And that smoothened your path to such a tremendous extent. The output you'll get will be:

```
10 ... 20
20 ... 10
20 ... 10
```

Simple? And uncannily convenient? That was referencing. Making a job cleaner, simpler and a lot more efficient.

In fact, the baubles that C++ is saturated with has one central and conspicuous theme: relieving programmer tension, increasing programmer efficiency and enhancing programmer productivity. The informality that C++ exhibits makes it the friendliest medium that a programmer could work in. Referencing was one of those sunny brushes. Function overloading is another instrument that has stress unloading as its primary goal.

Function Overloading

The idea behind function overloading is comfortingly simple. To appreciate its potential, however, let's first talk about C. In C, two function definitions with the same name in the same scope would generate an error. If you, therefore, wanted a display of an *int*, a *long* and a *string*, you'd need three separate functions to indicate the same function albeit with different datatypes. You'd probably incorporate a *displayi( )* for the *int*, *displayl( )* for the *long* and *displays( )* for the *string*. And that would be the simplest collection you'd ever encounter. Think about the number of function names you'd have to remember if you had a fatter collection of datatypes to be displayed. You'd be better off remembering the birthdays of every person you ever met.

The C++ compiler, on the other hand, is a fatherly old chap. It understands the pressures that a programmer has to contend with, and goes about smoothening the path in every way it can. Function overloading is one such road roller. Let's take a program for a practical stint before we get into lengthy explanations:

PROGRAM 43

```c
#include <stdio.h>

void display(int);
void display(long);
void display(char *);

main( )
{
    int i = 10;
    long j = 600000;
    char *str = "Hello";

    display(i);
    display(j);
    display(str);
}

void display(int var)
{
    printf("%d\n",var);
}

void display(long var)
{
    printf("%ld\n",var);
}

void display(char *var)
{
    printf("%s\n",var);
}
```

display( ) is the single function name that displays three data types, an *int*, a *long* and a *string*. The C++ compiler simply considers the job set aside for the *display( )* function, and decides on which particular *display( )* function should be executed, depending on the parameter(s) passed. The output you'll get when you run this program will be:

```
10
600000
Hello
```

That is, one single *display( )* function to give you the three printouts you asked for.

Function overloading not only reduces memorization units, but also does away with lengthy and redundant code. Take the function, *itoa( )* and *ltoa( )* in C. How much simpler would life be if we could have a single function to stand for both? A function like *ntoa( )*, standing for "number to alphabet", *int* or *long*, or what have you. That's what function overloading in C++ is all about. Another gloss to the C shine.

A point of consideration, however, is that C++ does not distinguish between different return values. For function overloading to work effectively, you should remember, the differences should be in parameters passed, not in return types. Where return values are concerned, the C++ compiler suffers from acute myopia. It does not even recognize the personage called 'return values'. Thus, if you wanted an overloaded function like *aton( )* to represent *atoi( )* and *atol( )*, you'd meet a stone wall.

Let's check that out through a program:

PROGRAM 44

```
#include <stdio.h>
#include <stdlib.h>

int aton(char *);
long aton(char *);

main( )
{
    char *ptri = "25";
```

```
char *ptrl = "6000000";

printf("%s\n",ptrl);
printf("%s\n",ptrl);

int num;
long num2;

num = aton(ptrl);
num2 = aton(ptrl);

printf("%d\n",num);
printf("%ld\n",num2);
}
```

That's our own *aton( )* function, the one we wanted to write, to represent two data types - *int* and *long*. But we've also written a program that won't work. The two *aton( )*s have been defined with the same type of parameters, and the same number of parameters. The selectively blind C++ compiler cannot differentiate between them because it cannot see the different return values that distinguish them to the normal human eye. So, the error.

Keep that in mind when you use function overloading. Pass different parameters to distinguish between two functions with the same name. Don't rely on return values to differentiate them.

While you were getting to know C++ intimately, did you notice the uninhibited variable declaration patterns that C++ permitted. Take the example we just left. And marvel at the convenience. An executable line following declared variables without ever generating an error. Yes, C++ gives you the privilege of declaring variables as and when their need arises. C had a glaring limitation, in that all the variables you will ever need in the program, even if it is one instance in the last line of a 200 line program, have to be anticipated and declared right in the beginning. C++ liberates you from that straitjacket.

And another trick in the informality circus. The use of *cout* instead of the stiffer *printf( ). printf( )* demands a certain protocol. You have to state whether you want an *int* to be printed, a *string*, a character, etc. with the appropriate notation. You had to specify a *%d*, a *%s*, a *%c*, a *%u*, etc. *cout*, which we'll study in fastidious detail as we go along, does not require these specifications. It recognizes each datatype for what it's worth, and prints accordingly. Take this program:

PROGRAM 45

```
/* "iostream.h" is the header file
where cout has been defined */

#include <iostream.h>

main( )
{
    int i = 10;
    cout << "OOPs we're there"; // print a string
    cout << "i = " << i;  // print a string and an int
}
```

The '//' Comment

A trivial, yet noteworthy comment before we wind up C++ as an enhancement to C: the use of // instead of the starry /*...*/ to comment out a statement. Take the preceding program as a specimen.

You need the symbol // at that point of your line which you wish to comment out. The part prefixed by that symbol is hidden from the compiler as comment. Line 4 and 5 are examples.

If you wanted to keep an entire block out of the compiler's purview, however, you'd still use the C symbol /*...*/.

For single lines the newer // symbol is the better bet.

That covers most of C++ as an extension to C. Small additions and subtractions to the basic C structure, stretching C itself. Far beyond boundaries you never knew existed. Adorning the lithe body that C had, exercising it to peak form, to give programming a sprightlier look.

We've pumped enough irons now to graduate to the other aspect of C++. A language that incorporates the concept of object oriented programming or OOPs. It is, in fact, this aspect that gives C++ its aura of innovation. It is this that lifts it out of the C genre and gives it its exclusivity.

But the murky depths of OOPs don't look terribly inviting to most people. They are viewed as sinister and full of garbled and big words that most people do not want to test their strengths with.

Object Oriented Programming

That big word that puts the fear of death in most people. Most of us would avoid venturing into frontiers that seem alien and unfriendly. But are they really?

The big and portly words that characterize people's perception of Object Oriented Programming are just so much mumbo-jumbo, simple and down to earth ideas encased in elitist jargon. Object Oriented Programming, or call it by the more recallable name, OOPs, is a shift to more controlled, yet versatile programming, peppered with rather pompous tags. Its like a biologist describing the subtle points about Oryza sativas. And after a couple of nervous gulps you realize he's only talking about rice.

It is Object Oriented Programming, with its newness that gives C++ that ring of novelty. As Scott Robert Ladd, one of the most eloquent preachers of C++ defines it, Object Oriented Programming lets you organize data in your program the same way a biologist organizes his sativas and pudicas and different kinds of plants. Yes, Object Oriented Programming has to do with classes and families, genres and species.

Specifically the focus of OOPs is data. Data. That is the soul of any program. After all, we inhabit the world of data processing. In the melee for program modulation and program conciseness, however, we've lost sight of the actual building blocks - the data. We directed all our energies into the body beautiful and let the cells fester. In short, we took data for granted, often forgetting their role, in the larger pursuit.

Enter Object Oriented Programming. Not so much a revolutionary method as a revolutionary attitude. A re-defining of objectives. An introspective aftermath. Object Oriented Programming airs the data locked in modulation cupboards and sweeps off the mustiness around them. It recognizes the import of data as the nucleus of all programming, and attempts to define the relationship between data and operations.

Data is no longer the silent observer, suffering quietly in its shell, while functions walked away with the applause and the credit. Data has finally been lifted out of its innocuous existence and put on par with functions. Object Oriented Programming stresses the dependency of one on the other. Functions cannot exist without data, and data need functions to give it shape.

Objectivity In OOPs

Let's steep ourselves into this radical method of thinking, an attitude which is fast becoming a cult.

A program to initiate us into the new mould:

```
PROGRAM 46
#include <stdio.h>

struct Integer
{
    private:
    int i;
};

main( )
{
    struct Integer num;
    num.i = 10;
    printf("%d\n",num.i);
}
```

This program will not go beyond the drawing board. All because of the *private* in the code. *private: int i* builds a barbed wire around the variable *i*. It is like a "Private Property. No thoroughfare" placard keeping trespassers out.

Although *i* is a member of the structure *num*, *main( )* cannot invade its private precincts, however correct the rest of the code is. The data thus secured cannot be touched or tampered with, even accidentally.

Let's take another program with a related concept: *public*. We'll broadcast the explanation after we've seen a program.

PROGRAM 47

```
#include <stdio.h>

struct Integer
{
    public:
    int i;
};

main( )
{
    struct Integer num;
    num.i = 10;
    printf("%d\n",num.i);
}
```

This program will work without a whimper, because *i* here is public property, like the water fountain in the public square. Everyone can draw from it, whatever their mission. In the program above, the function *main( )* assigns a value to the member *i* and calls *printf( )* to output that value.

To summarize the two programs that we breezed through, a *private* member of the structure is guarded against outside interference, while a *public* member is for all to use. When we label a member *private* we literally hide it from the public eye, protecting its substance.

This is the essence of that much touted phrase 'data encapsulation'.

Does that mean that a *private* member cannot be accessed at all? That it has to necessarily remain rigid and fixed throughout its existence? Certainly not.

Entry is prohibited to trespassers only. But an authorized member can be given the key to the 'private' zone.

The 'struct' Keyword

Take a look at this program. And the minuscule change:

```
PROGRAM 48
#include <stdio.h>

struct Integer
{
    public:
    int i;
};

main( )
{
    Integer num;
    num.i = 10;
    printf("%d\n",num.i);
}
```

The moral of this program is that it is not necessary to prefix the structure tag *Integer* with the keyword *struct*. The C++ compiler takes care of these minor subtleties. Once you've defined the structure tag there's no need to keep informing the compiler about it.

Functions Within Structures

Take this example:

```
PROGRAM 49
#include <stdio.h>

struct Integer
{
    private:
    int i;
    public:
```

```
    void print(void)
    { i = 10; printf("%d\n",i); }
};

main( )
{
    Integer num;
    num.print( );
}
```

We have here a *private* member, *i* and a *public* function, *print(void)*. This function can be invoked by us, to access the restricted areas of the structure. This is the other side of the data handling coin. Called data abstraction, it is actually another manifestation of 'data encapsulation'. The encapsulated data is hidden from the general view but visible to functions within the same structure. That is a new concept to us. Including functions as members of a structure. In C, we had data members. Now we also have member functions. Functions which stand sentry between the private members and the outsiders.

In the program above, thus, *int i* is the private member to which *main( )* initializes a value through the public member function *print( )*.

Let's replace the word *struct* with *class*, a much abused term, bandied and thrown around like words from an enlightened sire.

PROGRAM 50

```
#include <stdio.h>

class Integer
{
    private:
    int i;
    public:
    void print(void) { i = 10; printf("%d\n",i); }
};

main( )
{
```

```
    Integer num;
    num.print( );
}
```

The output will be exactly the same as the previous program. *i* will be initialized through the member function *print( )* and displayed. Both *i* and *print(void)* are members of the class *Integer*.

Data Encapsulation and Classes

Well, welcome to Object Oriented Programming. Data encapsulation, data abstraction, classes and objects, words you were afraid to decipher, are actually simple concepts dressed in fancy sequins. The big words are just that - big words for simple ideas.

Getting back to the program, the question is: Are *struct* and *class* two names of the same entity or aren't they??? On the face of it they are exactly similar, in fact they can be used interchangeably. But...

Run this program:

```
PROGRAM 51
struct Integer
{
    int i;
};

main( )
{
    Integer num;
    num.i = 5;
}
```

Worked?

Now replace *struct* with its OOPs brother, *class* and run the program:

PROGRAM 52

```
class Integer
{
    int i;
};

main( )
{
    Integer num;
    num.i = 5;
}
```

Error?

The difference? The *class* program did not work because all members of a *class* are private by default, while all members of a structure are public. In the earlier, *struct* program, thus, the variable *i* was accessible. We reached a dead end with the *class* program because its data member became private and bound within abstract walls.

Having pinpointed that not-so-subtle difference, we'd like to inform you that from now on we'll use the Object Oriented terminology *class* alone. Only we'll use it with caution, declaring the private and the public members carefully. Like this:

PROGRAM 53

```
#include <iostream.h>

class Integer
{
    private:
    int i;
    public:
    void set(int a) { i = a; }
    void print( ) { cout << i; }
};

main( )
{
    Integer num;
```

```
    num.set(15);
    num.print( );
}
```

This is a typical OOPs program. So, let's talk OOPs. First of all, let's once and for all do away with terms in the code that are a mouthful, especially when we are familiar with pithy and pert words that perform the same function. We'll replace *printf( )* with the lighter *cout*.

Let's OOPs now. We've declared our private variable and the public functions that we require as go-betweens. Let's zip to the *main( )*. The statement *Integer num* intimates that we can now create our own datatypes among other exciting things. Theoretically speaking, a class is merely a user-defined datatype which ensconces data members, and functions which manipulate or act on these data. A data item is an object. And every object belongs to a class. By that definition, therefore, *num* is an object of the class *Integer*. Projecting that backwards, we can thus call all the *ints*, and *chars*, *floats* and *doubles*, classes and the variables that we suffixed to them, their objects.

A function associated with an object is called a method. Invoking a method of the object is known as "sending a message to the object". So, let's look at our example.

num.set(15). The function *set( )* is, in OOPs terminology "sending a message to the object to do something to itself". *set( )*, a public function opens the private member *I* to initialize it to the value passed to it, which is 15. The next method simply prints out that value of *I*.

Let's see what happens when member functions of a class are privatised as well.

PROGRAM 54

```
#include <iostream.h>

class Integer
{
```

```
        private:
        int i;
        void set(int a)
        { i = a; }
        void print( )
        { cout << i; }
};

main( )
{
    Integer x1;
    x1.set(105);
    x1.print( );
}
```

This will simply give you an error because member functions that need to be called from outside the object have to be public.

The 'this' Pointer

Take this program:

```
PROGRAM 55
#include <iostream.h>

class Integer
{
    private:
    int i;
    public:
    void set(int a) { i = a; }
    void print( )
    { cout << i << "\n"; }
};

main( )
{
    Integer num,digit;

    num.set(15);
    digit.set(10);
```

```
    num.print( );
    digit.print( );
}
```

num and *digit* are two objects of the class *Integer*. So, how does the computer know which *i* has been initialized by the method *set( )*? And how does *print( )* print the right *I*? How are the right messages sent and received? Is there any overwriting? What does happen?

Each object that is declared has its own set of data members. When a method is invoked, and a message is sent to the object, implicitly, the first parameter passed to the method will be a pointer to the object to which the message is being passed. By default each method is passed a pointer which points to the right object.

Coming back to our example, when *num.set( )* is invoked, the message is sent to the object *num*, and the first parameter passed to *set( )*, transparent to us, will be a pointer to the object *num*. The next *set( )* will have the pointer to the object *digit*.

Let's see that in clear black-and-white:

PROGRAM 56

```
#include <iostream.h>

class Integer
{
    private:
    int i;
    public:
    void set(int a)
    { this->i = a; }
    void print( )
    { cout << this->i << "\n"; }
};

main( )
{
    Integer num,digit;
```

```
    num.set(15);
    digit.set(10);

    num.print( );
    digit.print( );
}
```

The built-in pointer we spoke about in the last program is called *this*. To recap, the *this* pointer points to the object being processed. And is used to access the data members of the object. *this -> i* will thus access the private member *i* of the individual objects in our program.

Constructors And Destructors

From those little puddles, let's jump to a deeper inlet. Constructors. What is a constructor? And when is it used? These are the questions we'll answer first. Take the following program:

PROGRAM 57

```
#include <iostream.h>

class Integer
{
    private:
    int i;
    public:
    Integer(void)
    {
        cout << "\nThis is in constructor of class Integer";
    }

    void print( ) { cout << i << "\n"; }
};

main( )
{
    Integer num;
}
```

Note the similarity between the class name and the name of the method. Such methods, as have the same name as that of the classes they are part of, are called constructors.

A constructor lies beyond our control. We have no powers to invoke it. The constructor is called as soon as you declare an object of the class.

Take the output that this program will give you: This is in constructor of class Integer. That means, the minute you define the object, the constructor will arrive into the program. The constructor is the only method among a host of methods that does not need to be explicitly called, in fact you cannot call it even if you wanted to. Take the example above.

If we wanted *print( )* to perform some task for us, we'd have to call it, in so many words. We'd have to put a statement like *num.print( )* which would invoke the function. But a method that is a constructor gets called when the object of the class is being built.

The most obvious and elementary use of a constructor is to initialize the elements of an object while creating it, instead of writing a separate method and calling it to initialize the data member.

You'll also notice that constructors do not return a value unlike methods called by us. After all, a constructor is not ours to call so we do not have the option of providing a receptacle to receive a returning value.

Take another program on constructors:

PROGRAM 58

```
#include <iostream.h>

class Integer
{
    private:
    int i;
```

```
    Integer(void)
    {
        cout << "\nThis is in constructor of class Integer";
    }
};

main( )
{
    Integer num;
}
```

Why did this program generate an error? Simply because a constructor cannot be shut inside private estates. That is, of course, pretty obvious logic. The declaration of the object in that class will be in the *main( )*, i.e. outside the class definition. The constructor, thus has to be made publicly accessible.

Let's take a program to initialize a data member through a constructor:

PROGRAM 59
#include <iostream.h>

```
class Integer
{
    int i;
    public:
    Integer(void)
    {
        i = 10;
        cout <<"\nThis is in constructor with i = " << i;
    }
};

main( )
{
    Integer num;
}
```

The minute you create the object *num*, the constructor will initialize the member *i* to 10. The output you'll get will be:

This is in constructor with i = 10

That's the obvious utility of constructors we spoke about in the beginning.But this is a stupid program, to say the least. By hard-coding the value of i in the constructor definition, we are under-utilizing the immense extent of constructors. We are restricting the range of this far-reaching tool. The ideal way to use constructors would be:

Overloading Constructors

```
PROGRAM 60
#include <iostream.h>

class Integer
{
    int i;
    public:
    Integer(void)
    {
        i = 10;
        cout <<"\nThis is in constructor with i = " << i;
    }

    Integer(int para)
    {
        i = para;
        cout << "\nThis is an int constructor with i = " << i;
    }
};

main( )
{
    Integer num,digit(5);
}
```

To make the constructor more flexible, we've overloaded it, just as we overloaded simple functions earlier. In the program above, thus, when you declare *num*, the *void* constructor will get called, and *num.i* will be initialized to 10. Since *digit* has been declared with the value 5 attached to it by the brackets, the *int* constructor will be invoked. So, *digit.i* will get the value 5.

Everything that is born has to die. That is the story of life. The object that was born midwifed by the constructor lives its span and finally dies. In its death throes, a destructor is called. The destructor is represented by a 'tilde' - ~. Just as a method with the same class name is a constructor, a method with the same class name, but prefixed by a tilde, is a destructor. Let's meet the destructor in a program:

PROGRAM 61

```
#include <iostream.h>

class Integer
{
    int i;

    public:
    Integer(void)
    { cout << "\nIn constructor"; }

    void print(void)
    {
        i = 10;
        cout << "\n In print i = " << i;
    }

    ~Integer(void)
    {
        cout << "\nIn destructor";
    }
};

main( )
{
    Integer num;
    num.print( );
}
```

This program will give you the following output:

```
In constructor
In print i = 10
In destructor
```

Destructors, like constructors, are extremely useful tools. Further, like constructors they are not in our command. That is, we cannot call a destructor. When the object is on its last leg, the destructor visits like the proverbial messenger of Death.

We'll go to the destructor's party a little later, when we've understood some more about living objects.

More About Classes And Methods

Let's linger on some complexities now:

```
PROGRAM 62
#include <iostream.h>

class Integer2
{
    int i,j;

    public:
    Integer2(int para1 = 0, int para2 = 0)
    { i = para1; j = para2; }

    void change(int p1, int p2)
    { i = p1; j = p2; }

    void change(int p1)
    { i = p1; j = p1; }

    void print(void)
    { cout << i << " " << j <<"\n"; }
};

main( )
{
    Integer2 num,digit(10);

    num.print( );
    digit.print( );

    num.change(5,6);
```

```
    num.print( );

    digit.change(8);
    digit.print( );
}
```

The class *Integer2* has two data members *i* and *j*, and four public member functions, or methods. The first method is a constructor which has been defined with two default values. Next we have overloaded the *change* methods, one to accept two parameters, and the other to accept one. The last method *print( )*, as usual, prints the values of the data members *i* and *j*.

Let's shift gears to the *main( )*. Since *num* has been defined without any parameters, *i* and *j* will get the values 0 and 0 by default. *digit* has been declared with one parameter, 10, so its *i* will be 10 and *j*, by default, 0. *num.print( )* will, thus, output 0 0 and *digit.print( )*, 10 0.

The next method *change( )* will send a message to its object *num* and the values of *i* and *j* will be changed to 5 and 6, resply. *num.print( )* will output the revised values of *i* and *j*.

digit.change(8) will reinitialize the members *i* and *j* of *digit* to 8 and 8. *digit.print( )* will output the values of *i* and *j* as 8 and 8, resply.

Into Further Complexities

PROGRAM 63

```
#include <iostream.h>

class Integer2
{
    int i,j;
    public:
    Integer2(int para1 = 0, int para2 = 0)
    { i = para1; j = para2; }
```

```
    void add(int p1)
    {
        cout << (i+p1) << " " << (j+p1) << "\n";
    }

    void add(Integer2 p1)
    {
        cout << (i+p1.i) << " " << (j+p1.j) << "\n";
    }

    void print(void)
    { cout << i << " " << j <<"\n"; }
};

main( )
{
    Integer2 num(3,4),digit(10,20);

    num.print( );
    digit.print( );

    num.add(5);
    num.add(digit);

    num.print( );
}
```

Actually, a run of the program will prove that the complexity is only in the outward gloss. Basically, the program is no big deal. It only goes to show that not only can regular, in-built datatypes be passed to a method, but so can datatypes created by us.

Let's uncoil the program. Like the earlier one, we have a class with two data members, *i* and *j* and four methods. Only, instead of the method *change*, we have the method *add*. There are two *add* methods, one passed an *int* parameter and the other, our own datatype. *print( )* will, as usual, output the values of *i* and *j*.

Let's bludgeon into the *main( )*.

Both the objects *num* and *digit* have been passed two parameters. Thus *num.print( )* will output 3 4, and *digit.print( )* will output 10 20.

num.add(5) will add 5 to the existing value of *i* in *num*, and 5 to the value of *j* as well. This, of course, does not change the intrinsic value of *i* and *j*, but displays the sum. *cout* of the method *add( )* will, thus, display the result of *i* and *j* as 8 and 9, resply.

num.add(digit). A message is sent to *num* to add the values of the *i* of *digit* to the *i* of *num*, and the *j* of *digit* to the *j* of *num*. Thus the display outputted by *cout* will be 13 and 24, resply. When *print( )* is invoked again, the values of *i* and *j* will be printed as 3 and 4 itself, proving that the values of *i* and *j* have not changed after all that work in the middle.

Methods And Their Return Values

PROGRAM 64

```
#include <iostream.h>

class Integer2
{
    int i,j;
    public:
    Integer2(int para1 = 0, int para2 = 0)
    { i = para1; j = para2; }

    int add(int p1)
    { return(i+j+p1); }

    int add(Integer2 p1)
    { return(i+p1.i+j+p1.j); }

    void print(void)
    { cout << i << " " << j <<"\n"; }
};

main( )
{
```

```
Integer2 num(3,4),digit(10,20);

num.print( );
digit.print( );

int r1 = num.add(5);

cout << r1 << "\n";

int r2 = num.add(digit);

cout << r2 << "\n";
}
```

For the first time since we embarked on this journey, we are defining a method that returns a value. All this while, we returned a void, in other words, zilch.

add( ) is overloaded to accept either an int or an object of the type Integer2. Both of them return an int. Now let's get down to the business of the main( ).

The first two invocations of print( ) are simple enough. num.print( ) will output 3 and 4, the values of i and j. And digit.print( ) will print 10 and 20.

When you call the method add( ) it sends a message to num. The method results in the addition of the values of i and j to 5. That gives you 12. This value will be returned to r1. r1 will thus be 12.

int r2 = num.add(digit). Translating that, the method add( ) sends a message to the object num to add its values of i and j to those of digit. The sum, 37, will be returned to r2.

cout will, of course, do a printf( ) on them.

Let's take another program of "returning values".

PROGRAM 65

```
#include <iostream.h>
```

```
class Integer2
{
    int i,j;
    public:
    Integer2(int para1 = 0, int para2 = 0)
    { i = para1; j = para2; }

    Integer2 add(int p1)
    {
        Integer2 tmp;
        tmp.i = i+p1 ;
        tmp.j = j+p1 ;
        return(tmp) ;
    }

    Integer2 add(Integer2 p1)
    {
        Integer2 tmp;
        tmp.i = i+p1.i;
        tmp.j = j+p1.j;
        return(tmp);
    }

    void print(void)
    { cout << i << " " << j <<"\n"; }
};

main( )
{
    Integer2 num(3,4),digit(10,20);

    num.print( );
    digit.print( );

    Integer2 r1 = num.add(5);
    Integer2 r2 = num.add(digit);

    r1.print( );
    r2.print( );
}
```

int was an in-built datatype so returning it was a straight-forward operation. Returning an object of the class, however, calls for creating the object to be returned. In the program above, that's what we are attempting.

To return *Integer2*, we have to create another object within the method. The new object that we've created is *tmp*. Let's push into *main( )* to get the program going.

The first two method invocations are routine enough. They'll output: 3 4 and 10 20, resply. Take the next pair of statements, one at a time. *Integer2 r1 = num.add(5)*. By that, we are sending a message to *num* to take its values *i* and *j* and add 5 to them separately. The result of that calculation is passed to the newly created object, *tmp*, which is then returned to *Integer2 r1*.

The next statement adds the corresponding values of *num* and *digit*. That means, the *i* of *num* will be added to the *i* of *digit*, and so will the *j*s be added separately.

r1.print( ) and *r2.print( )* will output the values of *r1* and *r2* like this:

8 9
13 24

Operator Overloading

Remember the time when we learnt to count on our fingers and toes, then graduated to abacuses when the numbers got bigger, and moved to abstractions, the symbols of arithmetic. Soon, 5 + 3 was just as easily understood and accomplished as pebble stashing. Apples were added to Apples and then to Oranges without any conspicuous pressures on the grey matter.

And we slipped into adding *ints* to *ints* and *chars* to *chars*. If *int abc = 5* and *int xyz = 3* had to be added, we did it with such practiced ease, we didn't have to think twice. We simply abstracted the relationship - *abc + xyz* - and arrived at 8. Simple and straight-forward.

Binary Operator Overloading

Within this climate of abstractions and legibility, why should you have an enigmatic notation like *num.add(digit)?* Why can't we just say *num + digit* and stop wasting time decoding an inscription?

Like this:

```
PROGRAM 66
#include <iostream.h>

class Integer2
{
    int i,j;
    public:
    Integer2(int para1 = 0, int para2 = 0)
    {
        i = para1; j = para2;
    }
    void print(void)
    {
        cout << i << " " << j <<"\n";
    }
};

main( )
{
    Integer2 num(3,4),digit(10,20);

    num.print( );
    digit.print( );

    Integer2 r1 = num + 5;
    Integer2 r2 = num + digit;

    r1.print( );
    r2.print( );
}
```

It won't work. The operator cannot be applied to these operand types in function main( ). That's the message you'll be discouraged with. Why? Because the operands you used are your own datatypes. Datatypes that the compiler does not recognize. To make matters plain and simple therefore, you have some dirty work to do yourself. Overload the operator. So C++ can acknowledge the operands, and extend the operator to them.

Take this program:

```
PROGRAM 67
#include <iostream.h>

class Integer2
{
    int i,j;
    public:
    Integer2(int para1 = 0, int para2 = 0)
    { i = para1; j = para2; }

    Integer2 operator + (int p1)
    {
        Integer2 tmp;
        tmp.i = i+p1 ;
        tmp.j = j+p1 ;
        return(tmp) ;
    }

    Integer2 operator + (Integer2 p1)
    {
        Integer2 tmp;
        tmp.i = i+p1.i;
        tmp.j = j+p1.j;
        return(tmp);
    }

    void print(void)
    { cout << i << " " << j <<"\n"; }
};

main()
{
```

```
Integer2 num(3,4),digit(10,20);

num.print( );
digit.print( );

Integer2 r1 = num + 5;
Integer2 r2 = num + digit;

r1.print( );
r2.print( );
}
```

Now you can have your simple readable abstraction. *num + 5* will result in 5 being added to the *i* and *j* of *num*, to return 8 and 9 to *r1*. *r2* will get the values 13 and 24 *(num + digit)*. Which means, we've added two objects using the familiar + operator, instead of defining a method to perform that operation. We've moved once again to legible abstractions.

But how are the operands identified in the operator overloading statement? The operator has been defined with an *int* parameter and an *Integer*. + is a binary operator, but in the operator definition, only one parameter is passed at a time. That parameter is the one to the right of the operator. So, how is the other operand identified? If you recall, we have spoken about the default parameter that a method is passed. The *this* pointer. The left operand is the one pointed to by *this* - *num*, in this case. The right operand is the one you have to elucidate.

If we can enumerate the operands and state the relationships between them, then surely we can manipulate the operands. Put the *int* before the *Integer*, juxtapose their positions. Let's try that out with the earlier program. It would generate an error because of the way you overloaded the operator. The *int* parameter you passed to the operator was representative of the operand to the right of the operator. So, if you wanted to use an *int* on the left of the operator, would it work if you specified the first parameter, while overloading the operator, as in:

PROGRAM 68

```
#include <iostream.h>

class Integer2
{
    int i,j;
    public:
    Integer2(int para1 = 0, int para2 = 0)
    { i = para1; j = para2; }
    Integer2 operator + (int p1, Integer2 p2)
    {
        Integer2 tmp;
        tmp.i = p1+p2.i ;
        tmp.j = p1+p2.j ;
        return(tmp) ;
    }
    Integer2 operator + (Integer2 p1)
    {
        Integer2 tmp;
        tmp.i = i+p1.i;
        tmp.j = j+p1.j;
        return(tmp);
    }
    void print(void)
    { cout << i << " " << j <<"\n"; }
};

main( )
{
    Integer2 num(3,4),digit(10,20);
    num.print( );
    digit.print( );
    Integer2 r1 = 5 + num;
    Integer2 r2 = num + digit;
    r1.print( );
    r2.print( );
}
```

Integer2 operator + (int p1, Integer2 p2) seems a highly logical method. You certainly wouldn't have expected the error you got: 'Integer2 operator + (int p1, Integer2 p2)' must be declared with one argument. That means, like it or not, the first parameter is fixed . It is inherently the *this* pointer. If you pass it two parameters, therefore, the total number of parameters read will be 3, and the + operator is a binary operator. Hence the error.

What you need, mate, is a friend. To pamper you, to indulge your stubborn wishes. So if you insist on having your own way, go get yourself a friend first.

Friend Operators

PROGRAM 69

```
#include <iostream.h>

class Integer2
{
    int i,j;

public:

Integer2(int para1 = 0, int para2 = 0)
{ i = para1; j = para2; }

friend Integer2 operator + (int p1, Integer2 p2)
{
    Integer2 tmp;
    tmp.i = p1+p2.i ;
    tmp.j = p1+p2.j ;
    return(tmp) ;
}

Integer2 operator + (Integer2 p1)
{
    Integer2 tmp;
    tmp.i = i+p1.i;
    tmp.j = j+p1.j;
    return(tmp);
}

void print(void)
```

```
   { cout << i << " " << j <<"\n"; }
};

main( )
{
   Integer2 num(3,4),digit(10,20);
   num.print( );
   digit.print( );
   Integer2 r1 = 5 + num;
   Integer2 r2 = num + digit;
   r1.print( );
   r2.print( );
}
```

A *friend* can access all the members of a class, without being restricted to the rules governing the other members of the class. All member functions are passed the *this* pointer as the first parameter. The *friend* function is passed no such default parameter. So, now if you want to place the *int* to the left of the operator, remember you can call a friend. *friend integer2 operator + (int p1, Integer2 p2)* will allow the program to proceed without a hitch.

Unary Operator Overloading

Let's jaunt through these examples:

PROGRAM 70

```
#include <iostream.h>

class Integer2
{
   int i,j;
   public:
   Integer2(int para1 = 0, int para2 = 0)
   { i = para1; j = para2; }
   void operator ++ ( )
   {
      i++;
      j++;
```

```
    }
    void operator - ( )
    {
        i--;
        j--;
    }

    void print(void)
    { cout << i << " " << j <<"\n"; }
};

main( )
{
    Integer2 num(3,4),digit(10,20);
    num.print( );
    digit.print( );
    num++;
    digit--;
    num.print( );
    digit.print( );
}
```

That's a unary operator we are playing with. A unary operator does not ask for a parameter to be passed to it, simply because the default parameter takes over. The output here will surely cause you no worries. *num.print( )* will give you 4 and 5. *digit.print( )* will give you 9 and 19.

What is interesting is that the operators are completely under your thumb. The class is defined by you, and so all operations on the datatypes of the class are also defined by you. You can get them to do what you wish. Make the '++' operator do a '--' job, or a division job. Anything you wish to do. They're all yours to pick.

That's a lot of power at your disposal. Like a powerful dictator, you can puppet a host of datatypes around. All we can advise is, don't let that power corrupt. Don't loosen your girdles and slacken your socks. If you want to have fun making your '++' do a multiplication, cheer your '--' while it clambers through a division hoop, you're in the wrong business. Programming is no big-tent circus. So, use the power carefully. Only then can you draw the applause with it.

Sermon over! Let's sober down and go ahead:

PROGRAM 71

```
#include <iostream.h>

class Integer2
{
    int i,j;
    public:
    Integer2(int para1 = 0, int para2 = 0)
    { i = para1; j = para2; }

    void operator ++ ()
    {
        i++;
        j++;
    }
    void print(void)
    { cout << i << " " << j <<"\n"; }
};

main( )
{
    Integer2 num(3,4),digit(10,20);
    num.print( );
    digit.print( );
    Integer2 r1 = num++;
    r1.print( );
}
```

This program will result in an error, because while overloading the operator we have declared that the particular function will return a *void*. Therefore, *r1* cannot be assigned the return value of the operation *num++*.

We've checked return values before, but let's reiterate with one small program:

```
PROGRAM 72
#include <iostream.h>

class Integer2
{
   int i,j;
   public:
   Integer2(int para1 = 0, int para2 = 0)
   { i = para1; j = para2; }

   Integer2 operator ++ ( )
   {
      Integer2 tmp;
      tmp.i = ++i;
      tmp.j = ++j;
      return(tmp);
   }

   void print(void)
   { cout << i << " " << j <<"\n"; }
};

main( )
{
   Integer2 num(3,4),digit(10,20);
   num.print( );
   digit.print( );
   Integer2 r1 = num++;
   num.print( );
   r1.print( );
}
```

We have defined the *++* operator to return an object of type *Integer2*. Therefore *r1* will now get the value of the operation *num++*. *num.print( )* will thus be 4 and 5, and so will *r1.print( )*.

Saying '*this'

This is a better way of returning objects:

PROGRAM 73

```cpp
#include <iostream.h>

class Integer2
{
    int i,j;
    public:
    Integer2(int para1 = 0, int para2 = 0)
    { i = para1; j = para2; }

    Integer2 operator ++ ()
    {
        i++;
        j++;
        return(*this);
    }

    void print(void)
    { cout << i << " " << j <<"\n"; }
};

main()
{
    Integer2 num(3,4),digit(10,20);

    num.print();
    digit.print();

    Integer2 r1 = num++;

    num.print();
    r1.print();
}
```

Now that we know all about the *this* pointer, we can replace the object with the pointer explicitly, instead of dragging in another object which will then return the value to *r1*. *return(*this)* is the same as saying *return(num)*, in this example. *num.print( )* and *r1.print( )* will both output 4 and 5.

More Overloading

If you thought '++' and '--' were the only operators that could be overloaded easily, you've got another program coming:

PROGRAM 74

```
#include <iostream.h>

class Integer2
{
    int i,j;
    public:
    Integer2(int para1 = 0, int para2 = 0)
    { i = para1; j = para2; }

    int operator <= (Integer2 p)
    { return (i <= p.i && j <= p.j); }

    int operator >= (Integer2 p)
    { return (i >= p.i && j >= p.j); }
};

main()
{
    Integer2 num(3,4),digit(10,20);
    cout << (num <= digit) << "\n";
    cout << (num >= digit) << "\n";
}
```

That's the <= and >= operators we are dealing with. How do you overload them? By using the && logical operator in the overloading definition. In effect, what you're saying is if the *i* of *num* is less than the *i* of *digit* and if the *j* of *num* is lesser than the *j* of *digit*, only then will the statement *num <= digit* be true. *cout* will thus output 1 in the first instance and 0 in the second, since the statement *num >= digit* will be false.

The Copy Constructor

With that preamble, we come to a very important issue. Let's monitor the progress of the elements we studied. Bring all that you've gleaned so far to the program we're about to do. Open your minds and take off:

PROGRAM 75

```
#include <iostream.h>

class Integer2
{
    int i,j;
    public:
    Integer2(void)
    {
        i = 0; j = 0;
        cout << "In void constructor\n" ;
    }

    Integer2(int para1, int para2)
    {
        i = para1; j = para2;
        cout << "In int constructor\n" ;
    }

    Integer2(Integer2 &p1)
    {
        i = p1.i; j = p1.j;
        cout << "In copy constructor " << i << " " << j << "\n";
    }

    Integer2 operator + (Integer2 p1)
    {
        Integer2 tmp;
        tmp.i = i+p1.i;
        tmp.j = j+p1.j;
        return(tmp);
    }

    void print(void)
```

```
        { cout << i << " " << j <<"\n"; }
};

main( )
{
    Integer2 num(3,4),digit(10,20);

    num.print( );
    digit.print( );

    Integer2 r2;
    r2 = digit + num;

    r2.print( );
}
```

We've come back to our favorite + operator. Now, let's go on an exciting clippety-cloppety ride. Let's tackle it from the *main( )*. As soon as *Integer2* is defined two *int* constructors are called. The next two *print( )* methods will, of course, output the values of *num* as 3 and 4 and of *digit* as 10 and 20.

Integer2 r2 will result in the call of the void constructor. *r2 = digit + num* is the most exciting part of the monitoring program. *digit*, as we've learnt, will be passed as the *this* pointer, by virtue of its position to the left of the + operator. How is *num* taken by the computer? We've lectured on and pictured stacks at great length. That is what we have to pull in here.

num will be stacked away, before the operator is executed. In the operator overloading definition, we have created another object *tmp*. So, the void constructor will be called again. Now, because the object *tmp* is being returned, the copy constructor will be energized again. The job of the copy constructor now is to copy the entire object on to the stack. To visualize the way this was accomplished, we've written our copy constructor the way we have. The final output you get is a telling comment on the constructors called and when:

In int constructor
In int constructor

```
3 4
10 20
In void constructor
In copy constructor 3 4
In void constructor
In copy constructor 13 24
13 24
```

Take another meticulous monitor:

PROGRAM 76

```cpp
#include <iostream.h>

class Integer2
{
    int i,j;
    public:
    Integer2(void)
    {
        i = 0; j = 0;
        cout << "In void constructor\n" ;
    }

    Integer2(int para1, int para2)
    {
        i = para1; j = para2;
        cout << "In int constructor\n" ;
    }

    Integer2(Integer2 &p1)
    {
        i = p1.i; j = p1.j;
        cout << "In copy constructor" << i << " " << j << "\n";
    }

    Integer2 operator + (Integer2 &p1)
    {
        Integer2 tmp;
        tmp.i = i+p1.i;
        tmp.j = j+p1.j;
        return(tmp);
    }
```

```
        void print(void)
        { cout << i << " " << j <<"\n"; }
};

main( )
{
    Integer2 num(3,4),digit(10,20);

    num.print( );
    digit.print( );

    Integer2 r2;
    r2 = digit + num;

    r2.print( );
}
```

The output now will be:

```
In int constructor
In int constructor
3 4
10 20
In void constructor
In void constructor
In copy constructor 13 24
13 24
```

How did one In copy constructor get eaten away? There's only one reason. In the operator overloading definition, we have passed a reference of the object rather than the object itself. There is no need, therefore, to create a temporary object on the stack. The copy constructor will be called only to copy the newly created object, *tmp*, on to the stack, because it has to be returned.

Is it possible then to use referencing for parameters and return values? Let's check that out:

PROGRAM 77

#include <iostream.h>

class Integer2

```
{
    int i,j;
    public:
    Integer2(void)
    {
        i = 0; j = 0;
        cout << "In void constructor\n" ;
    }

    Integer2(int para1, int para2)
    {
        i = para1; j = para2;
        cout "In int constructor\n" ;
    }

    Integer2(Integer2 &p1)
    {
        i = p1.i; j = p1.j;
        cout << "In copy constructor" << i << " " << j << "\n";
    }

    Integer2 operator + (Integer2 &p1)
    {
        Integer2 tmp;
        tmp.i = i+p1.i;
        tmp.j = j+p1.j;
        return(&tmp);
    }

    void print(void)
    { cout << i << " " << j <<"\n"; }
};

main( )
{
    Integer2 num(3,4),digit(10,20);

    num.print( );
    digit.print( );

    Integer2 r2;
    r2 = digit + num;
```

```
    r2.print( );
}
```

This program will generate an error. You cannot pass a reference to a local object, *tmp* in our example. The principles that local objects are subject to are the same as those that govern local variables in C. The local object dies when the function is exited from. It makes absolutely no sense therefore to pass back the address of an object that is going to die the minute you leave the function. When you return the object itself, on the other hand, the smart C++ compiler, with enough foresight, copies these values in the correct destinations before the object meets its end.

Here's some more food for thought:

PROGRAM 78

```cpp
#include <iostream.h>

class Integer2
{
    int i,j;
    public:
    Integer2(void)
    {
        i = 0; j = 0;
        cout << "in void constructor\n" ;
    }

    Integer2(int para1, int para2)
    {
        i = para1; j = para2;
        cout << "in int constructor\n" ;
    }

    Integer2(Integer2 &p1)
    {
        i = p1.i; j = p1.j;
        cout << "in copy constructor" << i << j << "\n";
    }

    Integer2& operator + (Integer2 &p1)
    {
```

```
        Integer2 *tmp = new Integer2;
        tmp->i = i+p1.i;
        tmp->j = j+p1.j;
        return(*tmp);
    }

    void print(void)
    { cout << i << " " << j <<"\n"; }
};

main( )
{
    Integer2 num(3,4),digit(10,20);
    num.print( );
    digit.print( );

    Integer2 r2;
    r2 = digit + num;
    r2.print( );
}
```

The copy constructor never gets called in this case. If you look at the operator overloading definition, you'll know why. We're not creating an object, but a pointer to an object. And memory for the object has been allocated using *new*. So, what we return is not the object, but the address of that object. The address gets copied on the stack and not the object. So the copy constructor has no role to play, and therefore does not get called at all.

Here's the output for your perusal:

```
In int constructor
In int constructor
3 4
10 20
In void constructor
In void constructor
13 24
```

The int constructor will be called twice, once for *num* and once for *digit*. And the void constructor, for *r2* and *new*.

The Initializer

Take this program for this facet of the copy constructor:

PROGRAM 79

```
#include <iostream.h>

class Integer2
{
    int i,j;
    public:
    Integer2(void)
    {
        i = 0; j = 0;
        cout << "in void constructor\n" ;
    }

    Integer2(int para1, int para2)
    {
        i = para1; j = para2;
        cout << "In int constructor\n" ;
    }

    Integer2(Integer2 &p1)
    {
        i = p1.i; j = p1.j;
        cout << "In copy constructor" << i << " " << j << "\n";
    }

    Integer2& operator + (Integer2 &p1)
    {
        Integer2 *tmp = new Integer2;
        tmp->i = i+p1.i;
        tmp->j = j+p1.j;
        return(*tmp);
    }

    void print(void)
    { cout << i << " " << j <<"\n"; }
};
```

```
main( )
{
    Integer2 num(3,4),digit(10,20);

    num.print( );
    digit.print( );

    Integer2 r2 = digit + num;

    r2.print( );
}
```

At first glance you'll get no inkling of the difference between this program and the earlier one. So what was behind the output you got?

```
In int constructor
In int constructor
3 4
10 20
In void constructor
In copy constructor 13 24
13 24
```

r2 = digit + num. That is where the difference lies. In the earlier program, the void constructor was called before the assignment was made. *r2* was individually defined, and by the time the assignment was made, an object called *r2* was already created. So, when you passed a pointer to the object, there was no need to copy the object.

In this case, however, following convention, the operation to the right of the assignment operator will be evaluated first. The result of the operation has to be returned to an object which hasn't been born yet. Since *r2*, the receiving object has not been created, the copy constructor will be called to copy the sum on to a stack before returning to *r2*.

The important point is, whenever an object does not exist, and you are assigning it some value, the object has to first be created. We've always called a phenomenon like this initialization. An assignment can only be made to something that already exists. So, shouldn't this constructor be called an initialization constructor rather than a copy constructor? We leave that little decision to you.

The Assignment Operator

Did it cross your mind that you've been using the assignment operator between two objects that you've created? We went into one lengthy discourse about how we have to overload an operator to make it legible to the compiler. So why don't we spell out the assignment operator to C++ too? Simply because if we don't build our own assignment operator, C++ builds one by default. Just like the copy constructor. In all the above examples we elucidated it merely to monitor its presence.

Let's get those details absolutely clear:

PROGRAM 80

```
#include <iostream.h>

class Integer2
{
    int i,j;
    public:
    Integer2(void)
    {
        i = 0; j = 0;
        cout << "In void constructor\n" ;
    }

    Integer2(int para1, int para2)
    {
        i = para1; j = para2;
        cout << "In int constructor\n" ;
    }

    Integer2(Integer2 &p1)
    {
        i = p1.i;
        j = p1.j;
```

```
        cout << "In Initialization constructor" << i << " " << j << "\n";
    }

    Integer2& operator + (Integer2 &p1)
    {
        Integer2 *tmp = new Integer2;
        tmp->i = i+p1.i;
        tmp->j = j+p1.j;
        return(*tmp);
    }

    void operator = (Integer2 &p1)
    {
        i = p1.i;
        j = p1.j;
        cout << "In assignment operator" << i << " " << j << "\n";
    }

    void print(void)
    { cout << i << " " << j <<"\n"; }
};

main( )
{
    Integer2 num(3,4),digit(10,20);

    num.print( );
    digit.print( );

    Integer2 r2 ;
    r2 = digit + num;
    r2.print( );

    Integer2 x3 = digit + num;
    r3.print( );
}
```

Check the output first. And we'll know when the assignment operator is called and when the copy constructor.

```
In int constructor
In int constructor
3 4
```

```
10 20
In void constructor
In void constructor
In assignment operator 13 24
13 24
In void constructor
In Initialization constructor 13 24
13 24
```

The first two *int* constructors are for *num* and *digit*. The first two void constructors take care of *r2* and the *new* object in the + operator. The next one is an assignment operator, because *r2* now exists, courtesy the void constructor. You have a void constructor again, since *new* will create a new object again. The next one in line is the initialization constructor because the object *r3* has not been created yet.

What if we wanted to execute a statement like *r2 = digit = num* in the same program? Try it out:

PROGRAM 81

```cpp
#include <iostream.h>

class Integer2
{
    int i,j;
    public:
    Integer2(void)
    {
        i = 0; j = 0;
        cout << "in void constructor\n" ;
    }

    Integer2(int para1, int para2)
    {
        i = para1; j = para2;
        cout << "in int constructor\n" ;
    }

    Integer2(Integer2 &p1)
    {
        i = p1.i; j = p1.j;
```

```
        cout << "in copy constructor" << i << j << "\n";
    }

    Integer2& operator + (Integer2 &p1)
    {
        Integer2 *tmp = new Integer2;
        tmp->i = i+p1.i;
        tmp->j = j+p1.j;
        return(*tmp);
    }

    void operator = (Integer2 &p1)
    {
        i = p1.i; j = p1.j;
        cout << "in assignment operator" << i << " " << j << "\n";
    }

    void print(void)
    { cout << i << " " << j <<"\n"; }
};

main( )
{
    Integer2 num(3,4),digit(10,20);
    num.print( );
    digit.print( );
    Integer2 r2 ;

    r2 = digit = num;

    r2.print( );
}
```

Error! That's because we have asked the assignment operator to return a void. The equation *digit = num* will evaluate fine. But the evaluation cannot go any further. The part *digit = num* of the expression *r2 = digit = num* returns a void to *r2*. And so the error.

The only way out is to return an *Integer2*. The question is how best to. When we returned values of the + operator, we had to create an object, albeit through a pointer, because the sum of the operation was different from the individual operands. The =

operator, instead, changes the value of the operand to the left of the = sign, which is to be returned. So, all you need to return is the object to the left of the = sign. Let's work that out through a program:

PROGRAM 82

```
#include <iostream.h>

class Integer2
{
    int i,j;
    public:
    Integer2(void)
    {
        i = 0; j = 0;
        cout << "in void constructor\n" ;
    }

    Integer2(int para1, int para2)
    {
        i = para1; j = para2;
        cout << "in int constructor\n" ;
    }

    Integer2(Integer2 &p1)
    {
        i = p1.i; j = p1.j;
        cout << "in copy constructor" << i << j << "\n";
    }

    Integer2& operator + (Integer2 &p1)
    {
        Integer2 *tmp = new Integer2;
        tmp->i = i+p1.i;
        tmp->j = j+p1.j;
        return(*tmp);
    }

    Integer2& operator = (Integer2 &p1)
    {
        i = p1.i; j = p1.j;
        cout << "in assignment operator" << i << " " << j << "\n";
```

```
        return(*this);
    }
    void print(void)
    { cout << i << " " << j <<"\n"; }
};

main( )
{
    Integer2 num(3,4),digit(10,20);
    num.print( );
    digit.print( );

    Integer2 r2 ;
    r2 = digit = num;
    r2.print( );
}
```

We simply return the object pointed to by the *this* pointer. *this* as we know so well points to the object to the left of the assignment operator. So what you do is return the object through the *this* pointer.

Reiterations And Revisions

Let's reiterate some salient points. Take this program with its array and constructors:

PROGRAM 83

```
#include <iostream.h>
#include <string.h>

class Chars
{
    char str[20];
    public:
    Chars(void)
    { str[0] = '\0'; }

    Chars(char *s)
    { strcpy(str,s); }
```

```
        void change(char *c)
        { strcpy(str,c); }

        void print( )
        { cout << str << "\n"; }
};

main( )
{
    Chars s1("Hello"),s2;
    s2 = s1;
    s1.print( );
    s2.print( );

    s1.change("Bye");
    s1.print( );
    s2.print( );
}
```

We've defined here a class called *Chars* which has the following members: two constructors, two methods and an array.

Let's view them through *main( )*. For *s1*, the constructor which accepts an address (*char **) will be called. This constructor copies the string, Hello, into the array. *s2* will cause the void constructor to be called. This constructor will put a ´\0´ in the first element of the array.

s2 = *s1*. That equation will result in the array in *s2* also being initialized to Hello. *s1.print( )* and *s2.print( )* will both, thus output, Hello.

We next call the method *change( )* which copies a new string, Bye into *s1*. *s1.print( )* will thus output Bye, and *s2.print( )*, still, Hello.

So? What's the point we're trying to make? What is it we're getting at? Let's check the next program to find out:

Flawed Logic

The next couple of programs are extremely crucial. So, put the T.V. off and concentrate.

PROGRAM 84

```
#include <iostream.h>
#include <string.h>

class Chars
{
    char *str;
    public:
    Chars(void)
    { str = new char[1]; str[0] = '\0'; }

    Chars(char *s)
    { str = new char[strlen(s)+1]; strcpy(str,s); }

    void change(char *c)
    { strcpy(str,c); }

    void print()
    { cout << str << "\n"; }
};

main()
{
    Chars s1("hello"),s2;
    s2 = s1;
    s1.print();
    s2.print();

    s1.change("Bye");
    s1.print();
    s2.print();
}
```

We have again a class called *Chars* with one data member and four methods.

Before we analyze the program contents, let's get the concept above board. We have to first recall the concept of *malloc( )* which we pondered over at great length. Instead of *malloc( )* we've been using *new*, which is less complicated in its functioning. Before we get into the newness here, there's one point to understand.

In the earlier program, the array fixed the number of memorylocations that were stored. That was a limiting factor in a way, restricting the length of the string that could be used. And that kind of limitation is what we've always been fighting against. We need the facility of allocating memory dynamically as well.

Now let's go to the program, working it, of course, from the *main( )*. For *s2*, the void constructor will be called. *new* allocates memory for one *char*, just as *malloc( )* would have. The address is put into *str*. And the first element is initialized to '\0'.

s1 has a string Hello. Therefore, the *char* * constructor is called. *new* allocates a fresh chunk of memory. The number of locations allocated is calculated by *strlen(s) + 1*, in our example this will be six. The address is returned to *str* and the string is then copied into *str* by *strcpy( )*.

s2 = s1 is the most interesting aspect of the program and the concept. The = assignment operator now equates *s1.str* to *s2.str*. The address stored in *s1.str*, in other words, is put into *s2.str*. So, *s1.print( )* and *s2.print( )* will both output Hello.

The method *change( )* will next be called. *change( )* is also passed a pointer. *strcpy( )* copies the new string at the address pointed to by *str*, that means, Hello is overwritten by Bye at that memory location.

s1.print( ) will, of course, print Bye this time around. And *s2.print( )* will print ... Bye as well. Why? Because the data members, *s1.str* and *s2.str*, both point to the same address.

Now that was what we'd call bad bad bad programming and bad bad bad advice. First of all, the method *change( )* has been carelessly worded. What if you'd changed the string to ByeBye. The number of locations that Hello was allocated through the constructor will not be enough for the string ByeBye. Which implies that we would be overwriting memory that did not belong to us. Forget about ethics, it's absolutely stupid to do that.

Secondly, by equating addresses, you're laying your own booby trap. Instead of giving each object its own memory space to store a string, the default assignment operator merrily assigns the address of the same storage space to both the objects. After the assignment if you ever wanted to change one of the strings, the change would be reflected in any other object which received the string because of the =.

Here's another manifestation of that irresponsible code:

PROGRAM 85

```
#include <iostream.h>
#include <string.h>

class Chars
{
    char *str;
    public:
    Chars(void)
    { str = new char[1]; str[0] = '\0'; }

    Chars(char *s)
    { str = new char[strlen(s)]; strcpy(str,s); }

    void change(char *c)
    { strcpy(str,c); }

    void print( )
    { cout << str << "\n"; }

    ~Chars(void)
    { delete str; }
};
```

```
main( )
{
    Chars s1("hello"),s2;

    s2 = s1;
    s1.print( );
    s2.print( );

    s1.change("Bye");
    s1.print( );
    s2.print( );
}
```

First, let's understand the statement ~*Chars(void) { delete str; }*. If you recall, we had to send the function *malloc( )* packing with *free( )*, then we closed a file with *fclose( )* once we opened it with *fopen( )* - all instances of neat programming practices - we have to let go of *new* with *delete*. *delete* frees the memory allocated by *new*.

Getting back to the program, if you run it, you'll be saddled with results you never expected. Sure, the program will run, but consider the output:

Hello
Hello.
Bye
Bye
Null pointer assignment

So, where's the catch? Where did the last phrase pop in from?

The only reason for this ineptness is the fact that the pointers of both the objects are pointing to the same location. The destructor is called the first time itself, i.e. when *s1* is dying. The destructor, as embodied by *delete*, releases the space allocated by *new*. So, when *s2* emerges to call the destructor again, it just gives a 'Sorry-no-such-location-exists' shrug and outputs the bawdy message Null pointer assignment.

So, what's the best way to copy a string into another object, keeping the identity of each intact?

Why Overload The Assignment Operator?

PROGRAM 86

```
#include <iostream.h>
#include <string.h>

class Chars
{
    char *str;
    public:
    Chars(void)
    { str = new char[1]; str[0] = '\0'; }

    Chars(char *s)
    { str = new char[strlen(s)+1]; strcpy(str,s); }

    void print()
    { cout << str << "\n"; }

    void operator = (Chars &p)
    {
        delete str;
        str = new char[strlen(p.str)+1];
        strcpy(str,p.str);
    }

    void change(char *c)
    {
        delete str;
        str = new char[strlen(c)+1];
        strcpy(str,c);
    }

    ~Chars(void) { delete str; }
};

main()
{
    Chars s1("Hello"),s2;
```

```
s2 = s1;

s1.print( );
s2.print( );

s1.change("Bye");

s1.print( );
s2.print( );
}
```

How did this program work? Let's analyze it carefully.

The most crucial issues here are the overloading of the assignment operator and the *change( )* method. That's where you should concentrate your attention. But before we get there, let's start from the beginning.

To begin with, *s1* will cause the (char *) constructor to copy the string Hello into the space allocated for it by *new*. That address is then put into *str*, the member of the object *s1*.

Now, the void constructor will be invoked for *s2*. The steps followed for the creation of *s2* are the same as in the previous program. *new* allocates one element, initializes it to '\0' and returns that address to *str*.

Now, instead of allowing the default assignment operator to take over, we are writing our own assignment operator. Here's where the crux of the matter lies. Let's go to the operator equation.

The expression *s2 = s1* calls the assignment operator. The operand to the left has to be assigned the string of the operand to the right. The object to the left is passed as the *this* pointer, and the object to the right is passed by reference.

We'll first free this location with *delete str*. If you remember, *s2.str* contained the address of a memory location which contained a '\0'. The next step brings in *new* again. *new* allocates a fresh memory chunk equivalent to the string length of the string pointed to by *p.str* plus 1 for the '\0'. That is, Hello. The address of this new location is put into *str*. The string pointed to by *p.str* is now copied into the location pointed to by *str*.

That gives us two separate copies of the string Hello.

Now we go to the method *change( )*, the other big brother in the program.

change( ) is called by the object *s1*. So, the method *change( )* will wring changes in the object *s1*. *delete str*, thus refers to the deallocation of the memory block pointed to by *s1.str*. In effect, therefore, the Hello of *s1* is destroyed. That is not the end of the *change( )* method.

new next allocates a fresh chunk of memory, the amount equivalent to the length of the new string passed, Bye, in this example. The address of that location is passed to *str*, and the new string is copied into that location.

Now, *s1.str* will point to Bye and *s2.str* will point to Hello. Everything will now work perfectly. The destructor will not flag an error like the earlier one, since the pointers in both the objects are pointing to different memory locations. The two blocks will thus be destroyed separately when the objects die.

That was a short and swift drill that built the platform of OOPs. Object Oriented Programming - nothing but a refurbishing of old ideas. A more eloquent and terse version of the C and C++ orientation. Big words that embody conceptually lucid themes. Exciting not only in terms of their contents, but the potential they carry.

With those basics thoroughly soaked into our repertoire, let's tackle another pearl in the oyster. Inheritances.

The Laws Of Inheritances

Where would species, races, families be without the principles of inheritance? Can you imagine a world inhabited by creatures totally diverse and unconnected with each other. The chaos and the confusion, the proliferation of so many units, keeping track of everyone and everything would have been the sole purpose of life. Three cheers for inheritance!

Inheritance brings order into the world. The continuity of species, the classification, the order that exists is a function of inheritance. It is the perfect tool. Preserving the essence of a species and yet maintaining the individuality of each member in the group.

The principles of inheritance in C++ have been borrowed from real life. The ordering of objects, their place in an hierarchy, the resemblances and the distinctness each object exhibits relative to the other members of its class. From parent and child relationships in real life, it's a lateral movement to the base and derived classes of C++.

The parent class is referred to, in C++ parlance, as the base class and the class inherited from it, the child, the derived class. Let's understand the nuances involved as we examine the following programs.

Deriving Classes

Here's the first program, a simple demo of how one class is derived from another.

PROGRAM 87

```
#include <iostream.h>

class BClass
{
    public:
```

```
        int i;
        int j;
};

class DClass : BClass
{
    public:
    void init(void)
    {
        i = 5; j = 10;
        cout << i << " " << j;
    }
};

main( )
{
    DClass var;
    var.init( );
}
```

class DClass : BClass is the statement that defines the inheritance relationship. *BClass* is the base class from which the derived class *DClass* has been inherited.

In the *main( )*, thus, *var* is an object of *DClass*, the derived class. The method *init( )*, also belonging to *DClass*, initializes *i* and *j*, and *cout* outputs the result, 5 and 10.

Take another program:

```
PROGRAM 88
#include <iostream.h>

class BClass
{
    private:
    int i;
    int j;
};

class DClass : BClass
{
```

```
     public:
     void init(void)
     {
        i = 5; j = 10;
        cout << i << " " << j;
     }
};

main( )
{
    DClass var2;
    var2.init( );
}
```

This program will flag an error. In what way did it, then, differ from the earlier example?

The members *i* and *j* of the base class in the earlier example were public. And therefore the derived class could inherit both these characteristics. In this example, however, both the members have been declared private, and members private to the base class are not inherited by the derived class.

The point, in a nutshell, is that the child class does not inherit all the characteristics of the parent class. Only those members that have been declared public are transmitted from parent to child.

Now try this program out. What would be the outcome?

PROGRAM 89

```
#include <iostream.h>

class BClass
{
    int i;
    public:
    int j;
};

class DClass : BClass
{
    public:
```

```
    void init(void)
    { i = 5; j = 10; }
};

main( )
{
    DClass var2;
}
```

Error! Mainly because only the variable *j* of the base class will be inherited by the derived class. This is because *i* has been declared as private to *BClass*. All members are taken as private unless stated otherwise. So you'll fall flat if you try to initialize *i* in the derived class.

What do you think this program will do?

PROGRAM 90

```
#include <iostream.h>

class BClass
{
    public:
    int i;
    int j;
};

class DClass : BClass
{
    public:
    void init(void)
    {
        i = 5; j = 10;
        cout << i << " " << j;
    }
};

main( )
{
    DClass var;
    var.init( );
```

```
    var.i = 20;
    var.j = 30;

    cout << "\n" << i << " " << j;
}
```

Error, of course. *DClass* derived from *BClass* will inherit both *i* and *j*, public members of the base class. The problem does not lie here, though. Look at the *main( )* to pinpoint the error.

The public members inherited from a base class become private to the derived class unless otherwise specified. So, no access is available to *i* and *j* from *main( )*.

Access Specifiers

Is there any way we can make those objects public in the derived class as well? There is:

PROGRAM 91

```
#include <iostream.h>

class BClass
{
    public:
    int i;
    int j;
};

class DClass : public BClass
{
    public:
    void init(void)
    {
        i = 5; j = 10;
        cout << i << " " << j;
    }
};

main( )
{
```

```
DClass var;
var.init();

var.i = 20;
var.j = 30;

cout << "\n" << i << " " << j;
}
```

By specifying the access of the derivation as public, we can ensure that all the public members that the derived class inherits from the base class stay public. Access specifiers, like objects, by default are private, unless specifically tagged as public. In the examples before this one, we dealt with private accesses only. That is why all the objects and methods that the derived class inherited from the base were private to the derived class.

Incorporating Inheritances

But where and how does the concept of inheritances fit into the C++ scheme?

Consider this analogy. You have a base class 'dog', from which you derive a specific class 'poodle'. The base class will comprise those elements that encompass all the characteristics of the family 'dog'. 'color', 'weight', 'height' could be some of the data members of the class 'dog'. 'run', 'bite', 'bark' could be some of the methods incorporated into the base class.

Coming to the derived class 'poodle', since it is specific to the family 'dog', there is no need to redefine its basic traits. If you wanted a 'labrador' to keep your 'poodle' company, you'd certainly not go into rebuilding the class from scratch. You'd simply derive it from the parent class.

That is what inheritance is all about. Having a generic base class from which you keep deriving specific classes, classes which have all the qualities of the base class plus special attributes of their own.

Assume, for example, a base class that's an Editor. From this base class are derived two classes, the wordprocessor and the browser. The browser does not allow you do anything the Editor does, yet it is derived from it. The only meeting point between the two is that the browser lets you peruse through the document. But take the wordprocessor instead. The wordprocessor derived from the Editor inherits all the qualities of the Editor and more.

With those logistics plain and clear behind us, let's take a demonstrative program and come to some conclusions.

PROGRAM 92

```cpp
#include <iostream.h>

class Dog
{
    char color;
    public:
    Dog(void)
    {
        color = 'w';
        cout << " Color is " << color << "\n";
    }
    void chcol(char col)
    {
        color = col;
        cout << "Color changed to " << color << "\n";
    }
};

class Poodle : Dog
{
    public:
    void change(char splash)
    { chcol(splash); }
};

main( )
{
    Poodle Silky;
    Silky.change('b');
}
```

Silky, the pet poodle, in a chivalrous attempt to win his lady love jumped right into the can of paint that his master so carelessly left outside the kennel. And Silky's milky white coat got splotched with fast, water-proof black blotches. How does dotted Silky now fit into the class of pure white *Dog* he was derived from?

The method *change( )* changes the color of Silky's coat from *w* to *b. color* is a private member of the base class *Dog*. This member has to be accessed by the method *change( )* to effect the change in Silky's appearance. *change( )*, the public method of the derived class *Poodle*, in turn calls the method *chcol( )* inherited from *Dog*.

chcol( ) will now change the *color* to *b*. The entire exercise simply demonstrates how classes are designed, and the interconnections between encapsulated data, methods, derived classes, base classes, and of course, inheritance.

Further, the derived class itself can give birth to a child class. The derived class, thus becomes the base class of the newly derived class. The whole arrangement is a close duplication of traditional family trees.

Let's check access through the tree from third generation class to the root.

PROGRAM 93

```
#include <iostream.h>

class BClass
{
    private:
    int i;
    public:
    void print(void)
    { i = 5; cout << i << "\n"; }
};

class DClass : BClass
{
    public:
```

```
    void print1(void)
    { print( );}
};

class TGClass : DClass
{
    public:
    void print2(void)
    { print1( );}
};

main( )
{
    TGClass tg;
    tg.print2( );
}
```

DClass is the class derived from *BClass*, and class *TGClass* is further derived from *DClass*. The base class, *BClass* has a private member *i* and a public method *print( )*. So *DClass* inherits this method.

DClass, further, has a public method, *print1( )* which accesses the *print( )* method of the base class. *TGClass*, the child class of *DClass* inherits the public method *print1( )*. It, further, has its own public method *print2( )*, which can be accessed by the *main( )*.

main( ) accesses *print2( )*, which accesses *print1( )*, which accesses *print( )*, which initializes *i* and outputs its value as 5. Thus, the class *TGClass* inherits the characteristic of the base class *BClass* through a traceable hierarchy.

Inheritance And Constructors

How do constructors behave in an hierarchy? Run this program and see the answer outputted:

PROGRAM 94

#include <iostream.h>

```
class BClass
{
   public:
   BClass(void)
   { cout << "constructor -> BClass" << "\n";}
};

class DClass : BClass
{
   public:
   DClass(void)
   { cout << "constructor -> DClass" << "\n";}
};

main( )
{
   DClass y1;
}
```

```
constructor -> BClass
constructor -> DClass
```

The line followed by the constructor is, thus, straight down from the base to the derived. Whenever you define an object in the derived class, the constructor of the base class is first called, and then the constructor of the derived class.

Let's see how the constructor call traverses in multiple derivations:

PROGRAM 95

```
#include <iostream.h>

class BClass
{
   public:
   BClass(void)
   { cout << "constructor -> BClass" << "\n";}
};

class DClass : BClass
{
```

```
    public:
    DClass(void)
    { cout << "constructor -> DClass" << "\n";}
};

class TGClass : DClass
{
    public:
    TGClass(void)
    { cout << "constructor -> TGClass" << "\n";}
};

main( )
{
    TGClass tg;
}
```

When the object of the third generation *TGClass* is defined, the constructor of the base class *BClass* is called first, then the constructor of the class derived from this, *DClass*, and last of all the constructor of the newest derivative, *TGClass*.

The output:

```
constructor -> BClass
constructor -> DClass
constructor -> TGClass
```

Let's understand constructor calling even better:

PROGRAM 96

```
#include <iostream.h>

class BClass
{
    public:
    BClass(void)
    { cout << "constructor -> BClass" << "\n";}
};

class DClass : BClass
{
```

```
    public:
    DClass(void)
    { cout << "constructor -> DClass" << "\n";}
};

class TGClass : DClass
{
    public:
    TGClass(void)
    { cout << "constructor -> TGClass" << "\n";}
};

main( )
{
    BClass x1;
    cout << "\n";

    DClass  y1;
    cout << "\n";

    TGClass tg;
}
```

The printout here is what is significant.

```
constructor -> BClass

constructor -> BClass
constructor -> DClass

constructor -> BClass
constructor -> DClass
constructor -> TGClass
```

Inheritance And Destructors

The definition of an object in each of these classes results in the calling of the constructors in the right hierarchical line. If the constructor call goes down the line from the base to the derived, the destructor call is felt in the reverse order, from the derived class up, to the base class.

PROGRAM 97

```
#include <iostream.h>

class BClass
{
    public:
    BClass(void)
    { cout << "constructor -> BClass" << "\n"; }
    ~BClass(void)
    { cout << "destructor -> BClass" << "\n"; }
};

class DClass : BClass
{
    public:
    DClass(void)
    { cout << "constructor -> DClass" << "\n"; }
    ~DClass(void)
    { cout <<"destructor -> DClass"<< "\n"; }
};

main( )
{
    DClass y1;
}
```

When the object of the derived class is defined, the constructor call takes this order:

constructor -> BClass
constructor -> DClass

The destructor call traverses like this:

destructor -> DClass
destructor -> BClass

Let's understand that difference with a program:

PROGRAM 98

```
#include <iostream.h>
```

```
class BClass
{
    public:
    BClass(void)
    { cout << "constructor -> BClass" << "\n"; }
    ~BClass(void)
    { cout << "destructor -> BClass" << "\n"; }
};

class DClass : BClass
{
    public:
    DClass(void)
    { cout << "constructor -> DClass" << "\n"; }
    ~DClass(void)
    { cout <<"destructor -> DClass"<< "\n"; }
};

class TGClass : DClass
{
    public:
    TGClass(void)
    { cout << "constructor -> TGClass" << "\n"; }
    ~TGClass(void)
    { cout <<"destructor -> TGClass"<< "\n"; }
};

main()
{
    BClass x1;
    cout << "\n";

    DClass y1;
    cout << "\n";

    TGClass tg;
    cout << "\n";
}
```

The output will be eloquent enough:

constructor -> BClass

```
constructor -> BClass
constructor -> DClass

constructor -> BClass
constructor -> DClass
constructor -> TGClass

destructor -> TGClass
destructor -> DClass
destructor -> BClass
destructor -> DClass
destructor -> BClass
destructor -> BClass
```

Protected Members

Public and private members and access specifiers. That was the focus so far. Consider an hierarchy of three classes, each derived from the one preceding it in the derivative tree. If the members in the base class are declared public, they are inherited by the derived class. If the access specifier declares the derivation to be public, these members stay public in the derived class and can be passed on to the next generation class. If this class also has a public access, then those members can be further passed on. But that makes them open property to any Tom, Dick and Harry function that looks for access.

Is it possible therefore to maintain the inner sanctum sanctorum of a group of classes? To ensure that data members can be inherited only within and among the classes of a family, keeping the outsiders out? Yes, it is.

Enter the will and testimony of the family - the "protected" label tagged to a data member of a base class. A member declared protected can be passed on from class to derived class as long as the derivation is public. It is protected, however, from access by an outside function.

Take this program:

PROGRAM 99

```
class BClass
{
    protected:
    int i;
};

main( )
{
    BClass x1;
    x1.i = 10;
}
```

Consider the class *BClass*. It has a protected member *i*. An attempt is made to access the member *i* through *main( )*. The program will register an error because *i* cannot be accessed through *main( )*.

Protected Members And Access Specifiers

There is, though, an option available that opens a protected member to access by an outside function. Through a public method.

PROGRAM 100

```
#include <iostream.h>

class BClass
{
    protected:
    int i;
    public:
    void print(void)
    { i = 10; cout << i << "\n";}
};

main( )
{
    BClass x1;
    x1.print( );
}
```

BClass has a protected member *i* and a public method *print( )*. The method initializes the member *i* to 10. *main( )* is allowed to call the function *print( )*, through which it can grab the protected property *i*.

Protected Members And Derived Classes

Those were examples with a single class. Let's check derived classes and the behavior of protected members within them. The protected members of a base class are inherited as protected members in the derived class. Take the program below:

PROGRAM 101

```
#include <iostream.h>

class BClass
{
    protected:
    int i;
};

class DClass : public BClass
{
    public:
    void print(void)
    { i = 10; cout << i << "\n"; }
};

main( )
{
    DClass y1;
    y1.print( );
}
```

i is the protected member of the base class *BClass* from which has been derived the class *DClass*. The derivation access has been declared as public, so all public and protected members of the base class become public and protected members of the derived class.

The method *print( )* in the derived class is specifically stated as public. So it can be accessed by *main( )*. The duty of this method is to initialize the protected member *i* to 10. Thus, *main( )*, through the method *print( )* can access the protected member.

If the access specifier was private, however, the public and protected members that the derived class inherited would have been private.

What we are leading to is that at the first level of derivation, the kind of access does not affect the security of protected members. If access is private, they become private members of the derived class, and if it is public, they stay as protected members. Either way, inaccessible to outsider functions.

Look at this program:

PROGRAM 102

```
#include <iostream.h>

class BClass
{
    protected:
    int i;
};

class DClass : BClass
{
    public:
    void print(void)
    { i = 10; cout << i << "\n";}
};

main( )
{
    DClass y1;
    y1.print( );
}
```

The access specifier is private by default. When it comes to protected members, the access specifier is of little consequence in single derivations. In the case of multiple inheritances, however, the access specifier makes a telling difference. The protected members of the base class become private to the derived class when the access specifier is private. So the third generation classes derived from this second level will have no access to the protected members.

Let's take a couple of programs to make our point clear.

PROGRAM 103

```cpp
#include <iostream.h>

class BClass
{
   protected:
   int i;
};

class DClass : public BClass
{
   public:
   void printDClass(void)
   { i = 10; cout << i << "\n";}
};

class TGClass : public DClass
{
   public:
   void printTGClass(void)
   { i = 20; cout << i << "\n";}
};

main( )
{
   DClass y1;
   TGClass tg;

   y1.printDClass( );
   tg.printTGClass( );
}
```

Since the access is public here, the protected member *i* from the base class is inherited by the derived class *DClass* and further by the third generation class *TGClass*. The member *i* is protected through its passage from one class to another. *main( )* can thus access these protected members through the public methods inherent in the classes. The output you'll get:

```
10
20
```

If you are wondering, as we did, whether the *i* of both the objects are the same entity, we have this to say to you: add the function that will print the value of *y1.i* again. The output you'll now get will be:

```
10
20
10
```

What does that prove? That each object inherits its own group of data members. So the *i* of *y1* obviously is different from the *i* of *tg*.

But when it comes to multiple inheritances, the access specifier plays a significant role:

PROGRAM 104

```cpp
#include <iostream.h>

class BClass
{
    protected:
    int i;
    public:
    void print(void)
    { i = 10; cout << i <<"\n"; }
};

class DClass : BClass
{
    public:
    void print1( )
```

```
    { i = 5; cout << i; }
};

class TGClass : DClass
{
    public:
    void print2( )
    { i = 15; cout << i; }
};

main( )
{
    DClass y1;
    TGClass tg;

    y1.print1( );
    tg.print2( );
}
```

The program wouldn't get past the conveyor belt of the compiler. Because the access is private by default, the protected member in the base class will be inherited as a private member in the derived class. The third generation class *TGClass* will not inherit the member *i* at all. And so the error.

Multiple Inheritances

That was the story of linear inheritances. Wealth from one side of the family. But there are some lucky blokes around who inherit wealth from other sides as well. Multiple inheritances. It's time we met these children of fortune.

PROGRAM 105

```
#include <iostream.h>

class King
{
    public:
    King(void)
    { cout << " This is in base class King\n";}
};
```

```
class Queen
{
   public:
   Queen(void)
   { cout << " This is in base class Queen\n";}
};

class Prince : public King,public Queen
{
   public:
   Prince(void)
   { cout << " This is in derived class Prince\n";}
};

main( )
{
   Prince Lucky;
}
```

Prince is the privileged class derived from a composition of *King* and *Queen*. *Prince* will thus inherit from both *King* and *Queen*.

The printout outputted by the above program will be:

```
This is in base class King
This is in base class Queen
This is in derived class Prince
```

Now that we have acknowledged the existence of multiple inheritances, let's go ahead imbibing its nuances.

Take this program:

PROGRAM 106

```
#include <iostream.h>

class BClass1
{
   int i;
   public:
   void get(void)
```

```
   { i = 5; cout << i << "\n"; }
};

class BClass2
{
   int i;
   public:
   void get(void)
   { i = 10; cout << i << "\n"; }
};

class CClass : public BClass1, public BClass2
{
   public:
   void get1(void)
   { get();}
};

main( )
{
   CClass c;
   c.get1( );
}
```

Both *BClass1* and *BClass2* have the function *get( )*. *main( )* accesses the method *get1( )* of the derived class *CClass*. *CClass*, in turn, invokes the method *get( )*. But which *get( )* is that? The method of the base class *BClass1* or the method of the base class *BClass2*?

The specific error message flagged Field 'get' is ambiguous in 'CClass' in function 'CClass::get1( )' is an eloquent comment. So how do we tide over that problem?

PROGRAM 107

```
#include <iostream.h>

class BClass1
{
   int i;
   public:
   void get(void)
```

```
    { i = 5; cout << i << "\n"; }
};

class BClass2
{
    int i;
    public:
    void get(void)
    { i = 10; cout << i << "\n"; }
};

class CClass : public BClass1, public BClass2
{
    public:
    void get1(void)
    { BClass1::get( ); }
};

main( )
{
    CClass c;
    c.get1( );
}
```

All that need be done is qualify the name of the method with the name of the class. As in *BClass1::get( )*. That is, the derived class now specifically knows which method should be invoked. The output you'll get will be 5.

That is the gist of multiple inheritances. We'll see its performance in the programming realm as we go along.

About Friends And Peers

Take this program and get introduced to a friend of the class.

```
PROGRAM 108
#include <iostream.h>

class FClass;

class RDale
```

```
{
   int i;
   public:
   friend  FClass;
   void print(void)
   { cout << i << "\n"; }
};

class FClass
{
   public:
   void get( RDale& x )
   { x.i = 5; cout << x.i << "\n"; }
};

main( )
{
   FClass Jug;
   RDale Arch;
   Jug.get(Arch);
   Arch.print( );
}
```

How do you think this program will work? *I* is, after all, a private member of the class *RDale*. So, will *main( )*, the outsider function, or for that matter even *FClass* which is not even derived from it, be able to access it?

A look at the output tells you that it was. *RDale* let *FClass* into its private circle and allowed it special privileges.

Once you declare a friend to a class, the friend is given the right to access all members, data and methods, of the class befriending it. In our example, *Jug* is an object of the friend class *FClass*. *Arch* is the object of the main class we're talking about. The method *get( )*, the public method of the friend class has been passed one parameter, a reference to the object of the class *RDale*. *Jug.get(Arch)* will thus initialize the private member of *Arch* to 5. The statement *Arch.print( )* checks that out for you.

Take another program in the friend category:

PROGRAM 109

```
#include <iostream.h>

class RDale
{
    int i;
    friend class FClass;
    public:
    void print(void)
    { cout << i << "\n"; }
};

class FClass
{
    public:
    void get( RDale& x )
    { x.i = 5; cout << x.i << "\n"; }
};

main( )
{
    FClass Jug;
    RDale Arch;
    Jug.get(Arch);
    Arch.print( );
}
```

This program does the same thing as the earlier one. The only point that we're trying to make is that it is immaterial where you declare the friend class. You can declare it in the private or the public section of the befriended class. Another piece of information is that you need not even declare the friend class before you define the befriended class. The statement *friend class FClass* in the class definition is sufficient to underline the friendship.

Pointers And Friends

The next sojourn, of course, is with our good old ally, pointers. Pass a pointer to the method in the friend class and see what it gives you:

PROGRAM 110

```
#include <iostream.h>

class FClass;

class Class
{
    int i;
    friend  FClass;
};

class FClass
{
    public:
    void get (Class *x1 )
    { x1->i = 5; cout << x1->i << "\n"; }
};

main( )
{
    FClass pal;
    Class x1;
    pal.get(&x1);
}
```

To the method of the friend we've passed a pointer to the object, rather than the object itself. And in the *main( )*, we passed the reference of the object of the befriended class. The output will be no different from the previous examples. *i* will be initialized to 5, this time through a pointer.

A bit of advice: avoid using pointers when you can just as easily use references. Pointer notation is quite an eyesore - at least that's what we think. We prefer to use the friendlier references. Like this:

PROGRAM 111

```
#include <iostream.h>

class FClass;

class Class
```

```
{
    int i;
    friend FClass;
};

class FClass
{
    public:
    void get ( Class &x )
    { x.i = 10; cout << x.i << "\n"; }
};

main( )
{
    FClass pal;
    Class x1;
    pal.get(x1);
}
```

Easier? OK, let's move ahead.

You can also make a derived class a friend class of the base class. The private members of a base class cannot be accessed by the derived class. Declaring the derived class as a friend to the base class, instead, does the trick. When a friend class is derived from a base class, the friend class inherits all the members of the base class. That idea is best expressed by the fact that you do not need to pass the object of the base class to the method of the friend class to give you the same output.

The question that would arise in your mind now is why did we not make the members of the base class public or protected so they could be inherited by the derived class?

The fact is that a base class can give birth to a lineage of derived classes. Making the members public or protected would leave them open to every derived member down the line. So you restrict their access by naming a few friends. Only the friend derived classes can access all the members of the base class. That's eating your cake and having it too.

So let's encapsulate that in a program:

```
PROGRAM 112
#include <iostream.h>

class FClass;

class Class
{
    int i;
    friend  FClass;
};

class FClass : Class
{
    public:
    void get(void)
    { i = 5; cout << i << "\n"; }
};

main( )
{
    FClass pal;
    pal.get( );
}
```

That was a good example of holding the reins to data in your own hands. Having understood those basics, let's go into newer streams.

Friends Forever

Multiple inheritances and the way friend classes behave in long lineages. That's the realm we're shifting to. Take this program to get you going:

```
PROGRAM 113
#include <iostream.h>

class ClassOne
{
```

```
    int i;
    friend  class FClass;
};

class ClassTwo
{
    int i;
    friend  class FClass;
};

class FClass :  public ClassOne,public ClassTwo
{
    public:
    void get(void)
    { i = 5; cout << i << "\n"; }
};

main( )
{
    FClass pal;
    pal.get( );
}
```

FClass is the friend to both the base classes, *ClassOne* and *ClassTwo*. So when the method *get( )* of the friend class is invoked, there is ambiguity about the data member to be accessed. It is flummoxed about which *i*, among the *i*s of the two base classes is being referred to.

How can this error be corrected? Through the symbol ::, of course.

PROGRAM 114

```
#include <iostream.h>

class ClassOne
{
    int i;
    friend  class FClass;
};

class ClassTwo
{
```

```
    int i;
    friend  class FClass;
};

class FClass : public ClassOne,public ClassTwo
{
    public:
    void get(void)
    {
       ClassOne::i = 5;
       cout << ClassOne::i << "\n";
    }
};

main( )
{
    FClass pal;
    pal.get( );
}
```

Now the method of the friend class knows exactly which *i* is being talked about, and it will access the right *i* of the right base class. The output you'll get, 5, is testimony to that fact.

Nested Classes

Having got so close to friends of classes, let's leave them for a while and go exploring other regions. For instance, classes within classes, so appropriately called nested classes.

Here's a small program to get us started:

PROGRAM 115

```
#include <iostream.h>

class Class
{
    private:
    int i;
    class Cosy
    {
        int j;
```

```
    public:
    void setvali(Class x)
    { x.i = 5; cout << x.i << "\n"; }
};
    public:
    void setvalj(Cosy y)
    { y.j = 15; cout << y.j; }
};

main( )
{
    Class Home;
    Cosy bed;
    Home.setvalj(bed);
    bed.setvali(Home);
}
```

Nestled in the bosom of the class *Class* is a private class called *Cosy*. *Class* contains, apart from another class, a private data member *i* and a public method *setvalj( )*. *Cosy* has a private member *j* and a public method *setvali( )*. So far, so good.

Try initializing the private data member of the nested class through the method of the class it is nesting in, or vice-versa, and you'll get an error. Which proves that by nesting a class within a class, does not leave the involved classes open to manipulation by each other.

Access would still be possible if you wrote a program like this:

PROGRAM 116

```
#include <iostream.h>

class Class
{
    private:
    int i;
    class Cosy
    {
        int j;
        public:
        void setvalj(void)
```

```
        { j = 10; cout << j << "\n"; }
    }bed;
    public:
    void setvali(void) { bed.setvalj( );}
};

main( )
{
    Class x;
    Cosy y;
    x.setvali( );
    y.setvalj( );
}
```

Cosy is, of course, the class nestling in the class *Class*. *Cosy* has a private member *j*, a public method *setvalj( )* and an object declared in the class definition itself, *bed*.

The class that *Cosy* is nested in - for our purpose, let's refer to it as the home class, has a public method which accesses the data member of the class *Cosy* through its method *setvalj( )*. This method can be accessed only because of the data member *bed* which is an object of the class *Cosy*. Thus *x.setvali( )* indirectly accesses the member of the nested class, while *y.setvalj( )* accesses it directly.

We won't go into impossible details about classes nested cosily in their home classes. Just remember that they are there to be picked, and as and when you feel their need, pluck them out of the text and use them.

Local Classes

Here's one more statement we'd like to make, one more little something you must see before you get into deeper waters. Local classes and what they mean.

PROGRAM 117

#include <iostream.h>

void get(void)

```
{
    class Class
    {
      public:
      void show(void)
      { cout << "Hello World"; }
    };
    Class x;
    x.show( );
}

main( )
{
    get( );
}
```

Hello World. That is achieved through a very simple sequence of events. You have a function *get( )*, which is called in the *main( )*. *get( )* has a local class defined within it, *Class*. That class has a public method *show( )*. *show( )* sends a message to the object *x* of the class *Class* and Hello World is duly printed at the end of that chain of reactions.

The local class, of course behaves like all local variables. The class dies a silent death when the function is exited.

All we're trying to emphasize is that Object Oriented Programming is really no big deal. Old features in new garbs. Keep that in mind as we go along to tougher sounding nuts and pompous-looking *isms*. But we'll go slowly, so we can acclimatize leisurely, get ready for the tough stretch.

Slight 'isms'

First, a simple program:

PROGRAM 118
#include <iostream.h>

class BClass
{

```
   public:
   void print(void)
   { cout << "In class BClass\n"; }
};

class DClass : public BClass
{
   public:
   void print(void)
   { cout << "In class DClass\n"; }
};

main( )
{
   DClass y1;
   y1.print( );
}
```

When the base class and the derived class have methods with the same name, how do the methods behave? Who gets precedence and who leads the march? If you look at the printout that you get at the end of this run,

```
In class DClass
```

it should be quite obvious that the method in the derived class simply overrides the method in the base class.

Now let's visualize that at multiple levels:

```
PROGRAM 119
#include <iostream.h>

class BClass
{
   public:
   void print(void)
   { cout << "In class BClass\n"; }
};

class DClass : public BClass
{
```

```
    public:
    void print(void)
    { cout << "In class DClass\n"; }
};

class TGClass : public DClass
{
    public:
    void print(void)
    { cout << "In class TGClass\n"; }
};

main( )
{
    BClass x1;
    DClass y1;
    TGClass tg;
    x1.print( );
    y1.print( );
    tg.print( );
}
```

We have here three objects of three classes in an hierarchical tree. Each class has its own *print( )* method. And each object will call its own personal *print( )* to give you the following output:

```
In class BClass
In class DClass
In class TGClass
```

In the concept of inheritances, that was one important patch we've framed completely. Let's go to another. And the joy of all things in C, pointers.

Pointers To Objects

How do pointers figure in C++ and OOPs? To begin with, like we had pointers pointing to integers and characters and strings, we now have pointers pointing to objects. Objects are, after all, instances of user-defined datatypes, just as variables were instances of standard datatypes. Most of Object Oriented Programming is only so much jargon, remember?!

PROGRAM 120

```
#include <iostream.h>

class Class
{
    int i;
    public:
    void print(void)
    { i = 5; cout << i <<"\n";}
};

main( )
{
    Class *x1;
    x1 -> print( );
}
```

You'll know without having to be told that *x1* is a pointer to a class, *Class*. If *x1* had been an object of the class, it would be appropriate to use *x1.print( )*. Since it is a pointer, we use the notation *x1 -> print( )*. The answer to this problem would, of course, be 5.

But do you think that code is sensible. Sure, it didn't generate an error. But we think code should be more carefully written. We'd prefer to use a pointer to a class, like this:

PROGRAM 121

```
#include <iostream.h>

class BClass
{
    int i;
    public:
    void print(void)
    { i = 5; cout << i <<"\n";}
};
```

```
main( )
{
    BClass *x1;
    BClass x;
    x1 = &x;
    x1 -> print( );
}
```

What we do is first define an object, pass the address of the object to the pointer and then access the methods of the object through the pointer. The output here will be no different from the first one. But then all we're saying is, that's our style.

Now consider pointers to classes at two levels: the base class and the derived class.

PROGRAM 122

```
#include <iostream.h>

class BClass
{
    public:
    void print(void)
    { cout << "In class BClass\n"; }
};

class DClass : public BClass
{
    public:
    void print(void)
    { cout << "In class DClass\n"; }
};

main( )
{
    BClass x1,*bp;
    DClass y1;
    bp = &x1;
    bp -> print( );
    bp = &y1;
    bp -> print( );
}
```

We have methods in the base and the derived classes with the same name. When you accessed the methods directly through the derived class objects, the method of the derived class overrode the method of the base class. Do pointers behave any differently?

Look at the printout you get before you answer that:

```
In class BClass
In class BClass
```

Which means that however painstakingly you give the pointer another address, it will continue to access the methods of the base class.

Now let's follow the movements of a pointer through a multitiered hierarchy:

PROGRAM 123

```
#include <iostream.h>

class BClass
{
    public:
    void print(void)
    { cout << "In class BClass\n"; }
};

class DClass : public BClass
{
    public:
    void print(void)
    { cout << "In class DClass\n"; }
};

class TGClass : public DClass
{
    public:
    void print(void)
    { cout << "In class TGClass\n"; }
};

main( )
```

```
{
    BClass *bp,x1;
    DClass y1;
    TGClass tg;
    bp = &x1;
    bp -> print( );
    bp = &y1;
    bp -> print( );
    bp = &tg;
    bp -> print( );
}
```

The printout you'll get will be:

```
In class BClass
In class BClass
In class BClass
```

Which means that the logic for single derivations is the same as that for multiple derivations. The pointer will keep accessing the method of the object of the base class.

Casting Pointers

How do we tide over that small issue? How do we get the pointer to access a method of the derived class?

Take this program:

PROGRAM 124

```
#include <iostream.h>

class BClass
{
    public:
    void print(void)
    { cout << "in class BClass\n"; }
};
```

```
class DClass : public BClass
{

public:
   void print(void)
   { cout << "in class DClass\n"; }
};

main( )
{
   BClass *bp,x1;
   DClass y1;

   bp = &x1;
   bp -> print( );

   bp = &y1;
   bp -> print( );
   ((DClass *)bp) -> print( );
}
```

What you can do is cast the pointer. Casting is certainly not an alien concept. In this instance we are casting the pointer to access the object of the derived class *DClass*. Now you'll get the right printout through the pointer.

The output:

```
In class BClass
In class BClass
In class DClass
```

The last printout is the result of the explicit casting you indulged in.

But while you're casting the pointer, you needn't even pass it the address of the derived class. The minute you cast it to access the object of the derived class, it does so without being given the address. Take this program. And run it to double-check.

PROGRAM 125

```
#include <iostream.h>

class BClass
{
    public:
    void print(void)
    { cout << "In class BClass\n";}
};

class DClass : public BClass
{
    public:
    void print(void)
    { cout << "In class DClass\n";}
};

main( )
{
    BClass *bp,x1;
    bp = &x1;
    bp -> print( );
    ((DClass *)bp) -> print( );
}
```

The output?

```
In class BClass
In class DClass
```

Now let's see typecasting at multiple levels:

PROGRAM 126

```
#include <iostream.h>

class BClass
{
    public:
    void print(void)
    { cout << "In class BClass\n";}
};
```

```
class DClass : public BClass
{
    public:
    void print(void)
    { cout << "In class DClass\n";}
};

class TGClass : public DClass
{
    public:
    void print(void)
    { cout << "In class TGClass\n";}
};

main( )
{
    BClass *bp,x1;

    bp = &x1;
    bp -> print( );

    ((DClass *)bp) -> print( );
    ((TGClass *)bp) -> print( );
}
```

To get the pointer to access the methods of the derived classes down the line, you cast the pointer to each object. It's absolutely elementary. The output will be:

```
In class BClass
In class DClass
In class TGClass
```

The 'ism' - Polymorphism

The stage is now set for another zinger of a term in Object Oriented lingo. More of a term surrounded by a lot of magic and mystique,alot of advertising hype glamorizing a very simple concept, rather than a new and revolutionary idea itself. Like the new improved variety of the same old detergent soap. Polymorphism.

Polymorphism has been the butt of a great many jokes by brave and fearless men like Jeff Dunteman who gagged, "(Polymorphism)... sounds more like a developmental defect in parrots than a programming technique...". As the dictionary would reveal, polymorphism comes from the Greek word for "having many forms".

Where have we seen a single entity with multiple forms in C++. Raise your eyes skyward and ... that's right, function overloading and operator overloading! That's polymorphism for you. A designer tag on recycled goods.

Seriously, polymorphism is nothing but the ability to access different implementations of a function using the same name.

There are two levels at which polymorphism operates. Compile-time polymorphism and run-time polymorphism. Without realizing it, we handled compile-time polymorphism like we would shuffle a pack of cards. Function overloading and operator overloading were the twin aces of compile-time polymorphism. Let's turn to run- time polymorphism now.

Virtual Functions And Polymorphism

Run-time polymorphism stands on two basic features: virtual functions and derived classes. We've touched upon derived classes at some length. Let's talk about virtual functions.

A program to set the path:

PROGRAM 127

```
#include <iostream.h>

class BClass
{
    public:
    virtual void print(void)
    { cout << "In class BClass\n";}
```

```
};

class DClass : public BClass
{
    public:
    void print(void)
    { cout << "In class DClass\n";}
};


main( )
{
    BClass *bp,x1;
    DClass y1;

    bp = &x1;
    bp -> print( );

    bp = &y1;
    bp -> print( );
}
```

Not only does the use of the word *virtual*, prefixed to the method in the base class, remove the necessity for typecasting the pointer to access the method of the object in the derived class, but it also increases runtime efficiency. Like function overloading, which decided at compile-time what function, among many with the same name, had to be called, a virtual function decides which method has to be called at runtime, depending on the type of object pointed to.

Take the program above. The pointer is now ready to accept the address of the object of the derived class because the method invoked has been declared a *virtual* one. C++, at runtime, executes the relevant version of the virtual function on the basis of the object pointed to.

The output you'll receive will be:

In class BClass
In class DClass

The same format works for multiple derivations as well. Take a program again:

PROGRAM 128

```
#include <iostream.h>

class BClass
{
    public:
    virtual void print(void)
    { cout << "In class BClass\n";}
};

class DClass : public BClass
{
    public:
    void print(void)
    { cout << "In class DClass\n";}
};

class TGClass : public DClass
{
    public:
    void print(void)
    { cout << "In class TGClass\n";}
};

main( )
{
    BClass *bp,x1;
    DClass y1;
    TGClass tg;

    bp = &x1;
    bp -> print( );

    bp = &y1;
    bp -> print( );

    bp = &tg;
    bp -> print( );
}
```

The output will be:

In class BClass
In class DClass
In class TGClass

That means that one single inscription of the term *virtual* attached to the declaration of the method in the base class, is enough to call the appropriate virtual function.

Take another example of multiple derivations:

PROGRAM 129

```
#include <iostream.h>

class BClass
{
    public:
    virtual void print(void)
    { cout << "In class BClass\n";}
};

class DClass : public BClass
{
    public:
    void print(void)
    { cout << "In class DClass\n";}
};

class TGClass : public DClass
{

};

main( )
{
    BClass *bp,x1;
    DClass y1;
    TGClass tg;
    bp = &x1;
    bp -> print( );
    bp = &y1;
```

```
    bp -> print( );
    bp = &tg;
    bp -> print( );
}
```

TGClass, here, does not have its own method *print( )*. So who will it borrow from? *BClass* or *DClass*? Look at the printout for the answer:

In class BClass
In class DClass
In class DClass

Let's tamper a little with the program:

PROGRAM 130

```
#include <iostream.h>

class BClass
{
    int i;
    public:
    virtual void print(void)
    { i = 5; cout << i <<"\n";}
};

class DClass : public BClass
{
    int i;
    public:
    int print(void)
    { i = 10; cout << i << "\n";return i;}
};

main( )
{
    BClass *x1,x2;
    DClass y1;
    x1 = &x2;
    x1 -> print( );
```

```
    x1 = &y1;
    x1 ->print( );
}
```

Error! Virtual function 'DClass::print( )' conflicts with 'BClass::print( )'.

That's because, while defining the virtual function, you have specifically stated that it will return a *void*. In the derived class, then, you cannot have the method return an *int*. That's where the error lies.

Pure Virtual Functions And Abstract Classes

Let's go to another area of virtual functions. Pure virtual functions. Look at the following program before we get into detailed theorization:

```
PROGRAM 131
#include <iostream.h>

class BClass
{
    public:
    virtual void print(void) = 0;
};

class DClass : public BClass
{
    public:
    void print(void)
    { cout << "in class DClass\n";}
};

main( )
{
    BClass x1
    DClass y1;
}
```

Not another error! To understand the error we have to first understand the concept of abstract classes.

A class that contains a pure virtual function is called an abstract class. Objects of an abstract class cannot be defined. But how does the compiler recognize a pure virtual function and an abstract class. The initialization of the virtual function to 0 is what tells the compiler that the virtual function referred to is a pure virtual function and the class it is enclosed within is an abstract class.

Thus, in our case, *virtual void print(void) = 0* intimates the compiler about this special function and class.

If objects cannot be defined for an abstract class, why do we need abstract classes at all?

Abstract classes are simply used to derive child classes. The derived class inherits all the members of the abstract class. And of what use is it practically? Well, that's what we'll see as we go through some non-erroneous programs.

PROGRAM 132

```
#include <iostream.h>

class BClass
{
    public:
    virtual void print(void) = 0;
};

class DClass : public BClass
{
    public:
    void print(void)
    { cout << "in class DClass\n";}
};

main( )
{
```

```
    BClass *bp;
    DClass y1;
    bp = &y1;
    bp -> print( );
}
```

You can define a pointer to an abstract class, even if you cannot define an object of its type. Through the pointer, as usual, you can go about using the tools of virtual functions and polymorphism.

Here's a program that you should read as carefully as if it were an instruction manual to a high voltage electrical unit.

PROGRAM 133

```
#include <iostream.h>

class BClass
{
    public:
    virtual void print(void) = 0;
};

class DClass : public BClass
{
    public:
    void print(void)
    { cout << "In class DClass\n";}
};

class TGClass : public BClass
{
    // error - pure function print( ) not overridden in TGClass
};

main( )
{
    BClass *bp;
    DClass y1;
    TGClass tg;

    bp = &y1;
```

```
    bp -> print( );

    bp = &tg;
    bp -> print( );
}
```

Before we go into detailed descriptions, let's understand the error. Classes derived from an abstract base class must have their own version of the virtual method.

The essence of polymorphism is, in fact, hidden in the annals of this erroneous program.

Consider a group of three objects derived from three different classes, each springing from the same root. The root is an abstract class defined with the virtual function *edit*. It is mandatory now for each of the derived classes to have their own *edit* method as well, each *edit* being unique to its class.

Whenever the message *edit* is sent, it is internally decided which *edit* among the three has to be invoked. Each *edit* is, after all, special to each object.

It's like a camel. To the Bedouin, the camel is a survival kit, to a citizen of New York City it's just something to gawk at in the zoo. So, when you refer to a camel in a Bedouinian context, you elicit a totally different recall from that generated in the urban American context.

That's polymorphism for you. Calling the right version of a function in the right context.

Some Homework

And now that we've understood the basics of polymorphism, virtual functions and derived classes, let's look at some brain-teasers:

PROGRAM 134

```
#include <iostream.h>
```

```
class obedient_robot
{
    public:
    void add(int a,int b)
    { cout << "Yes master the answer is " << a+b << "\n"; }
};

class disobedient_robot
{
    public:
    void add(int a,int b)
    { cout << "I don't feel like adding\n"; }
};

main( )
{
    obedient_robot no5;
    disobedient_robot hal;

    no5.add(40,2);
    hal.add(2,2);
}
```

The printout you'll get is:

Yes master the answer is 42
I don't feel like adding

The former was the outcome of the invocation of the method of the object *no5* of the class *obedient_robot*. The latter, the method of the object *hal* of the class *disobedient_robot*.

And another example:

PROGRAM 135

```
#include <iostream.h>

class obedient_robot
{
    public:
    void add(int a,int b)
    { cout << "Yes master the answer is " << a+b << "\n"; }
```

```
};

class disobedient_robot : public obedient_robot
{
    public:
    void add(int a,int b)
    { cout << "I don't feel like adding"; }
};

main( )
{
    obedient_robot no5;
    disobedient_robot hal;
    no5.add(35,7);
    hal.add(2,2);
}
```

Sure, the output will be the same as the previous one, but the route to the output is what is different. In the previous program, both the classes were distinctly unconnected. This one is an instance of a derived class.

The output is the result of an overriding of the method of the base class *obedient_robot*, by the method of the derived class *disobedient_robot*. So each object will invoke its own method *add( )* for the desired output:

Yes master the answer is 42
I don't feel like adding

Now solve this one on your own:

PROGRAM 136

```
#include <iostream.h>

class obedient_robot
{
    public:
    void add(int a,int b)
    { cout << "Yes master the answer is " << a+b << "\n"; }
};
```

```
class disobedient_robot : public obedient_robot
{
    public:
    void add(int a,int b)
    { cout << "I don't feel like adding"; }
};

main( )
{
    obedient_robot *no5 = new obedient_robot;
    obedient_robot *hal = new disobedient_robot;
    no5 -> add(40,2);
    hal -> add(2,2);
}
```

What will the output be?

Both the *obedient_robot* and the *disobedient_robot* will click their heels to give you the same answer:

Yes master the answer is 42

So how did the *disobedient_robot* talk like the *obedient_robot*? The answer is simple. The pointers, *no5* and *hal* were made to point to the base class with the idea that we could then shift them to the methods of objects of other derived classes as well. But if you remember, that's not the right way to do it. The pointer will continue to access the method of the object in the base class even if you give it the address of the derived class. Hence, the output you got.

What was the solution to that? One was casting the pointer to access the derived class. And the other, easier and more convenient - virtual functions. So let's look at a program with a virtual function:

PROGRAM 137
```
#include <iostream.h>

class obedient_robot
{
```

```
    public:
    virtual void add(int a,int b)
    { cout << "Yes master the answer is " << a+b << "\n"; }
};

class disobedient_robot : public obedient_robot
{
    public:
    void add(int a,int b)
    { cout << "I don't feel like adding"; }
};

main( )
{
    obedient_robot *no5 = new obedient_robot;
    obedient_robot *hal = new disobedient_robot;
    no5 -> add(40,2);
    hal -> add(2,2);
}
```

The term *virtual* prefixed to the method *add( )* in the base class solves the problem. Each object then gets its own *add( )* to work for it. The relevant version of the virtual function will be called for the concerned object. So the pointer will access the method differently for the two objects. The output you'll get, thanks to the principles of polymorphism, will be:

```
Yes master the answer is 42
I don't feel like adding
```

Arrays In Polymorphism

Let's use an array of pointers to do the same thing. Will it work or won't it?

PROGRAM 138

```
#include <iostream.h>

class obedient_robot
{
    public:
    void add(int a,int b)
```

```
    { cout << "Yes master the answer is " << a+b << "\n";}
};

class disobedient_robot :public obedient_robot
{
    public:
    void add(int a,int b)
    { cout << "I don't feel like adding"; }
};

main( )
{
    obedient_robot *clan[2];

    clan[0] = new obedient_robot;
    clan[1] = new disobedient_robot;
    clan[0] -> add(40,2);
    clan[1] -> add(2,2);
}
```

This again will not work in the way you want it to. Both the robots will mouth the same phrase:

Yes master the answer is 42

So what caused the circuit of the *disobedient_robot* to fuse? The fact is that *clan[ ]* is an array of pointers pointing to the base class, *obedient_robot*. Which means that both the pointers access the method of the object in the base class. It is absolutely essential thus to have the virtual function defined in the base class.

What do you think about this program? Go through it carefully. Will polymorphism operate or not?

PROGRAM 139

```
#include <iostream.h>

class robot
{
    public:
    virtual void greeting (void)
```

```
    { cout << "At your command master \n";}
};

class robot_from_2001 : public robot
{
    public:
    void greeting (int unused_arg)
    { cout << "Daisy, Daisy,...\n"; }
};

main( )
{
    robot *robbie = new robot;
    robot *hal = new robot_from_2001;

    robbie -> greeting( );
    hal -> greeting( );
}
```

The output?

At your command master
At your command master

Whoa! Where's the problem now? You've defined the function *greeting( )* in the base class as a virtual function. There does not seem to be any obvious overlooking or overloading of elements? Or is there?

The most irresponsible act here is passing different parameters to the method *greeting( )* in the base class and the derived class. The virtual function *greeting( )* has been passed a void, while the method *greeting( )* of the derived class *robot_from_2001* has an *int* passed to it. For polymorphism to be effective, not only should names of the methods be identical in the derived and base classes, but the parameters passed to them should be identical too.

robbie -> greeting( ) and *hal -> greeting( )* accessed the method of the same object, since *greeting(int unused_arg)* was looked at as another function altogether, and not another version of the virtual function declared in the base class.

Using The '::' Operator

Let's try working the other way around, from the tail up so to speak.

PROGRAM 140

```
#include <iostream.h>

class robot
{
    public:
    void greeting(void)
    { cout << "At your command master\n"; }
};

class robot_from_2001 : public robot
{
    public:
    void greeting(void)
    { cout << "Daisy,Daisy,.....\n"; }
};

main( )
{
    robot_from_2001 hal;
    hal.greeting( );
    hal.robot::greeting( );
}
```

Let's pin the output down before we get into the intricacies of this program:

Daisy, Daisy,.....
At your command master

For the actual program now. *hal* is an object of the derived class *robot_from_2001*. You've first called the method *greeting( )* of this object to give you the output Daisy, Daisy,..... But if you scrutinize the entire output, you'll realize that the method of the object of the base class also got invoked. How?

Because of the last line of the program, *hal.robot::greeting( )*. *::* indicates that the method of the level higher up, that is of the base class, should be invoked. If you recall, we used *::* to access the global variable. In a sense, then, isn't the base class also the umbrella of the derived class? The logic is the same. *::* helps you access the level above.

Let's see how that works for multiple levels:

PROGRAM 141

```
#include <iostream.h>

class robot
{
   public:
   void greeting(void)
   { cout << "At your command master\n"; }
};

class robot_from_2001 : public robot
{
   public:
   void greeting(void)
   { cout << "Daisy,Daisy,......\n"; }
};

class robot_in_Mars : public robot_from_2001
{
   public:
   void greeting(void)
   { cout << " Poppy Poop\n"; }
};

main( )
{
   robot_in_Mars hal;
   hal.greeting( );
   hal.robot_from_2001::greeting( );
   hal.robot::greeting( );
}
```

Starting with the youngest derived class, *robot_in_Mars*, we define an object *hal* of that class, and invoke the method *greeting( )* of the object of that class. Using *::* we can access the right level of the base class by inserting the name of the class we wish to access.

Thus, the above program will give you this output:

Poppy Poop
Daisy, Daisy,.....
At your command master

Smooth operator, this C++, isn't it!

That was the "what" of polymorphism. The "why" is unquestionably obvious. The "how" is what we have to tackle now.

Late Binding

Polymorphism functions through a process called late binding.

In the process of compiling a program, what you get is an *.OBJ* file, with the references to the various functions. At the linking stage, these externals are resolved to get an *.EXE* file. This type of linking is referred to as early binding.

As against early binding is late binding. The platform on which polymorphism rests. In this kind of binding process, the externals are resolved not at link-time, but at run-time. It is only at run-time that the decision about the function pointed to can be made. Without this facility polymorphism would have remained an exciting idea that would never have seen the light of day.

That's all there is to C++. That dreaded package that everyone is scared to prise open. There were no jack in the boxes or hidden daggers, were there? C++, in fact, makes programming a lark. The inherent issues and the morsels that coagulate to give it substance are so fascinatingly simple, they make life a rainbowed playground.

Your first lessons are over. You can now read on fluently. And carry on as effortlessly as strolling in the garden.

Streams

Let's get into the more elegant and sophisticated realm of C++. Most languages incorporating Object Oriented Programming, like SmallTalk, Actor, etc, arrive with a lot of useful luggage. These baggages, mostly handy classes that you may need along the way, take the load off your shoulders. They're designed to make your journey as light-weight as it possibly can get. Rather than being additional burdens that retard your progress, these extras make your steps a great deal lighter.

C++, in keeping with this tradition, brings with it an elegant array of classes that handle streams flowing in and out relentlessly. The signals that control this input/output traffic, abbreviated to I/O System, are housed in the header file iostream.h.

In the header, is a class called *streambuf*, a base class in a sense. The next class in the hierarchy is *ios*. *ios* is the structure that provides the means for formatting the streams. *istream*, *ostream* and *iostream* are three classes derived from this class. An input stream can be created from *istream*, an output stream from *ostream* and a double-edged stream that deals with both input and output, from *iostream*.

The Output Stream

Let's start with the *ostream* candidate *cout* and discover how it enriches our repertoire:

PROGRAM 142

```
#include <iostream.h>

main( )
{
    cout << " Hello World \n";
}
```

We've worked with *cout* before. We used it instead of the clumsier *printf( )*. The syntax that *cout* uses is also simple: the symbol << preceding the string, character or integer to be printed. Let's understand *cout* better.

Take another program:

PROGRAM 143

```
#include <iostream.h>

main( )
{
    int i = 35;
    char *str = "This is cout";

    cout << i << "\n" << str ;
}
```

The output?

```
35
This is cout
```

Which means that without being told in so many words, *cout* was able to recognize the integer and the string and print them out. *printf( )* would have needed a *%d* and a *%s* to do the same thing. *printf( )* is thus bulkier and in a sense, cruder than *cout*. The << isolates each segment to be printed. The three elements in the above example, *i*, *\n* and *str* are each appended into the stream by <<. That is all *cout* demands.

The Input Stream

iostream comes in handy for basic input-output operations. *cout* is associated with the output stream, i.e. it prints to the standard output device, the screen. Let's look at an instance of the input stream.

PROGRAM 144

```
#include <iostream.h>
```

```
main( )
{
    int a;
    cout << "Enter a number: ";
    cin >> a;
    cout << "The number is: " << a ;
}
```

cin takes input from the standard input device - the keyboard. So whatever you type in will be taken by *cin* into the variable provided for the purpose, *a* in our case. *cout*, of course, deals directly with the output stream, and you have the relevant message on your screen. Your output will resemble this:

```
Enter a number: 28
The number is: 28
```

28, of course, is the number we keyed in.

The Methods Of Formatting

Let's go into more detail:

PROGRAM 145

```
#include <iostream.h>

main( )
{
    cout.setf(ios::showpos);
    cout << "\n" << 546 << " " << 340.23 << " ";
    cout.setf(ios::scientific);
    cout << "\n" << 340.23 ;
}
```

The output you get is:

```
+546 +340.23
+3.4023e+02
```

Where did that spaced-out output come from? Where did that format materialize from?

That is the facility given to you by *cout* and the method *setf( )* defined in the header file *iostream.h.*

setf( ) is a method that allows you to format your output in various ways, depending on the parameters passed to it. Take *ios::showpos* in the above example. *showpos* is, in other words, a member of the class *ios*. *showpos* represents a certain value in the class. A value that lends a certain kind of format - the symbol + in front of positive numbers.

ios::scientific similarly gives you the scientific notation of a number. Various such formatting styles are available in the class *ios* - left alignment, upper case conversion, octal decimals and many others.

And because C - and therefore C++ - have always been flexible and programmer-friendly languages, allowing you to lessen lines and repetitions in the code, here's what you can also do:

PROGRAM 146

```
#include <iostream.h>

main( )
{
    cout.setf(ios::showpos | ios::scientific);
    cout << "\nHello world  " << 546 << " " << 340.23 << " ";
}
```

By using the *Or* symbol *|*, you restrict the function calls to one. This means that in one call to *setf( )*, you can set as many format styles as you want. Just use the *|* symbol to designate multiple formats at one time. The output you'll get when you run this program will be:

Hello World +546 +3.4023e+02

Now take another format type:

PROGRAM 147

```
#include <iostream.h>

main( )
{
    cout.setf(ios::showpos | ios::showpoint);
    cout << "\n" << 546 << " " << 340.23 << " ";
}
```

The output will be:

+546 +340.230000

This means that *showpoint* gave you up to six decimal places for the floating number. And so on and so forth. To be precise, 15 various formatting tendencies are recognized in *ios*.

Let's introduce ourselves to another method now:

PROGRAM 148

```
#include <iostream.h>

main( )
{
    cout.setf(ios::showpos);
    cout.setf(ios::left);
    cout.width(20);
    cout.fill('$');

    cout << "Hello world";
}
```

width( ) and *fill( )* are a couple of very interesting methods. *width( )* delimits an area within which the string is printed. *fill( )* stuffs the unused spaces within the field with whatever character you pass it. In the above program *width( )* chalks out 20 spaces for the field. The space left over by the printing of the string is planted with $ symbols by *fill( )*.

Hello World, for example, which takes up 11 spaces will be printed and the 9 spaces left over will be padded with $ signs.

Further, *left* in the function *setf( )* left-aligns the output. You'll have an output that will look like this:

Hello World$$$$$$$$$

Let's go further into other engrossing functions in the iostream header.

PROGRAM 149

```
#include <iostream.h>

main( )
{
    cout.precision(2);
    cout.width(10);

    cout << 123 << " " << 123.34823 << "\n";

    cout.fill('#');
    cout.width(10);

    cout << 123 << " " << 123.23;
}
```

cout.width(10) demarcates the width of the field for the printing to be done in. *cout.precision( )*, the new addition here, prints the floating number upto the prescribed decimal figure. In the program above, we have set that figure at 2, so up to 2 decimal places will be outputted. Take a look at the output:

```
    123 123.35
######123 123.23
```

What strikes the eye immediately is that the output is right justified. But there's no parameter you can recognize in the program that could possibly be responsible for this. Obviously then, the answer is "default". There are two kinds of alignments possible. To align output to the left, you have to explicitly call the relevant method. If you do not put your preference down, you'll get a right aligned output by default.

Another fact that hits you is that in both *cout*s only the first figure responds to the call of the *width( )* method. That's the way things work, though. That is, the first number in both the cases is formatted in keeping with the width set. The second numbers are printed minus the format. If you want the second number to be formatted, you'd have to state that specifically.

Let's put several of those elements together and work with them:

PROGRAM 150

```
#include <iostream.h>

main( )
{
cout.setf(ios::right);
cout << 546 << " " << 123.234506 << "\n";

cout.precision(2);
cout.fill('0');
cout.width(10);
cout << 546 << " " << 123.234506 << "\n";

cout.setf(ios::left);
cout.fill(' ');
cout.width(10);
cout << 546 << " " << 123.234506;
}
```

We've called the *setf( )* method twice here. First with a specific right alignment parameter and next, with a left aligned one. The program doesn't really need an explanation from us. So we'll take our voices away and leave you just the output to double check with:

```
546 123.234506
0000000546 123.23
546       123.23
```

That was a simple demonstration of a simple project.

Manipulators

Let's now understand what are called manipulators. In the precluding section, the object *cout* called the methods that formatted the output. Manipulators, on the other hand, allow you to add the functions into the stream itself, reducing program lines even further.

Output Manipulators

Let's get going with an example:

PROGRAM 151

```
#include <iostream.h>
#include <iomanip.h>

main( )
{
    cout << setprecision(2) << 1000.248 ;
    cout << setw(20) << "Hello there.";
}
```

Note the inclusion of another header file, iomanip.h. The manipulator tags have all been defined in this file.

setprecision( ) does exactly what *cout.precision( )* did. Set the number of decimal places to be printed. And *setw( )* performs the job of *cout.width( )*: defining the size of the field. There is no difference at all in the way they format the output. So without further ado, let's jump to the output:

1000.25   Hello there.

If we hadn't roped in *setw(20)*, Hello World would have looked like a code for a space program: 1000.25HelloWorld. So, thank God for little mercies like *setw( )* that helps us format the output in the appropriate fashion.

Here's another small program:

PROGRAM 152

```
#include <iostream.h>
#include <iomanip.h>

main( )
{
    cout << setprecision(2) << 1000.243 << endl;
    cout << setw(20) << "Hello there.";
}
```

endl is a manipulator that does the same job as a \n. It takes the rest of the stream on to the next line. *endl*, which is only used in association with the output stream, also flushes the stream if it is buffered.

The *setf( )* methods of formatting also come in some other interesting and abridged forms. Like this:

PROGRAM 153

```
#include <iostream.h>
#include <iomanip.h>

main( )
{
    cout << setiosflags(ios::showpos);
    cout << 123 << " " << 123.23;
}
```

setf( ), the method called by the object *cout*, is replaced by *setiosflags( )*. If you separate the weaves of that term, you'll realize that three distinct terms can be discerned: *set*, *ios* and *flags*. And that's exactly what it does. Sets the *ios* flags depending on the parameter passed. We've already dealt with *showpos*. Look at the output for reconfirmation:

+123 +123.23

That was all about output manipulators. But all these, except for *endl* which is purely an output manipulator, are also input manipulators. Before we close this discussion, it would be in order to spare a few words for the operation of the input manipulator.

Input Manipulators

PROGRAM 154

```
#include <iostream.h>

main( )
{
    char s[80];
    cin >> ws >> s;
    cout << s;
}
```

Run this program. Leave some silent white spaces and type in your name. Like this:

SantaClaus

This will be outputted as:

SantaClaus

Since when did Santa's reindeers become space eating monsters? Well, ever since you introduced *ws* in the program. *ws* is a pure input manipulator that chucks out leading spaces. Take *ws* out of the code and spaces and all will be left alone.

Customized Manipulators

We've been hangers-on long enough. But as connoisseurs of C, we're used to creativity. So how about building our own manipulators?

PROGRAM 155

```
#include <iostream.h>
#include <iomanip.h>

ostream &setup(ostream &st)
{
```

```
        st.setf(ios::left);
        st << setw(10) << setfill('$');
        return st;
}

main()
{
    cout << 10 << " " << setup << 10;
}
```

setup is the manipulator we've built. *setup* succeeds in performing multiple tasks. These tasks have been elucidated by us to include various formatting flags. A call to the function *setup* will bring the three functions enumerated - *setf( )*, *setw( )* and *setfill( )* - in its wake.

The output you'll get will be:

10 10$$$$$$$$

setf(ios::left) left-aligned the output, *setw( )* set the width of the output field and *setfill( )* hammered $ signs into the remaining spaces. And all this was done only for the second 10. Simply because we called *setup* to set the stage only for it.

That was an output manipulator we created. Let's create an input manipulator. The process for building it is the same as that used for the output manipulator.

PROGRAM 156

```
#include <iostream.h>
#include <iomanip.h>

istream &prompt(istream &st)
{
    st >> hex;
    return st;
}

main()
{
    int i;
```

```
cout << "\n Enter a HEX number : 0x";
cin >> prompt >> i;
cout << "\nThe number in decimal : " << i;
}
```

The input manipulator is *prompt*. All we did was change the *ostream* tag to *istream*. When the prompt to key in a hex number is followed and you've keyed in the number, the stream is returned. Consider that you've keyed in the hex number 10, 0x10, then the output you'll get will be:

The number in decimal: 16

That is, the decimal value of the hexa-decimal number 10, is 16.

Classes And Stream Objects

We've studied them all separately - the intricacies of the input-output streams, how to use standard manipulators and how to custom-build our own. Let's put all that knowledge to some practical use. Where would it fit in? In our master-plan of classes, of course. So, let's start with a small example:

PROGRAM 157

```
#include <iostream.h>

class Point
{
    public:
    int x,y,z;
    Point(int a,int b,int c)
    { x = a; y =b; z =c; }
};

ostream &operator << (ostream &myobj, Point obj)
{
    myobj << obj.x << " ";
    myobj << obj.y << " ";
    myobj << obj.z << "\n";
    return myobj;
}
```

```
main( )
{
    Point a(1,2,3), b(3,4,5), c(5,6,7);
    cout << a << b << c;
}
```

We've overloaded the binary operator << outside the class definition. The operator takes a reference to an object of type *ostream* as its first parameter and an object of type *Point* as its second. This renders the program more approachable. It allows us to work in a style we are comfortable and familiar with. We've become acclimatized to the use of *cout* and *cin* to output and input from and to the stream, respectively. To continue that tradition with user defined datatypes, we overload the

Coming back to the program, we've defined the three objects of the class *Point* with three parameters each. The overloading of the operator to accept the two objects allows us to view the individual data members of each object separately. Go carefully, line by single line, and you'll have all your explanations pat. In fact, you can read it like an easy text. The output:

```
1 2 3
3 4 5
5 6 7
```

Here's another way of writing the same thing:

PROGRAM 158

```
#include <iostream.h>

class Point
{
    public:
    int x,y,z;
    Point(int a,int b,int c)
    { x = a; y =b; z =c; }
};

ostream &operator << (ostream & myobj, Point obj)
```

```
{
    cout << obj.x << ", ";
    cout << obj.y << ", ";
    cout << obj.z << "\n";
    return myobj;
}

main( )
{
    Point a(1,2,3), b(3,4,5), c(5,6,7);
    cout << a << b << c;
}
```

The output will be the same as the previous one, but this is not an advisable script to use. By replacing *myobj* with *cout*, we've hard coded the program. Consider what would happen to the program if the stream was an input stream instead of the output one. The << operator could be used for any operation, couldn't it? So, by rigidly loading a *cout* on to it, you're cramping the operator. It's better therefore to use the object name that has been passed to it. It makes the program more flexible.

Insertors

One step better is:

PROGRAM 159

```
#include <iostream.h>

class Point
{
    int x,y,z;
    public :
    Point(int a,int b,int c)
    { x = a; y = b; z = c; }
    friend ostream &operator << (ostream & myobj, Point obj)
    {
        myobj << obj.x << ", ";
        myobj << obj.y << ", ";
        myobj << obj.z << "\n";
        return myobj;
```

```
    }
};

main( )
{
    Point a(1,2,3), b(3,4,5), c(5,6,7);
    cout << a << b << c;
}
```

Suppose you wanted to output details about the data members of your object. One way of doing it would be to define a separate function which accepted the object as a parameter. But that entails going back to the unsophisticated ways of C, where things happened around the data, not to the data, where functions and data were treated differently. But as regular C++ers, we should shed this naivete.

So that's not the best way to do it. Ideally, therefore, all the data and the methods acting on them should be encapsulated in a single can. That is why we discussed classes at all. So why shouldn't we dump our operators into the class too? And declare them as friend operators so they can access the private members of the class. Members we couldn't touch even if we wanted to write cumbersome code like *cout << a.x << b.x << c.x*. So, isn't that a piece of cake ... or what???

The output will be:

```
1 2 3
3 4 5
5 6 7
```

The overloaded << operator is also called an overloaded insertor since it makes insertions into the output stream.

A stop at insertors has to lead to a discussion on its diametrically opposed cousin. Extractors.

Extractors

```
PROGRAM 160
#include <iostream.h>

class Point
{
    int x,y,z;
    public:
    Point(int a,int b,int c)
    { x = a; y = b; z = c;}
    friend ostream &operator << (ostream &myobj, Point &obj)
    {
        myobj << obj.x << ",";
        myobj << obj.y << ",";
        myobj << obj.z << "\n";
        return myobj;
    }
    friend istream &operator >> (istream &myobj, Point &obj)
    {
        cout << "Enter X,Y,Z values: ";
        myobj >> obj.x >> obj.y >> obj.z;
        return myobj;
    }
};

main( )
{
    Point a(1,2,3);
    cout << a;
    cin >> a;
    cout << a;
}
```

An extractor takes material from the stream and writes to wherever you have designated it to be written.

When *cout* waits with the command Enter X,Y,Z values: and you key in three values, say, 8, 9 and 10, the overloaded >> operator works as an extractor and takes in these values. Then *cout*, with its insertor operator, prints it out.

File Handling

With all those nuances sponged into our systems, it's time we turned to that mandatory of all programming realms: file handling. File handling, the C++ way. That's what we'll now shift into.

The 'ofstream'

PROGRAM 161

```
#include <iostream.h>
#include <fstream.h>

main( )
{
    ofstream fpo("TEST");

    if(!fpo)
    {
        cout << "Cannot open file";
        return 1;
    }

    fpo << 10 << " " << 123.23 << "\n";
    fpo << "This is a short text file .";
    fpo.close( );
}
```

Let's start with opening a file. We declare an object *fpo* of the type *ofstream*. *ofstream* has been defined in the header file fstream.h. Assume that you want to open a file called TEST. The constructor will be called with the name of the file.

Look at the *if* statement. *if(!fpo)*. If the file cannot be opened, *fpo* will register a 0. The statement will be true and the line Cannot open file will be outputted.

But if the constructor is successful in opening the file, the *if* statement will be false and the next chunk will be activated. The file TEST will now contain the following:

10 123.23
This is a short text file.

Check it out for yourself after you've run the program.

Another way of doing the same thing follows:

PROGRAM 162

```
#include <iostream.h>
#include <fstream.h>

main( )
{
    ofstream fpo;
    fpo.open("PEST",ios::out,0);

    if(!fpo)
    {
        cout << "cannot open file";
        return 1;
    }

    fpo << 10 << " " << 123.23 << "\n";
    fpo << "This is a short text file .";
    fpo.close( );
}
```

The void constructor is called to create the object *fpo* of the type *ofstream*. Through the object thus created, we've called the method *open( )*. To *open( )* are passed three parameters - the name of the file, the format, *ios::out* standing for an output format and the attribute of the file, 0, which indicates that it is a normal file we're dealing with.

The rest of the program follows the same route as the previous one. So the output should come as no surprise to you.

All this while we were directing the output into a file. But it is just as essential to be able to read from a file. So let's move ahead and see how that can be done.

The 'ifstream'

PROGRAM 163

```
#include <iostream.h>
#include <fstream.h>

main(int argc, char *argv[ ])
{
    char ch;
    ifstream fpi(argv[1]);

    if( !fpi)
    {
        cout << "Cannot open file";
        return 1;
    }

    while(fpi)
    {
        fpi.get(ch);
        cout << ch;
    }
}
```

From the command line you specify the file you want opened. If the attempt is unsuccessful, there's nothing that can be done than output: Cannot open file. If successful, the *while* loop will be executed. Each character from the opened file will be picked and displayed using *get( )* and *cout*.

Here's another way of saying the same thing. What it does is exactly what the previous program did. Only the functions we use are different.

The 'filebuf'

PROGRAM 164

```
#include <iostream.h>
#include <fstream.h>

main(int argc,char *argv[ ])
{
```

```
filebuf fpi;
char ch;

fpi.open(argv[1],ios::in I ios::nocreate);

if(!fpi.is_open())
{
    cout << "Cannot open file";
    return 1;
}

while( (ch = fpi.sbumpc()) != -1 )
    cout << ch;

fpi.close();
}
```

In the previous program, the overloaded *!* operator was used. Internally, the method *is_open( )* is called. So what we did here was spell out the method in the program itself.

is_open( ) is used in conjunction with the method *open( )*. The first parameter taken by *open( )* is the name of the file as fed in from the command line. The second parameter *ios::in I ios::nocreate* states that the file should be opened to read and that the file should be one that already exists and not one that needs to be freshly created.

The other new method here is *sbumpc( )*. *sbumpc( )* does what *get( )* did in the previous program. It takes each character from the opened file, moving the file pointer one character ahead each time. *printf( )*, of course, outputs the characters one at a time.

Exactly the same? Absolutely.

Another interesting inclusion in the above program is the class *filebuf*. To be able to use *is_open( )* and *sbumpc( )*, the object we create should belong to the class *filebuf*.

More On Streams

Here's another simple program. And as comfortable C bodies you'll find this a cinch:

PROGRAM 165

```
#include <iostream.h>
#include <fstream.h>

main( )
{
    char *p = "Hello there";

    ofstream fpo("TEST");

    if(!fpo)
    {
        cout << "Cannot open file";
        return 1;
    }

    while(*p)
        fpo.put(*p++);

    fpo.close( );
}
```

We open the file TEST. And if the file can be opened, keep putting elements into it, one by one, through the pointer p.

First type the TEST file you've already made. Now run this program and see what happens to its contents. All that was in the file will be overwritten by the new message Hello there.

The 'fstream'

PROGRAM 166

```
#include <iostream.h>
#include <fstream.h>
#include <stdlib.h>

main(int argc, char *argv[ ])
```

```
{
    fstream fpo;
    fpo.open (argv[1],ios::in I ios::out);

    if(!fpo)
    {
        cout << "Cannot open file";
        return 1;
    }

    fpo.seekp(atol(argv[2]),ios::beg);
    fpo.put('X');
    fpo.close( );
}
```

We have here an object of the class *fstream*. *fstream* actually stands for the combination of the output and the input streams. The object *fpo* of the type *fstream* calls the method *open( )*, to which are passed two parameters. The first parameter accepts the name of the file to be opened from the command line. The second describes the mode in which the file has to be opened. In this case, it is the read and write mode.

If the file cannot be opened, the ride will stop after the message Cannot open file. This message is outputted when the *if* statement is activated.

What we're interested in is, of course, what happens after the file has been opened. So let's assume we have been successful.

seekp( ) is the method that moves the file pointer to a location you specify. The second parameter of the method *seekp( )*, *ios::beg* indicates that the pointer be moved to the beginning of the file. The first parameter, which specifies the location, is taken relative to the second. Read together, it would mean the location of the character you wish to change calculated from the beginning of the file.

seekp( ) in C++ is like *fseek( )* in C which allowed the file pointer to be moved from the beginning of the file, the current position, or the end of the file. *ios::beg* thus stands for the beginning of file, *ios::cur* represents current position and *ios::end* for end of file pointer position.

Getting back to the program at hand, *fpo.put('X')* replaces the character where the file pointer is positioned with X.

If you want to stand on your head and read the file backwards, you've got to step in here:

PROGRAM 167

```
#include <iostream.h>
#include <fstream.h>

main(int argc,char *argv[ ])
{
    fstream fpo;
    fpo.open(argv[1],ios::in I ios::ate I ios::binary);

    char ch;
    int i = fpo.tellg( );
    cout << "size of file is " << i <<"\n";

    for(int k=1;k<=i;k++)
    {
        fpo.seekg(-k,ios::end);
        fpo.get(ch);
        cout << ch;
    }
}
```

fopen( ) accepts the name of the file from the command line and another parameter *ios::in I ios::ate I ios::binary*. *ios::in* indicates that the file has been opened for reading. *ios::ate* takes the file pointer to the end of the file. *ios::binary* opens the file in binary mode.

tellg( ) is the next function to ponder over. *tellg( )* gives you the current position of the pointer. Now consider the *for* loop. The function *seekg(-k,ios::end)* in the *for* loop, moves the pointer from the end of the file backwards according to the value of *k*. *k* is negative because the pointer has to be shifted backward. *get(ch)* picks up the character pointed to and *cout* prints it all out.

Our file TEST comprised of this:

```
Hello
Hi
Bye
```

After we ran this program, the output looked like this:

```
size of file is 14
eyB
iH
olleH
```

We'll continue some more in the same vein.

PROGRAM 168

```
#include <iostream.h>
#include <fstream.h>
#include <stdlib.h>

main(int argc, char *argv[ ])
{
    char ch;

    ifstream fpi(argv[1]);
    if(!fpi)
    {
        cout << "Cannot open file";
        return 1;
    }

    fpi.seekg(atol(argv[2]), ios::beg);

    while(fpi.get(ch))
        cout << ch;
}
```

This program attempts to open the file you've specified from the command line. If successful, it goes to the location specified by you as one of the parameters you passed to *seekg( )*. From that location, each character is picked up and printed by *cout*, thanks to the *while* loop.

How do you use this?

Type the name of the file and the exact location from where you want the file to be displayed.

Let's move into making replicas:

PROGRAM 169

```
#include <iostream.h>
#include <process.h>
#include <fstream.h>

main(int argc,char *argv[ ])
{
    char ch;
    ifstream source;
    ofstream dest;

    source.open(argv[1]);

    dest.open(argv[2]);

    while(source.get(ch))
        dest.put(ch);

    cout << "FCOPY completed\n";

    source.close( );
    dest.close( );
}
```

This simply copies one file into another.

That apart, let's look at the objects we've defined here. *source* is the object of the class *ifstream*, and *dest*, the object of the *ofstream*. The former opens a file in the read mode, and the latter, one in the write mode. You elaborate the file names in the two *open( )* methods, *source.open( )* and *dest.open( )*.

The *while* loop results in each character from the source file being taken and put into the destination file. *cout* prints the message: FCOPY completed at the end of that operation. Both the files are then closed carefully.

Here's an interesting twist to that tale:

PROGRAM 170

```
#include <fstream.h>
#include <iostream.h>

main(int argc,char *argv[ ])
{
    filebuf fpo,fpi;
    char ch;
    fpi.open(argv[1],ios::in I ios::nocreate);
    fpo.open(argv[2],ios::out I ios::noreplace);

    if(!fpi.is_open( ) I I !fpo.is_open( ))
    {
        cout << " Error opening file(s)\n";
        return 1;
    }

    fpi.seekoff(10l,ios::beg,ios::in);

    while( (ch = fpi.sbumpc( ) ) != -1)
        fpo.sputc(ch);

    fpi.close( );
    fpo.close( );
}
```

What this program does is the following: opens two files, one to read and one to write. It then uses a function to seek a particular character - or, rather, byte - in the file and copies the file from that character onward into the "write only" file.

The methods that open the two files take slightly different second parameters. The method *fpi.open( )* states that the file should be opened in the "read" mode and the file should be one that already exists. The method *fpo.open( )*, on the other hand, insists that the file opened in the "write" mode should be one that does not exist and should therefore be created. Logical, isn't it?

seekoff( ) is the method used to propel the pointer to a particular byte in the file. The method accepts two parameters, the number that pinpoints the byte the pointer should be moved to and the position from which it should be moved.

The *while* loop reins *sbumpc( )* to pick the characters from the "read only" file, one at a time. And *sputc( )* to put it into the "write only" file.

Thus, in our example, the "read only" file will be copied in the "write only" file from the 10th character on.

Let's get ahead with some more exciting stuff and introduce a new header file. strstream.h.

The 'istrstream'

PROGRAM 171

```
#include <iostream.h>
#include <strstream.h>

main( )
{
    char s[ ]="20";
    int i,j;
    istrstream ist(s,sizeof(s));

    ist >> hex >> i;

    cout << "In hex i is " << i << "\n";

    ist.seekg(ios::beg);
    ist >> oct >> j;
```

```
        cout << "In octal j is " << j << "\n";
}
```

This program reveals some added facilities. You can do to memory what you just did to the file. Open an array, for example, take input from it and manipulate it just as you did with files.

ist is an object of the class *istrstream*. To create this object we pass it two parameters, the name of the array and the size of the array.

Just as we never needed to keep repeating the name of the file whenever we wanted to work in it, once we'd opened it, we do not need to continue mentioning the array once we've got our hooks into it.

ist >> hex >> i takes the string in the array, converts it into a hexa-decimal figure and puts it into the variable *i*. *cout* then outputs the value of *i*.

At this stage, the byte pointer has shifted to the end of the array. To move it back to the beginning, we drag in the method *seekg( )*, whose duty is to move the pointer to the position stated within the array.

Having accomplished that with *seekg(ios::beg)*, we get into the next act. Converting the string into an octal figure and putting it into *j*. *cout*, of course, does the rest.

```
In hex i is 32
In octal j is 16
```

Let's check something else. The other side of the coin. We'll write into the array now.

The 'ostrstream'
PROGRAM 172

```
#include <iostream.h>
#include <strstream.h>

main( )
```

```
{
    char s[45];
    int i = 90 ;

    ostrstream ost(s,sizeof(s));

    ost << hex << i;
    cout << "buffer s: " << s << endl;

    ost.seekp(ios::beg);

    ost << oct << i;
    cout << "buffer s: " << s << endl;
}
```

In the last program we merely read from the array. This time, let's write into it. *ostrstream* takes the place of *istrstream*. *ost* is an object of a class we've created with two parameters, the name of the array and its size.

ost << hex << i takes the value of *i*, converts it into a hexa-decimal number and dumps it into the array. *cout* then outputs its message. *endl* flushes the stream and places a \n at the end of the message. So whatever follows from then on will appear on the next line.

Likewise, *seekp( )* is used in place of *seekg( )* because we intend to write into the array rather than read from it. *ost.seekp(ios::beg)* takes the byte pointer to the beginning of the array to begin scripting into it.

i is now converted into an octal number. The same process is repeated and the octal value of 90 is fed into the array.

The output you'll receive will be:

buffer s: a oty6 579¥690f88gs7
buffer s: 12o o9g557Üdkk

What???!! Where did you go wrong?

You should have put a \0 at the end of your string. The array, of course, contained much more than the string filled in. The junk outputted reflects the contents of the rest of the elements of the array.

PROGRAM 173

```
#include <iostream.h>
#include <strstream.h>

main( )
{
    char s[45];
    int i = 90;

    ostrstream ost(s,45);

    ost << hex << i;
    ost << '\0';
    cout << "buffer s: " << s << endl;

    ost.seekp(ios::beg);

    ost << oct << i;
    ost << '\0';
    cout << "buffer s: " << s << endl;
}
```

Take another program. The moral is: What you can do to an array with numbers, you can do with a normal string of characters as well. Let's take a quick look at that:

PROGRAM 174

```
#include <iostream.h>
#include <strstream.h>

main( )
{
    char s[100];

    ostrstream ost(s,sizeof(s));

    ost << "Hello I am here";
```

```
ost << '\0';

cout << "buffer s: " << s << endl;
}
```

Again, we bring the class *ostrstream* into the picture because we wish to write into the array. *ost << "Hello I am here"* performs that duty. This time we've been wiser, of course. We've tagged on the \0 at the end of the string. So the output you'll get will be:

buffer s: Hello I am here

endl, of course, takes whatever follows after that on to the next line.

Now let's add some more color. And twist and turn things to suit our purpose.

PROGRAM 175

```
#include <iostream.h>
#include <strstream.h>

main( )
{
    char s[100];
    int i;

    ostrstream ost(s,sizeof s);

    ost << "Hello I am not here";

    ost << '\0';

    char *p = ost.str( );
    cout << p << endl;

    s[0]='C';

    i = ost.pcount( );

    cout << "buffer s: " << s << endl;
```

```
    cout << "i is  : " << i << endl;
}
```

We've first inserted the string, Hello I am not here into the array
s. And we've very sensibly appended the \0 to the string.

That takes us to an interesting bend. char *p = ost.str( ). str( ) is a
method defined in strstream that returns the address of the array.
cout is now brought in to print the string by using a pointer.

Let's get to the most interesting aspect. Change a character in the
array without too many hang-ups.

s[0]='C' rewrites the character in the first element of the array,
changing it from H to C. cout then confirms the alteration,
printing:

```
Hello I am not here
buffer s: Cello I am not here
i is  : 20
```

The number that is outputted is the length of the string as
achieved by the method pcount( ).

That was a brief and very sketchy illustration of a small part of
what's in store. There's a lot, a lot more you can do. This was as
brief as a pre-monsoon shower. Open the floodgates at leisure and
enjoy the torrents that you'll find gushing in.

Building Classes - The Window Class

That's it. You're a full-fledged C++er now. And it wasn't such a harrowing journey, was it? Object Oriented Programming was no big scary giant either. So, how about some practical applications to get your confidence soaring?

Here's a tip-of-the-iceberg demonstration, for all we can cover in this book is just a part of what you can do with the things you now know. The scope is tremendous, the potential great. So take a small bite to whet your appetite.

The Point Class

In this exercise, our attempt will be to start a class from scratch and build on it. Until we have a solid and meaningful body. Let's start from a point.

PROGRAM 176

```
#include <conio.h>

class Point
{
    int x, y;
    public:
    Point(int u, int v)
    { x=u; y=v; }
    Point(void) { x=20; y=20; }
    void print()
    { cprintf("x->%d  y->%d\n", x, y); }
};

main()
{
    Point p1(3,10);
    p1.print();
}
```

In this program, we have a class *Point* which has two private data members, *x* and *y*. It also has two methods with the same name as the class - if you remember, such methods are called constructors. So, what we have is a void constructor and an int constructor passed two parameters.

Having established those salient points, let's spell out what the program will achieve. It will result in the initialization of *x* to 3 and *y* to 10.

The 'ctor' Initializer

Now here's a program that should have you doing a double take. What's this new syntax doing there? Just let it seep into your C++ repertoire. You'll be using it soon enough.

PROGRAM 177

```
#include <conio.h>

class Point
{
    int x, y;
    public:
    Point(int u, int v) : x(u) , y(v) { }
    Point(void) : x(20),y(20) { }
    void print( )
    { cprintf("x->%d  y->%d\n", x, y); }
};

main( )
{
    Point p1(3,10);
    Point p2;
    p1.print( );
    p2.print( );
}
```

Point(int u, int v): x(u), y(u) { } is the same as saying *x = u* and *y = v*. This method of initializing is called the ctor initializer, pronounced c-tor.

The program, after this point, follows a route you're absolutely familiar with. The appropriate constructors will be called, the relevant methods executed, and the output printed. *p1.print( )* will give you 3 and 10, and *p2.print( )* will take the default values 20 and 20.

We're afraid we'll have to keep you in some suspense about where and why ctor is used. For now, let's get on with the business of building our class.

A Tiny Teaser

PROGRAM 178

```
#include <conio.h>

class Point
{
    int x, y;
    public:
    Point(int u, int v)
    { x=u; y=v; }
    Point (void)
    { x=20; y=20; }
    void print( )
    { cprintf("x->%d  y->%d\n", x, y); }
};

main( )
{
    Point p2( );
    Point p1(3,10);
    p1.print( );
    p1=p2( );
    p1.print( );
}

Point p2( )
{
    Point pp(10,10);
    return pp;
}
```

We're back to using our old method of initializing here. The point to note is that we have a function that returns an object of the type *Point*.

Let's consider the output before we go any further. *p1.print( )*, in its response to the first call, will print the values 3 and 10. The second time around, the values it will print will be 10 and 10, because in the statement *p1 = p2( )* we've initialized *p1* to the return values of *p2( )*.

Simple? Before you condemn this as a silly and inane program, however, we'd like you to stop and ask yourself one question. What will happen if you removed the brackets at the end of *p2*, in the statement *p1 = p2( )*. All that will happen is, you'll get an error. Why?

Because, dear seasoned C++ers, *Point p2( )* was the prototype of the function and not an object that required the services of the void constructor to be created. If you'd given that a second thought without jumping the gun, you'd have remembered that an object is declared without the *( )* suffixed to it - unless you were initializing it with some value(s).

Raising Floors

With that well under way, let's get on with the next level of the brick-house we're planning to build.

PROGRAM 179

```
#include <conio.h>

class Point
{
    int x, y;
    public:
    Point(int u, int v)
    { x=u; y=v; }
    void pchange(int a, int b )
    { x=a;y=b;}
    void xpchange( int a)
```

```
    { x = a;}
    void ypchange( int b)
    { y = b;}
    void print( )
    { cprintf("x->%d  y->%d\r\n", x, y); }
};

main( )
{
    Point p1(3,10);
    p1.pchange(10,20);
    p1.print( );
    p1.xpchange(5);
    p1.ypchange(1);
    p1.print( );
}
```

The three methods to note here are *pchange( )*, which changes the values of both the members, *xpchange( )*, which changes the value of one of the members, notably *x*, and *ypchange( )*, which changes the value of the other member, *y*.

There are no catches in this program. Honest. So if you've surmised that the output will be 10 20 and 5 1, you've surmised right.

Some more methodical blocks.

Inline Methods

In this process of building, let's introduce ourselves to one more technique. Inline methods.

PROGRAM 180

```
#include <conio.h>

class Point
{
    int x, y;
    public:
    Point(int u, int v)
```

```
    { x=u; y=v; }
    void print( )
    { cprintf("x->%5d  y->%5d\r\n", x, y); }
    Point operator +(Point);
    Point operator -(Point);
};

Point Point::operator + (Point p)
    { return Point(x+p.x, y+p.y); }

Point Point::operator - (Point p)
    { return Point(x-p.x, y-p.y); }

main( )
{
    Point p1(3,10), p2(20,15);
    p1.print( );
    p2.print( );
    cprintf("---sum----------\r\n");
    Point p3 = p1 + p2;
    p3.print( );
    Point p4 = p3 + p2 + p1;
    p4.print( );
    cprintf("---difference---\r\n");
    p3 = p2 - p1;
    p3.print( );
    p4 = p3 - p2 - p1;
    p4.print( );
}
```

The hint of newness here is in the chunk outside the class
definition. In the earlier programs we always encapsulated the
code within the definition of the class itself. The methods
embodied by such code are called inline methods. Inline methods
are like macros, in that no specific function calls are made. When
the methods are inline, the compiler uses its discretion and
decides whether the function should be treated as inline or not. If
the code is bulky, the complier will treat it as a normal function
and make the appropriate function calls as and when required.

In this example, we're taking the onus on ourselves. By describing
only the prototype in the class definition and defining the code for

the methods outside the class, we're the ones deciding that the function is not going to be an inline function. Inline functions and normal functions, each have their own significance. But on the face of it, normal functions definitely augur for better reading.

Take the output of the above program and work your way in:

```
x-> 3 y-> 10
x-> 20 y-> 15
---sum----------
x-> 23 y-> 25
x-> 46 y-> 50
---difference----
x-> 17 y-> 5
x-> -6 y-> -20
```

The overloaded operators, + and -, perform their designated duties to give you this logical output.

The use of a function that is not inline in character lends the code a very structured look. If you still want the compiler to treat the function as inline and yet keep the structured look, all you have to do is add the word *inline* before the function definition outside the class. Like this:

PROGRAM 181

```
#include <conio.h>

class Point
{
    int x, y;
    public:
    Point(int u, int v)
    { x=u; y=v; }
    void print()
    { cprintf("x->%5d  y->%5d\r\n", x, y); }
    Point operator +(Point);
    Point operator -(Point);
};

inline Point Point::operator + (Point p)
    { return Point(x+p.x, y+p.y); }
```

```
inline Point Point::operator - (Point p)
    { return Point(x-p.x, y-p.y); }

main( )
{
    Point p1(3,10), p2(20,15);
    p1.print( );
    p2.print( );
    cprintf("---sum----------\r\n");
    Point p3 = p1 + p2;
    p3.print( );
    cprintf("---difference----\r\n");
    p3 = p2 - p1;
    p3.print( );
}
```

The output you get will be:

```
x-> 3 y-> 10
x-> 20 y-> 15
---sum----------
x-> 23 y-> 25
---difference----
x-> 17 y-> 5
```

In the two programs we just ran, we overloaded the operators, +
and -, with *Point* objects on either side, and what we returned was
also a *Point* object. Let's look at the next example, where we'll
overload the operators to accept *ints* as their right hand operands
and get them to return *ints*.

PROGRAM 182

```
#include <conio.h>
#include <stdio.h>

class Point
{
    int x, y;
    public:
    Point(int u, int v)
    { x=u; y=v; }
```

```
    void print( )
    { cprintf("x->%5d  y->%5d\r\n", x, y); }
    int operator +(int p)
    { return ( x+p);}
    int operator -(int p)
    { return ( x-p);}
};

main( )
{
    Point p1(3,10), p2(20,15);
    p1.print( );
    p2.print( );
    cprintf("---sum----------\r\n");
    int p3 = p1 + 10;
    printf("%d \n",p3);
    cprintf("---difference-----\r\n");
    int p4 = p2 - 10;
    printf("%d\n",p4);
    cprintf("---sum----------\r\n");
    int p5 = p1 + 10 + 20;
    printf("%d \n",p5);
}
```

The output?

```
x->   3 y->  10
x->  20 y->  15
---sum----------
13
---difference------
10
---sum----------
33
```

The only question that might niggle would be about the statement   *int p5 = p1 + 10 + 20*. We just might find ourselves pondering on the fact that we did not overload the + operator for two *ints*. But the fact is that *int* is an in-built datatype, and therefore the addition will proceed in the normal way: 10 and 20 will first be added and their sum added to the value of the *x* of *p1* - 3. Resulting in the final output: 33.

Using Friends

Let's wedge ourselves deeper into the concepts we've been studying:

PROGRAM 183

```
#include <conio.h>
#include <stdio.h>

class Point
{
    int x, y;
    public:
    Point(int u, int v)
    { x=u; y=v; }
    void print( )
    { cprintf("x->%5d  y->%5d\r\n", x, y); }
    friend int operator + (Point ,int );
    friend int operator + (int , Point);
};

int operator + (int p , Point a)
{ return ( a.x+p); }

int operator + (Point a,int p)
{ return ( a.x+p); }

main( )
{
    Point p1(3,10);
    p1.print( );
    cprintf("---sum----------\r\n");
    int p3 = p1+10;
    printf("%d \n",p3);
    p3 = 10+p1;
    printf("%d\n",p3);
}
```

The important point to consider in this program is the introduction of the friend operator. Look at Lines 9 and 10 of the program. Why do we need a friend operator?

Take the friend out from Line 9 along with the first parameter, *Point*, and it won't make a difference to the program. But erase the friend from Line 10 and your program won't even compile. Why?

If you recall, the operand to the left of the operator is implicitly passed the *this* pointer. All member functions, by default, will receive *this* as their first parameter. In the first case, therefore, we needn't even define the first parameter. But in the second case, since we require the first parameter to be an *int*, we have to explicitly state that information. And without the friend, we would end up passing three parameters to a binary operator. And that will never do.

So we tide over that little hurdle by bringing in a friend and then stating the two parameters explicitly.

The output of the program needs no explanation beyond that.

```
x->  3 y->  10
—sum—————
13
13
```

Fooling Around

Here's another program to tickle your sense of C and C++.

```
PROGRAM 184
#include <conio.h>

class Point
{
    int x, y;
    public:
    Point(int u, int v)
    { x=u; y=v; }

    void print( )
    { cprintf("x->%5d  y->%5d\r\n", x, y); }
```

```
    void putch(char c)
    { gotoxy(x, y); ::putch(c); }

    Point operator + (Point p)
    { return Point(x+p.x, y+p.y); }

    Point operator - (Point p)
    { return Point(x-p.x, y-p.y); }

    Point operator += (Point p)
    { return Point(x+=p.x, y+=p.y); }

    int operator <= (Point p)
    { return x<=p.x && y<=p.y; }

    int operator == (Point p)
    { return x==p.x && y==p.y; }

};

main( )
{
    clrscr( );
    for (Point p1(3,10); p1 <= Point(40,10); p1 += Point(1,0))
    {
        p1.putch('x');
    }
    gotoxy(1,24);
}
```

The multitude of operators defined here is what makes it look so mind-boggling. If you look at them keenly, you'll realize that it's not as complicated as it looks.

Take the function *putch( )*. There are two *putch( )* functions to contend with - one, a standard function defined in the header file *conio.h*. And the other, a method of the class *Point*. The method *putch( )* calls the function *putch( )*. The *::* before the function *putch( )* is absolutely essential to differentiate between the two *putch( )*s, unless of course you want your computer to hang. Without the *::*, the method *putch( )* will keep calling itself in an endless spell of inactivity.

That understood, let's get on with the nuances of this program. First of all, the program does not use all the operators declared. But that's a minor issue. So let's go to the important details. The *for* loop.

The first part of the *for* loop defines the object *p1* of the type *Point*. The second part is the condition which determines the duration of the loop. The loop will continue until the coordinates of *p1* remain less than or equal to those of *Point(40,10)*. In the third part, the y-coordinate in *p1* is kept constant and the x-coordinate is increased by 1 each time. At the end of every round of the loop, *putch( )* puts the character *x* on the screen.

gotoxy( ) at the end of the loop takes the cursor to the first column, 24th row. At this point you're at the end of the program. The output you'll see is a string of 38 *x*s from the 3rd column, 10th row on.

Take the next program. Another long list of operators that look confusing, a lot of noise about nothing really.

PROGRAM 185

```
#include <conio.h>

class Point
{
    int x, y;
    public:
    Point(int u, int v)
    { x=u; y=v; }

    void print( )
    { cprintf("x->%5d  y->%5d\r\n", x, y); }

    void putch(char c)
    { gotoxy(x, y); ::putch(c); }

    Point operator + (Point p)
    { return Point(x+p.x, y+p.y); }

    Point operator - (Point p)
```

```
{ return Point(x-p.x, y-p.y); }

int operator <= (Point p)
{ return x<=p.x && y<=p.y; }

int operator == (Point p)
{ return x==p.x && y==p.y; }

Point operator += (Point p)
{
    int a = x+p.x;
    int b = y+p.y;
    return Point(a, b);
}
};

main()
{
    clrscr();
    for (Point p1(3,10); p1 <= Point(40,10); p1 += Point(1,0))
    {
        p1.putch('x');
    }
    gotoxy(1,24);
}
```

This program will get stuck at the 3rd column, 10th row, like a needle in the groove of an old gramophone record. The reason behind this defect lies in the code that defines the working style of the += operator. Let's analyze that code:

```
Point operator += (Point p)
{
    int a = x+p.x;
    int b = y+p.y;
    return Point(a, b);
}
```

By elucidating code like this, what you are, in effect, saying is take the value of x as pointed to by the *this* pointer, add it to the value of the parameter passed, i.e. $p.x$, and put the sum of this operation into the local variable a. So also with y.

A *+* operator, obviously, does not change the value of the individual operands. Therefore, the value of *x* and *y* remain unchanged, and even though we are explicitly returning a new *Point* object with the new values, the code is not designed to allow *p1* to accept these values. So the needle stays where it is.

The point is, scripting code like this should be avoided, or you'll be pushed into changing your correct *for* statement into something as ridiculous as: p1 = p1 += Point(1,0).

Those were just little preliminaries to lead us somewhere. Let's do something really practical now. Like draw a rectangle on the screen, to start with.

Our class is ready, just waiting to be picked. The best ingredients have been added and we're ready to store it with its elements. The diary here is the header file. So let's script the class into the header *point.h*, so we can pick from it as and when required.

```
// Header file for point class
// Point.h

#include <conio.h>

class Point
{
    int x, y;
    public:
    Point( int u, int v ) : x(u), y(v) {}

    Point( )
    { x=0; y=0; }

    void print( )
    { cprintf("x->%5d  y->%5d\r\n", x, y); }

    Point operator + (Point p)
    { return Point(x+p.x, y+p.y); }

    Point operator - (Point p)
    { return Point(x-p.x, y-p.y); }
```

```
void putch(char c)
{ gotoxy(x, y); ::putch(c); }

int operator <= (Point p)
{ return x<=p.x && y<=p.y; }

int operator > (Point p)
{ return x>p.x && y>p.y; }

int operator < (Point p)
{ return x<p.x && y<p.y; }

int operator == (Point p)
{ return x==p.x && y==p.y; }

Point operator += (Point p)
{ return Point(x+=p.x, y+=p.y); }

int getx()
{ return x; }

int gety()
{ return y; }
};
```

That's the culmination of all the little programs we did earlier. Recognize the various methods and operators here? There are some new methods besides the ones we've studied in detail. Like *getx( )* and *gety( )*. Those are also simple methods. You can add your own methods to the file to make it as complex as you might feel the need to.

Point To Rectangle

Let's now use this *Point* class to draw a rectangle:

PROGRAM 186
```
#include "point.h"

class Rectangle
{
```

```
        protected:
        Point origin, corner;
        public:
        Rectangle(Point p, Point q) : origin(p), corner(q) { }   // ctor initializer

        void print( )
        { origin.print( ); corner.print( ); }

        void draw( );
};

enum Frame
{
        TopLeft=218,   Top=196,   TopRight=191,
        Left=179,                 Right=179,
        BottomLeft=192, Bottom=196, BottomRight=217
};

void Rectangle::draw( )
{
    Point p = origin;

    // top
    p.putch(TopLeft);
    for ( p+=Point(1,0); p<corner; p+=Point(1,0))
        p.putch(Top);
    p.putch(TopRight);

    // right
    for (p+=Point(0,1); p<(corner+Point(1,0)); p+=Point(0,1))
        p.putch(Right);

    // bottom
    p.putch(BottomRight);
    for (p+=Point(-1,0); p>origin; p+=Point(-1,0))
        p.putch(Bottom);
    p.putch(BottomLeft);

    // left
    for (p+=Point(0,-1); p>(origin-Point(1,0)); p+=Point(0,-1))
        p.putch(Left);
}
```

```
main( )
{
    clrscr( );
    Rectangle r1(Point(5,2), Point(40,12));
    r1.draw( );
    gotoxy(1,15);
    r1.print( );
}
```

Here, we've declared a class *Rectangle*, which has two protected members, *origin* and *corner* of the type *Point*. Going to the public section of the class, the first stop is the constructor which accepts two parameters, *p* and *q*, which are also objects of the type *Point*.

Next, we use the ctor initializer to initialize the objects *origin* and *corner*. After which, comes the method *print( )*. *print( )* simply calls the method *print( )* of the *Point* class through *origin.print( )* and *corner.print( )*. The final method is *draw( )*, the crucial method in the program.

Before we get down to the actual drawing of the rectangle, let's tackle that chunk called *enum Frame*. Don't let the unnerving appearance of that chunk throw you off balance. It's so simple really, you'll be surprised. Each variable here is initialized with a value. In fact, it is like a *#define*. Each time the variable is used, it is replaced with its corresponding value. Look carefully and you'll recognize them even before you get into the method *draw( )* where they feature.

Let's study the definition of the method *draw( )* now.

draw( ) has a *Point* object *p* which has been initialized with the values of *origin*. *origin* contains the starting coordinates of the rectangle which are now stored in *p*, which is then used to draw the actual outline of the rectangle.

Now let's go into the gruesome details. The method *putch( )*, as we're familiar, prints a character on the screen. In the first instance, *putch( )* is passed the parameter *TopLeft*. As we've stated earlier, *TopLeft* actually represents the number 218. The character printed by *putch( )* will thus be ⌐ .

That is the top left corner of the rectangle taken care of.

Which brings us into the *for* loop. The first part of the *for* loop uses the overloaded *+=* operator. The intricacies of this operator have been defined in our header file *point.h*. So let's restrict ourselves to a discussion of the outcome of this operation.

The second part of the *for* loop houses the condition *p<corner*. *corner* refers to the x- and y-coordinates that define the outer limits. The third part of the *for* loop increases the x-coordinate by 1, while keeping the y-coordinate constant. We've encountered that in our earlier programs.

Each round of the *for* loop results in the execution of the method *putch( )* with the parameter *Top*. *Top* holds the value 196, which is the ASCII code for a straight horizontal line. So, at the end of the *for* loop, you'll have a figure like this:

⌐‾‾‾‾‾‾‾‾‾‾‾‾‾‾‾

DIAGRAM 5.1

After exiting the *for* loop, i.e. when the value contained in the x-coordinate of *p* becomes equal to the value of the coordinate in the object *corner*, the maximum value of x, the method *putch( )* with the parameter *TopRight* is called.

TopRight, with the value 191, will draw the top right corner . At the end of this operation, your figure will be:

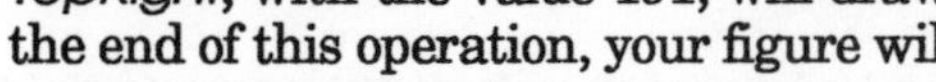

⌐‾‾‾‾‾‾‾‾‾‾‾‾‾‾‾‾‾‾‾‾‾‾┐

DIAGRAM 5.2

That takes us to the next *for* loop. This time the value of the x-coordinate stays the same, while the value of the y-coordinate keeps increasing by 1. At the end of every round of the *for* loop, *putch( )* will be called with *Right* and you'll get your vertical line on the right hand side of the box.

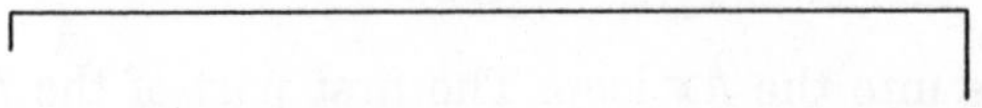

DIAGRAM 5.3

And so on with the other *for* loops until you have your entire rectangle on the screen.

The last function in the program, *gotoxy( )*, takes your cursor to the 1st column, 15th row of the screen, where the method *r1.print( )* will print the coordinates of the rectangle on the screen.

That lengthy explanation must have sounded like a stuck record. But we did want to reiterate one more time. We promise we'll keep a lower profile from now on.

Consider the user for a minute. He'd prefer to express his coordinates in integer form, rather than in object-of-a-class form. Shouldn't we make allowances for that? That's what we'll do in the next program:

PROGRAM 187

```
#include "point.h"

class Rectangle
{
    protected:
    Point origin, corner;
    public:
    Rectangle ( int a,int b,int c,int d) : origin(a,b),corner(c,d) { }

    Rectangle(Point p, Point q)
    { origin=p ; corner=q; }
```

```
    void print( )
    { origin.print( ); corner.print( ); }

    void draw( );
};

enum Frame
{
    TopLeft=218,  Top=196,  TopRight=191,
    Left=179,              Right=179,
    BottomLeft=192, Bottom=196, BottomRight=217
};

void Rectangle::draw( )
{

    Point p = origin;

    // top
    p.putch(TopLeft);
    for ( p += Point(1,0); p<corner; p+=Point(1,0))
        p.putch(Top);
    p.putch(TopRight);

    // right
    for (p+=Point(0,1); p<(corner+Point(1,0)); p+=Point(0,1))
        p.putch(Right);

    // bottom
    p.putch(BottomRight);
    for (p+=Point(-1,0); p>origin; p+=Point(-1,0))
        p.putch(Bottom);
    p.putch(BottomLeft);

    // left
    for (p+=Point(0,-1); p>(origin-Point(1,0)); p+=Point(0,-1))
        p.putch(Left);
}

main( )
{
    clrscr( );
    Rectangle r1(5,2,40,12);
```

```
        r1.draw();
        gotoxy(1,15);
        r1.print();
}
```

The four *int*s that a user specifies are taken into reckoning by this part of the program:

```
Rectangle ( int a,int b,int c,int d) : origin(a,b),corner(c,d) { }
```

Do you recognize the significance of the ctor initializer now. It was possible to pass the coordinates correctly to the objects because of the ctor initializer. You could never have said *origin = a,b*, could you?

The rest of the program follows the same route as the earlier one. You thus have the rectangle with the layman's interface.

Rectangle To Window

Let's derive another class, a window, from the rectangle. It's really extremely simple.

PROGRAM 188

```
#include "point.h"

class Rectangle
{
    protected:
    Point  origin, corner;
    public:
    Rectangle(Point p, Point q) : origin(p) , corner(q)  { } // ctor initializer
    void print()
    { origin.print(); corner.print(); }
    void draw();
};

enum Frame
{
    TopLeft=218,   Top=196,   TopRight=191,
    Left=179,               Right=179,
    BottomLeft=192, Bottom=196, BottomRight=217
```

```
};

void Rectangle::draw( )
{
    Point p = origin;

    // top
    p.putch(TopLeft);
    for ( p += Point(1,0); p<corner; p+=Point(1,0))
        p.putch(Top);
    p.putch(TopRight);

    // right
    for (p+=Point(0,1); p<(corner+Point(1,0)); p+=Point(0,1))
        p.putch(Right);

    // bottom
    p.putch(BottomRight);
    for (p+=Point(-1,0); p>origin; p+=Point(-1,0))
        p.putch(Bottom);
    p.putch(BottomLeft);

    // left
    for (p+=Point(0,-1); p>(origin-Point(1,0)); p+=Point(0,-1))
        p.putch(Left);
}

class Window : public Rectangle
{
    public:
    Window(Point p, Point q) : Rectangle(p,q) { }
};

main( )
{
    Window w1(Point(6,3), Point(41,13));
    w1.draw( );
    gotoxy(1,18);
    w1.print( );
}
```

You've derived the class *Window* from the class *Rectangle*. All that the class *Window* has is one constructor, which accepts two *Point* objects, and calls the two-point constructor of *Rectangle*.

Note that the class *Rectangle* is not a derived class, but the class *Window* has been derived from the class *Rectangle*. The window will have the coordinates passed to it: 6,3 and 41,13.

On your screen will be depicted the rectangle drawn by *Window* with the relevant coordinates.

That was the class registered in the header file *point.h*. We'll now put the *Rectangle* class that we created in the file *rect.cpp*. And we'll build our entire *Window* class on the basis of this header file.

RECT.CPP
```
// listing of include file rect.cpp
#include "point.h"

class Rectangle
{
    protected:
    Point  origin, corner;
    public:
    Rectangle(Point p, Point q) : origin(p) , corner(q) { }   // ctor initializer

    Rectangle(int a, int b, int c, int d) : origin(a,b) , corner(c,d) { }

    void print( )
    { origin.print( ); corner.print( ); }

    void draw( );
};

enum Frame
{
    TopLeft=218,   Top=196,   TopRight=191,
    Left=179,                 Right=179,
    BottomLeft=192, Bottom=196, BottomRight=217
};
```

```
void Rectangle::draw( )
{
    Point p = origin;

    // top
    p.putch(TopLeft);
    for ( p += Point(1,0); p<corner; p+=Point(1,0))
        p.putch(Top);
    p.putch(TopRight);

    // right
    for (p+=Point(0,1); p<(corner+Point(1,0)); p+=Point(0,1))
        p.putch(Right);

    // bottom
    p.putch(BottomRight);
    for (p+=Point(-1,0); p>origin; p+=Point(-1,0))
        p.putch(Bottom);
    p.putch(BottomLeft);

    // left
    for (p+=Point(0,-1); p>(origin-Point(1,0)); p+=Point(0,-1))
        p.putch(Left);
}

// end of rect.cpp
```

PROGRAM 189

```
#include "rect.cpp"
void fullScreen( )
{
    window(1,1,80,25);
}

class Window : public Rectangle
{
    public:
    Window(Point p, Point q)  : Rectangle(p, q) { }

    void select( )
    {
        window(origin.getx( )+1, origin.gety( )+1,
```

```
            corner.getx( )-1, corner.gety( )-1);
        }

        void open( )
        {
            select( );
            clrscr( );
            fullScreen( );
            draw( );
            select( );
        }

        void close( );

        void print( )
        {
            cprintf("%5d %5d %5d %5d ",
                    origin.getx( ), origin.gety( ),corner.getx( ), corner.gety( ));
        }

        Window& operator <<(char *s)
        {
            cputs(s);
            return *this;
        }
};

main( )
{
    clrscr( );
    Window w1(Point(6,3), Point(41,13));
    w1.open( );

    fullScreen( );
    gotoxy(1,18);
    w1.print( );

    w1.select( );

    for (int i=0; i<100; i++)
        w1 << "–Testing–";
    w1 << " Here is" << " the last line\n";
```

```
fullScreen();
gotoxy(1,24);
}
```

What this program will give you is a long train of the message *Testing* running across the little window that you opened - rather like a gaggle of geese going home.

Let's get back to base and take the program apart.

Let's start from *main( )*. The first thing to do is clear the screen so we can start on a fresh slate. *clrscr( )* is the function that takes care of that.

Now let's really get going. We have a class, *Window*, which has an object *w1* that is passed two initialized *Point* objects. The object then calls the method *open( )*. So let's charge to *open( )*.

open( ), in turn, calls another method of the class, *select( )*. *select( )* calls the standard function *window( )*. Basically, *window( )* demarcates an area on the screen which serves as a window. There are no barbed fences defining these edges. They are fixed in the computer's eye by the coordinates we've passed it. Coming to the *clrscr( )* function here, what is interesting is that the function will work on the area demarcated by the function *window( )*, rather than the entire screen, as it did all this time we called it.

fullScreen( ) is the next function in line. And the performance of *fullScreen( )* is delightfully logical and simple. To understand the intricacies, we need to first reiterate the fact that the function *window( )* that demarcated the little window on the screen did not draw any edges. The lines of the window, at this stage, are imaginary. To draw the window with its edges clearly penciled, we need to get back to the full screen mode. *fullScreen( )* calls the function *window(1,1,80,25)*, this time to demarcate the full screen. *draw( )* then waits to be executed.

We've seen what *draw( )* achieves for us. The rectangle. *select( )* is called again to get back into the old mode. So, only our window is active now. With those series of functions activated by *w1.open( )* now documented, it's time to leap into the *main( )* again and move with the program.

In the *main( )*, we go back to *fullScreen( )*, this time to print out the coordinates of the window at the right spots. *gotoxy( )* and *w1.print( )* are the arbitrators of this operation. *select( )* is called again to shift the action back into the window mode.

And we come to the *for* loop, which prints out the train Testing within the window. If you've noticed, the line *w1 << "-Testing-"* makes very convenient and, should we say, easy reading. You can read that as "print so-and-so string in so-and-so window". It definitely makes more reading sense than 'cout...etc.etc.'. This facility is available to us because we've overloaded the *<<* operator to write the string inside the text window currently active. The function *cputs( )* organizes the latter half.

After the *for* loop is exited, the line Here is the last line is similarly scripted into the window. We wind it all up with *fullScreen( )* and get the cursor to the end of the full screen.

We've kept the details to the minimum since you should now be able to read C++ code like a book of nursery rhymes.

Let's look at this from the user's point of view. Replace the *Point* objects with user-used terminology - *ints*. Simply note the subtle differences. Especially in the calling of the constructors and the ctor initializers. This program will give you two windows to demonstrate the result of the two kinds of input patterns.

PROGRAM 190

```
#include "rect.cpp"

void fullScreen()
{
    window(1,1,80,25);
}

class Window : public Rectangle
```

```
{
public:
Window(Point p, Point q) : Rectangle(p, q) { }

Window(int a, int b , int c , int d ) : Rectangle ( a,b,c,d) { }

void select( )
{
    window(origin.getx( )+1, origin.gety( )+1,corner.getx( )-1,
            corner.gety( )-1);
}

void open ( )
{
    select( );
    clrscr( );
    fullScreen( );
    draw( );
    select( );

void close ( );

void print ( )
{
    cprintf("%5d %5d %5d %5d ",origin.getx( ), origin.gety( ),
                corner.getx( ), corner.gety( ));
}

Window& operator <<(char *s)
{
    cputs(s);
    return *this;
}
};

main( )
{
    Window w1(6,3,41,12);
    Window w2(Point(20,14),Point(60,22));

    w1.open( );
    w2.open( );
```

```
w1.select( );
for (int i=0; i<100; i++)
    w1 << "-Testing-";
w1 << " Here is" << " the last line\n";

w2.select( );
for (i=0; i<100; i++)
    w2 << "-Resting-";
w2 << " Here is" << " the last job\n";

fullScreen( );

gotoxy(1,24);
}
```

We've defined two windows here, one by using *ints*, and the other with the *Point* class. After opening both the windows, one after the other, each is *select( )*ed and the appropriate message written into it. One window goes screeching the buzzword Testing, while the other with the same hyper-activity screams Resting.

Wasn't that fascinating? From a small and innocuous point, we've built an exciting window. Not one, but two. And as if that was not enough, we wrote messages inside them. Think about the ramifications. The amazing range of opportunities that this puts close at hand. A whole world lies in that little point. Just learn to harness it, and you'll be king.

Building Classes - The String Class

When it came to numbers, C was absolutely the last word. The polish and finesse exhibited was spell-binding. But when it came to strings, C left a lot to be desired. There were little handicaps and minor inadequacies that brought us short of tagging the label "absolute and perfect" to C. Strings was C's weak point.

'const' Parameters

What we are going to look at, is corrective surgery for this handicap. With C++ and its class-building ability. Using all the skills that we've acquired, let's go about building a class. Slowly and carefully because this is going to be a culmination of all the arduous hours of learning we've gone through.

Are we ready to go?

PROGRAM 191

```
#include <string.h>

class String
{
    private:
    char *str;
    int size;
    public:
    String(const char *s);
};

String::String(const char *s)
{
    size = strlen(s);
    str = new char[size + 1];
    strcpy(str, s);
}
```

```
main( )
{
    String s("String a string along.\n");
}
```

Nothing in this program is beyond your comprehension. So we'll just cap it with a small explanation.

The class *String* has been defined with two private members, a pointer, *str*, and an *int, size*. Among the public member is a constructor which has been designed to accept a pointer to a constant string. In fact, that is the lesson in this program. The word <$IF51MIconstF51MIconst, and why it should be used. By prefixing *const* to the pointer you are safeguarding the string from any modification within the function, whatever else.

The rest of the program is familiar enough. The string length is calculated, *new* is called to allocate space for the string, including the \0 that comes at the end, and *strcpy( )* is called to copy the string *s* into *str*.

The next stop in our itinerary:

PROGRAM 192

```
#include <iostream.h>
#include <string.h>

class String
{
    private:
    char *str;
    int size;
    public:
    String(const char *s);
    String(void);
};

String::String(void)
{
    size = 0;
    str = 0;
```

```
}

String::String(const char *s)
{
    size = strlen(s);
    str = new char[size + 1];
    strcpy(str, s);
}

main( )
{
    String s("String a string along.\n");
    String s1;
}
```

We're just reiterating a small point. We've called two constructors, a string constructor and a void constructor. For *s* the string constructor will be summoned and for *s1*, the void constructor. The void constructor initializes *size* and *str* to 0.

'const' Methods

Those were little inconsequential drops in the ocean. Let's go into some important inlets:

Take this program:

PROGRAM 193

```
#include <iostream.h>
#include <string.h>

class String
{
    private:
    char *str;
    int size;
    public:
    String(void);
    String(const char *s);
    void print(void);
};
```

```
String::String( )
{
    size=0;
    str=0;
}

String::String(const char *s)
{
    size = strlen(s);
    str = new char[size + 1];
    strcpy(str, s);
}

void String::print(void)
{
    char *ptr = "Hello";
    delete str;
    size = strlen(ptr);
    str = new char[size + 1];
    strcpy(str, ptr);
    cout << str;
}

main( )
{
    String s1;
    String s("String a string along.\n");
    s.print( );
    s1.print( );
}
```

What you'll get is an echo like this:

HelloHello

The method *print( )* that you defined led to this unwanted echo. It deleted the string assigned to *str* and assigned a new address to *str* and copied the string pointed to by *ptr* into it.

Should you have the method *print( )* do something other than what is its apparent function? If you wanted to change a string, you could have built another method let's say *change( )* and left *print( )* to simply print things.

If you recall, the first parameter is, implicitly the *this* pointer. It's obvious that you can do as you please with an object in your control. You can keep its contents steadfast by qualifying it with a *const*. But can you do that to an object that is implicitly passed? An object that is not within your control? C++ provides you an answer. By trailing the method with the word *const*, it is possible to ensure that the method is not allowed to change the contents of the first parameter through the *this* pointer.

Let's suffix *print( )* with *const* and see if we can do the trick:

PROGRAM 194

```cpp
#include <iostream.h>
#include <string.h>

class String
{
    private:
    char *str;
    int size;
    public:
    String(void);
    String(const char *s);
    void print(void) const;
};

String::String()
{
    size=0;
    str=0;
}

String::String(const char *s)
{
    size = strlen(s);
    str = new char[size + 1];
    strcpy(str, s);
}
```

```
void String::print(void) const
{
    char *ptr = "Hello";
    delete str;
    size = strlen(ptr);
    str = new char[size + 1];
    strcpy(str, ptr);
    cout << str;
}

main( )
{
    String s1;
    String s("String a string along.\n");
    s.print( );
    s1.print( );
}
```

Error! It won't go beyond the compiling stage. That's because once you've declared a method to be a constant, you have no right to give instructions to it to modify the object. The error flagged will be: Cannot modify a const object in function String::print( ) const.

Here's the right way of doing it:

PROGRAM 195

```
#include <iostream.h>
#include <string.h>

class String
{
    private:
    char *str;
    int size;
    public:
    String(void);
    String(const char *s);
    void print(void) const;
};

String::String( )
```

```
{
    size=0;
    str=0;
}

String::String(const char *s)
{
    size = strlen(s);
    str = new char[size + 1];
    strcpy(str, s);
}

void String::print(void) const
{
    cout << str;
}

main( )
{
    String s1;
    String s("String a string along.\n");
    s.print( );
    s1.print( );
}
```

Once you've tagged *const* to the method, just get that method to print the string.

The string of the object *s* will now be different from the string of the object *s1*. And all your problems have been solved.

Let's add one more element into the whole scheme:

PROGRAM 196
```
#include <iostream.h>
#include <string.h>

class String
{
    private:
    char *str;
    int size;
```

```
    public:
    String(void);
    String(const char *s);
    void print(void) const;
    ~String( );
};

String::String( )
{
    size=0;
    str=0;
}

String::String(const char *s)
{
    size = strlen(s);
    str = new char[size + 1];
    strcpy(str, s);
}

void String::print(void) const
{
    cout << str;
}

String::~String( )
{
    delete str;
}

main( )
{
    String s1;
    String s("String a string along.\n");
    s.print( );
    s1.print( );
}
```

The destructor. To tie up all ends. To wind up the show that
you've opened with the constructor. The destructor. Its purpose.
To free the memory allocated by *new*.

Overloaded 'int'

We get into another important area. Overloading. We're so used to operator overloading, we almost take it for granted. But hold on there. Here's something you've never done before. Cast a string into an *int*. Speaking in terms of equations, saying *int i = (int)s1*. Let's see how that is done:

PROGRAM 197

```
#include <iostream.h>
#include <string.h>

class String
{
    private:
    char *str;
    int size;
    public:
    String(void);
    String(const char *s);
    ~String( );
    void print( ) const;
    operator int( );
};

String::String( )
{
    size=0;
    str=0;
}

String::String(const char *s)
{
    size = strlen(s);
    str = new char[size + 1];
    strcpy(str, s);
}

void String::print(void) const
{
    cout << str;
}
```

```
String::operator int( )
{
    return size;
}

String::~String( )
{
    delete str;
}

main( )
{
    String s1;
    String s("String a string along.\n");
    s.print( );
    s1.print( );
    int i,j,k;
    i = s;
    j = (int)s;
    k = int(s1);
    cout << i << "\n" << j << "\n" << k;
}
```

This is called, technically, overloading the *int* operator. The statement that does this is:

```
String::operator int( )
{
    return size;
}
```

Remove that and the program will result in an error. The computer does not recognize the string, an object of a class born out of your imagination, as an *int*. Unless you specifically teach it to, by overloading the operator.

You can cast the *int* yourself like this: *j=(int)s* and *k=(int)s1*, but look at the statement *i=s*. Here, the computer will do the casting for us because we've loaded the *int*.

The output this program will give you:

```
21
21
0
```

Having learnt to overload the *int* operator, you can just as easily convert a string into a *long*, *float* or *char*. The computer understands the relationship between an *int* and a *long*, *char*, *float*, etc. So once you've loaded the *int* operator and taught it the relationship between an *int* and a string, the rest is taken care of by the computer.

PROGRAM 198

```cpp
#include <iostream.h>
#include <string.h>

class String
{
    private:
    char *str;
    int size;
    public:
    String(void);
    String(const char *s);
    ~String();
    void print(void) const;
    operator int();
};

String::String()
{
    size=0;
    str=0;
}

String::String(const char *s)
{
    size = strlen(s);
    str = new char[size + 1];
    strcpy(str, s);
}

void String::print(void) const
```

```
    {
        cout << str;
    }

String::operator int( )
    {
        return size;
    }

String::~String( )
    {
        delete str;
    }

main( )
    {
        String s("Strings should be easy to use.\n");
        s.print( );
        char h;
        int i;
        long j;
        float k;
        h = s;
        i = s;
        j = s;
        k = s;
        cout << h << "\n" << i << "\n" << j << "\n" << k;
    }
```

The output of this program will be:

```
21
21
21
```

First, the value 21, interpreted as an ASCII character, the second, the *int* value, the third, a *long* and the last, *float*.

Sliping In An Overloaded 'float'

What should the next program give you?

```
PROGRAM 199
#include <iostream.h>
#include <string.h>

class String
{
    private:
    char *str;
    int size;
    public:
    String(void);
    String(const char *s);
    ~String( );
    void print(void) const;
    operator int( );
    operator float( );
};

String::String( )
{
    size=0;
    str=0;
}

String::String(const char *s)
{
    size = strlen(s);
    str = new char[size + 1];
    strcpy(str, s);
}

void String::print(void) const
{
    cout << str;
}

String::operator int( )
{
    return size;
}

String::operator float( )
{
```

```
    return (float)size;
}

String::~String( )
{
    delete str;
}

main( )
{
    String s("String a string along\n");
    s.print( );
    long j;
    float k;
    j = s;
    k = s;
    cout << "\n" << j << "\n" << k;
}
```

An error. The question is: Should the string be converted into a *long* using the value of the overloaded *int* operator or should it be converted from the *float*? This confusion rampant in the mind of the compiler results in an error. The error messages are completely unambiguous:

Ambiguity between 'String::operator float( )' and 'String::operator int( )' in function 'main( )'. Cannot assign 'String' to long in function 'main( )'.

Let's skirt that error so:

PROGRAM 200

```
#include <iostream.h>
#include <string.h>

class String
{
    private:
    char *str;
    int size;
    public:
    String(void);
```

```
    String(const char *s);
    void print(void) const;
    operator int( );
    operator float( );
    ~String( );
};

String::String( )
{
    size=0;
    str=0;
}

String::String(const char *s)
{
    size = strlen(s);
    str = new char[size + 1];
    strcpy(str, s);
}

String::operator int( )
{
    return size;
}

String::operator float( )
{
    return (float)size;
}

String::~String( )
{
    delete str;
}

main( )
{
    String s("String a string along.\n");
    s.print( );
    long j;
    float k;
    j = (int)s;
    k = s;
```

```
    cout << "\n" << j << "\n" << k;
}
```

We've overloaded the *int* and the *float* operators, alright. But this time we're explicitly specifying the typecast. *j=(int)s* removes ambiguity and the compiler knows that the string has to be converted into an *int*. *k=s* is no problem at all because *k* has been defined as a *float*.

Overloaded Assignment Operator

Let's stick around the concept of overloading some more. Take this program and note the overloading of the = operator:

PROGRAM 201

```
#include <iostream.h>
#include <string.h>

class String
{
    private:
    char *str;
    int size;
    public:
    String(void);
    String(const char *s);
    ~String( );
    void print( ) { cout << str;}

    String& operator = (const char *s)
    {
        size=strlen(s);
        str=new char[size+1];
        strcpy(str,s);
        return *this;
    }

    String& operator = (String& s)
    {
        delete str;
        this->size = s.size;
        this->str = new char[s.size+1];
```

```
        strcpy(this->str,s.str);
        return *this;
    }

};

String::String( )
{
    size=0;
    str=0;
}

String::String(const char *s)
{
    size = strlen(s);
    str = new char[size + 1];
    strcpy(str, s);
}

String::~String( )
{
    delete str;
}

main( )
{
    String s;
    s = "String a string along.";
    String s1,s2;
    s2 = s1 = s;
    s.print( );
    s1.print( );
    s2.print( );
}
```

This program exhibits overloading of the = operator in two ways. Let's see how and why. We'll pick up the action from the *main( )*.

s is an object of the class string, and we're trying to equate it with a pointer to a string. To acquaint the computer with the equation of the two, we have the first overloaded operator. Let's look at it carefully:

```
String& operator = (const char *s)
{
    size=strlen(s);
    str=new char[size+1];
    strcpy(str,s);
    return *this;
}
```

Let's get into the overloading definition. We've initialized *size* to the length of the string. *new* then allocates memory for the string, and puts the address of the chunk into *str*. The string is then copied into *str*. And **this* is returned. Equating an object and a string.

s1 and *s2* are two other objects of the type *String*.

s2 = s1 = s is the next expression of note. The second = operator now takes centre-stage. This operator equates two objects. Owing to the overloaded = operator all the three objects *s*, *s1* and *s2* will contain the string String a string along.

Friend Assignment

We've assigned a string to an object with relative ease. Can we work the other way around? Assign an object to a string? You'd probably think declaring a friend operator will do the trick. Well, try it out.

PROGRAM 202

```
#include <iostream.h>
#include <string.h>

class String
{
    private:
    char *str;
    int size;
    public:
    String(void);
    String(const char *s);
    ~String( );
```

```
void print( )
{ cout << str;}

String& operator = (const char *s)
{
    size=strlen(s);
    str=new char[size+1];
    strcpy(str,s);
    return *this;
}

friend char *operator = (char *str,String& s)
{
    str=new char[s.size+1];
    strcpy(str,s.str);
    return str;
}

String& operator = (String& s)
{
    delete str;
    this->size = s.size;
    this->str = new char[s.size+1];
    strcpy(this->str,s.str);
    return *this;
}

};

String::String( )
{
    size=0;
    str=0;
}

String::String(const char *s)
{
    size = strlen(s);
    str = new char[size + 1];
    strcpy(str, s);
}
```

```
String::~String( )
{
    delete str;
}

main( )
{
    String s;
    s ="String a string along\n";

    char *p;
    p = s;
    s.print( );
    cout << p << "\n";
}
```

The simple truth of the matter is that the = operator cannot be defined as a friend. That's the rule, like it or not.

Overloaded '(char *)'

Does that mean assigning an object to a string is not possible? No. There is an opening out. Take this program:

PROGRAM 203

```
#include <iostream.h>
#include <string.h>

class String
{
    private:
    char *str;
    int size;
    public:
    String(void);
    String(const char *s);
    ~String( );
    void print( )
    { cout << str;}

    operator char *( )
    { return str; }
```

```
};
String::String( )
{
    size=0;
    str=0;
}

String::String(const char *s)
{
    size = strlen(s);
    str = new char[size + 1];
    strcpy(str, s);
}

String::~String( )
{
    delete str;
}

main( )
{
    String s("String a string along\n");
    s.print( );
    char *p;
    p = s;

    cout << "\n\n" << p << "\n" << *p;
}
```

Note the statement $p = s$. You are, in effect, overloading the (char *) operator. That means, you are assigning an object to a pointer. In a sense demoting it. It is like casting. $p = (char *)s$.

The output:

String a string along

String a string along
S

The first one is the output of *s.print( )*. The second, a result of *cout << "\n\n" << p*. And the third, the outcome of *cout << "\n" << *p*.

Overloaded '=='

Let's overload the comparison operator, ==. Read this program carefully and watch it work:

PROGRAM 204

```
#include <iostream.h>
#include <string.h>

class String
{
    private:
    char *str;
    int size;
    public:
    String(void);
    String(const char *s);
    ~String( );

    void print( )
    { cout << str;}
    int operator==(const String &s1);
};

String::String( )
{
    size=0;
    str=0;
}

String::String(const char *s)
{
    size = strlen(s);
    str = new char[size + 1];
    strcpy(str, s);
}

int String::operator==(const String &s1)
```

```
{
    return strcmp(str, s1.str)==0;
}

String::~String( )
{
    delete str;
}

main( )
{
    String s1("String a string along\n");

    String s2("This is different\n");

    String s3("String a string along\n");

    if ( s1 == s2 )
        cout << "The strings s1 and s2 are equal\n";
    else
        cout << "The strings s1 and s2 are not equal\n";

    if ( s1 == s3 )
        cout << "The strings s1 and s3 are equal\n";
    else
        cout << "The strings s1 and s3 are not equal\n";
}
```

The operator == has been overloaded to return an *int*. That apart, let's get into the gist of the program.

In the program *s1* is compared with *s2*, and then with *s3*. Let's take it from the first *if* statement. *if (s1 == s2)*. The object to the left, *s1* will be calling the operator. Would you like to recap the functioning of the == operator? *strcmp( )* compares the strings of the two objects passed to it, in our case, the first one is *s1*, passed implicitly by the *this* pointer, and the second *s2*. If these strings were equal *strcmp( )* would return a 0. 0 is equal to 0, so the statement will be true. 1 will be returned and accepted as the overloading statement specifies. The *if* statement will be true and so will be executed.

Since the two strings are not equal, the *if* statement will render untrue, so the *else* will be executed. *cout* will output the following legend:

The strings s1 and s2 are not equal.

if (s1 == s3). Since the two strings are equal, the *if* statement will be true and the output will be:

The strings s1 and s3 are equal.

Overloading Continued

Let's overload a range of those operators and bask in their logic:

PROGRAM 205

```
#include <iostream.h>
#include <string.h>

class String
{
    private:
    char *str;
    int size;
    public:
    String(void);
    String(const char *s);
    ~String();
    void print()
    { cout << str;}

    // compare class with pointer
    int operator==(const char *ptr)
        { return strcmp(str, ptr)==0; }

    // compare class with class
    int operator==(const String &s1)
        { return strcmp(str, s1.str)==0; }

    // compare pointer with class
    friend int operator==(char *ptr,const String &s1)
        { return strcmp(ptr, s1.str)==0; }
```

```
    // class less than pointer
    int operator<(const char *ptr)
        { return strcmp(str, ptr)<0; }

    // class less than class
    int operator<(const String &s1)
        { return strcmp(str, s1.str)<0; }

    // pointer less than class
    friend int operator<(char *ptr,const String &s1)
        { return strcmp(ptr, s1.str)<0; }

    // class greater than pointer
    int operator>(const char *ptr)
        { return strcmp(str, ptr)>0; }

    // class greater than class
    int operator>(const String &s1)
        { return strcmp(str, s1.str)>0; }

    // pointer less than class
    friend int operator>(char *ptr,const String &s1)
        { return strcmp(ptr, s1.str)>0; }
};

String::String( )
{
    size=0;
    str=0;
}

String::String(const char *s)
{
    size = strlen(s);
    str = new char[size + 1];
    strcpy(str, s);
}

String::~String( )
{
    delete str;
}
```

```
main( )
{
    String s1("Strings should be easy to use.\n");

    String s2("This is a different song \n");

    char *pointer = "This is a different song\n";

    if ( s1 == pointer )
        cout << "The string s1 is equal to pointer\n";

    if ( pointer == s2 )
        cout << "The pointer is equal to string s2\n";

    if ( s2 < pointer )
        cout << "The string s2 is less than pointer\n";

    if ( pointer > s2 )
        cout << "The pointer is greater than string s2\n";
}
```

We'll keep our discussion to the long line of operators only. Actually, even that should be a cake walk, but we'd like to reconfirm your ideas.

The first *if* statement compares an object with a string. If the strings are equal the *if* statement will become true and *cout* will be executed. Since that is not the case, the next *if* statement will be looked at.

The next *if* is something we'll have to look at a little more carefully. A string is compared with an object. The *if* statement regarding this piece of operation will be true, outputting The pointer is equal to string. The overloaded == for taking care of this operation must be a *friend* to be able to accept a string as its first parameter.

The chunk that follows uses the overloaded < operator. It checks whether the weight of the object is less than that of the string.

The last chunk deals with the overloading of the > operator. The same process is followed, and the output that you get will be: The pointer is equal to string

String Concatenation

That was all quite logical and simple. Can two strings be concatenated? How can two strings be added, if they can be added at all?

Let's take the following program:

PROGRAM 206

```
#include <iostream.h>
#include <string.h>

class String
{
    private:
    char *str;
    int size;
    public:
    String(void);
    String(char *s);
    String(const int length);
    ~String( );
    void print( )
    { cout << str << "\n";}
    String& operator+(const String &s1) const;
};

String::String( )
{
    size=0;
    str=0;
}

String::String( char *s)
{
    size = strlen(s);
    str = new char[size + 1];
```

```
    strcpy(str, s);
}

String::String(const int length)
{
    size = length;
    str = new char[size + 1];
    str[0] = '\0';
}

String::~String( )
{
    delete str;
}

String& String::operator+(const String &s1) const
{
    String *s2 = new String(strlen(str)+strlen(s1.str));
    strcpy(s2->str, str);
    strcat(s2->str, s1.str);
    return *s2;
}

main( )
{
    String s1("String a string along");
    String s2(" This is a different song");
    String s3;
    s3 = s1 + s2;
    s1.print( );
    s2.print( );
    s3.print( );
}
```

How is the overloading achieved? What is interesting here is the number of constructors called. And why? Look at the operator overloading definition, before you answer that.

new is being used to allocate a new object of type *String*. If you look at the statement carefully, you'll realize that *String* is, for the first time, passed a number. *strlen(str) + strlen(s1.str)* will result in a number. That is why you need the third and latest constructor.

The int constructor. The int constructor initializes the data members to the relevant values.

The address of the newly allocated object is put into *s2*. The first string is copied into *s2* -> *str*. The second string is appended to the first using the function *strcat( )*. And the object is returned.

Coming to the *main( )*, *s1.print( )* will output String a string along. *s2.print( )* will output This is a different song, and *s3.print( )*, String a string along This is a different song. The addition of two strings, never possible in C, achieved through a simple operator overloading technique!

Overloaded '[ ]'

When we dealt with arrays and pointers in C, the overwhelming thought was that arrays and pointers were essentially two sides of the same concept. Is it possible to extend that thought to C++? Let's check that out through a program:

PROGRAM 207

```
#include <iostream.h>
#include <string.h>

class String
{
    private:
    char *str;
    int size;

    public:
    String(void);
    String(char *s);
    void print(void) const;
    ~String( );
};

String::String( )
{
    size=0;
    str=0;
```

```
}
String::String( char *s)
{
    size = strlen(s);
    str = new char[size + 1];
    strcpy(str, s);
}

void String::print(void) const
{
    cout << str;
}

String::~String( )
{
    delete str;
}

main( )
{
    String s1("String a string along");
    s1[5];
}
```

Error! Because *s1* is an object and not a string. And so little details like arrays are not understood for the object. The error message: Operator cannot be applied to these operand types in function 'main( )'.

Is there an opening out? The answer, as you've probably guessed is Yes. All we have to do is overload the square brackets, [ ] how that is done is what we're going to see now.

PROGRAM 208

```
#include <iostream.h>
#include <string.h>

class String
{
    private:
    char *str;
```

```
    int size;

    public:
    String(void);
    String(char *s);
    void print(void) const;
    void operator[ ] (int i)
    ~String( );
};

String::String( )
{
    size=0;
    str=0;
}

String::String( char *s)
{
    size = strlen(s);
    str = new char[size + 1];
    strcpy(str, s);
}

void String::print(void) const
{
    cout << str;
}

void String::operator[ ] (int i)
{
    cout << "In [ ] " << i;
}

String::~String( )
{
    delete str;
}

main( )
{
    String s1("String a string along");
    s1[5];
}
```

All operators can be overloaded. That is the simple truth. And the brackets [ ] belong to the category of operators. So it's only a few small steps to overloading it.

We are overloading the operator to take an *int* as its explicit second parameter. So *s1[5]* will not flag an error now. The statement, if you haven't guessed already, is akin to a binary operator. *s1* is passed through the *this* pointer, and 5 is the *int* parameter that is accepted by the operator.

The output of this program will be:

In [ ] 5

Let's now ask for a *char* to be returned, instead of the void that the previous example returned.

PROGRAM 209

```
#include <iostream.h>
#include <string.h>

class String
{
    private:
    char *str;
    int size;

    public:
    String(void);
    String(char *s);
    void print(void) const;
    char operator[ ] (int i);
    ~String( );
};

String::String( )
{
    size=0;
    str=0;
}

String::String( char *s)
```

```
{
    size = strlen(s);
    str = new char[size + 1];
    strcpy(str, s);
}

void String::print(void) const
{
    cout << str;
}

char String::operator[ ] (int i)
{
    return str[i];
}

String::~String( )
{
    delete str;
}

main( )
{
    String s1("String a string along");
    cout << s1[5];
}
```

The operator is now designed to return the character specified by the *int* parameter. In our example, thus *return str[i]* will return the character of the data member *str* of the object passed implicitly.

The output you'll now get will be: 0g

You just printed the value already housed in the object. If you also wanted to change this value, how would you go about it?

PROGRAM 210
```
#include <iostream.h>
#include <string.h>

class String
{
```

```
        private:
        char *str;
        int size;

        public:
        String(void);
        String(char *s);
        void print(void) const;
        char operator[ ] (int i);
        ~String( );
};

String::String( )
{
    size=0;
    str=0;
}

String::String( char *s)
{
    size = strlen(s);
    str = new char[size + 1];
    strcpy(str, s);
}

void String::print(void) const
{
    cout << str;
}

char String::operator[ ] (int i)
{
    return str[i];
}

String::~String( )
{
    delete str;
}

main( )
{
    String s1("String a string along");
```

```
    s1[5] = 't';
    cout << s1[5];
}
```

If *s1* hadn't been an object, the equation *s1[5]* = 't' would have worked perfectly well. But there's no denying the fact that *s1* is an object. So *return str[i]* will return a *g* and stop at that. And *g* can certainly not be equal to *t*. The error message will be: Lvalue required in function main( ).

How do we solve that problem?

PROGRAM 211

```
#include <iostream.h>
#include <string.h>

class String
{
    private:
    char *str;
    int size;

    public:
    String(void);
    String(char *s);
    void print(void) const;
    char& operator[ ] (int i);
    ~String( );
};

String::String( )
{
    size=0;
    str=0;
}

String::String( char *s)
{
size = strlen(s);
str = new char[size + 1];
strcpy(str, s);
}
```

```
void String::print(void) const
{
    cout << str;
}

char& String::operator[ ] (int i)
{
    return str[i];
}

String::~String( )
{
    delete str;
}


main( )
{
    String s1("String a string along");
    s1[1] = 'p';
    s1.print( );
}
```

The idea is to return a reference. Enabling you to print the character as well as allowing you to change its value. The output this corrected program will give you:

Spring a string along

Here's another way of putting a 'Spring' in our string:

PROGRAM 212

```
#include <iostream.h>
#include <string.h>

class String
{
    private:
    char *str;
    int size;
```

```
    public:
    String(void);
    String(char *s);
    void print(void) const;
    char& operator[ ] (int i);
    ~String( );
};

String::String( )
{
    size=0;
    str=0;
}

String::String( char *s)
{
    size = strlen(s);
    str = new char[size + 1];
    strcpy(str, s);
}

void String::print(void) const
{
    cout << str;
}

char& String::operator[ ] (int i)
{
    return str[i];
}

String::~String( )
{
    delete str;
}

main( )
{
    String s1("String a string along");
    s1.operator[ ](1) = 'p';
    s1.print( );
}
```

Instead of saying *s1[1]* = 'p', we're complicating the equation by saying *s1.operator[ ](1)* = 'p'. It's the same thing worded differently. We're simply elaborating the fact that the [ ] is an operator by prefixing the word operator before it.

The output once again:

Spring a string along

Out-Of-the-Way '+='

Let's collate all that we've done so far. Take this program:

PROGRAM 213

```
#include <string.h>
#include <iostream.h>

class String
{
    private:
    int size ;
    char *str ;

    public:
    // constructors
    String(void);
    String(const char *ptr) ;
    String(String &s1) ;
    String(const int length);

    // create a character string from String method
    operator const char *( ) ;

    // assignment operator
    String operator = (String &s1) ;

    // concatenation methods
    String& operator+(const String &s1);
    String operator += (String &s1) ;

    // overloading the [ ]
    char& operator [ ] (int pos) ;
```

```
    // print method
    void print(void) const;

    // destructor
    ~String(void);

};

String::String(void)
{
    size = 0 ;
    str = 0 ;
}

String::String(const char *ptr)
{
    size = strlen(ptr) ;
    str = new char[size + 1] ;
    strcpy(str,ptr) ;
}

String::String(String& s1)
{
    size = s1.size ;
    str = new char[size + 1] ;
    strcpy(str,s1.str) ;
}

String::String(const int length)
{
    size = length;
    str = new char[size + 1];
    str[0] = '\0';
}

String String::operator = (String& s1)
{
    delete str ;
    size = s1.size ;
    str = new char[size + 1] ;
    strcpy(str,s1.str) ;
    return *this;
```

```
}

String& String::operator+(const String &s1)
{
    String *s2 = new String(strlen(str)+strlen(s1.str)+1);
    strcpy(s2->str, str);
    strcat(s2->str, s1.str);
    return *s2;
}

String String::operator += (String& s)
{
    int newsize;
    char *tmp;

    newsize = size + s.size;
    tmp = new char[newsize];
    size = newsize;

    strcpy(tmp,str);
    delete str;
    str = tmp;
    strcat(str,s.str);
    return *this;
}

char& String::operator [ ] (int pos)
{
    return str[pos];
}

void String::print(void) const
{
    cout << str << "\n";
}

String::~String(void)
{
    delete str;
}

main( )
{
```

```
String s1("OOPs it's happening");
s1.print( );

String s2("Long Live C++");
s2.print( );

char ret = s2[3];

cout << "Here's the character:" << ret << "\n";

s1 += s2;
s1.print( );
}
```

This long program does a very interesting thing. It brings all the operators that we've dealt with so far, under one roof. We've built it all under a single class.

The only addition here, is the overloading of the out-of-the-way operator, the *+=* operator. Let's look at that definition. For convenience, let's divide it into three distinct sections, the definition, the calculations and the copying aspect.

Let's tackle the calculation. The combined size of the two strings is first stored in *newsize*. A temporary variable is brought in to store the address of the newly allocated memory. The value of *newsize* is next assigned to *size*.

Now comes the copying bit. The first string, of the object pointed to by *this*, is copied into *tmp*. *str* is then deleted. The address in *tmp* is then transferred to *str*. And *strcat( )* concatenates the two strings. The output generated:

OOPs it's happening
Long Live C++
Here's the character: g
OOPs it's happeningLong Live C++

That was real cool, wasn't it?

String Along Some More

Let's have some fun with strings. Insert a character bang in the middle of a string or insert an entire string into another. You'll find a lot of use for this.

How is it done?

PROGRAM 214

```
#include <string.h>
#include <iostream.h>

class String
{
    private:
    int size ;
    char *str ;

    public:

    // constructors
    String(void);
    String(const char *ptr) ;
    String(String &s1) ;
    String(const int length);

    // create a character string from String method
    operator const char *( ) ;

    // assignment operator
    String operator = (String &s1) ;

    // concatenation methods
    String& operator + (const String &s1);
    String operator += (String &s1) ;

    // to insert a substring
    void StrInsert(int pos , char ch) ;
    void StrInsert(int pos , String& s1) ;

    char& operator [ ] (int pos) ;
```

```
    // print method
    void print(void) const;

    // destructor
    ~String(void);

};

String::String(void)
{
    size=0;
    str=0;
}

String::String(const char *ptr)
{
    size = strlen(ptr);
    str = new char[size + 1];
    strcpy(str,ptr);
}

String::String(String& s1)
{
    size = s1.size;
    str = new char[size + 1];
    strcpy(str,s1.str);
}

String::String(const int length)
{
    size = length;
    str = new char[size + 1];
    str[0] = '\0';
}


String String::operator = (String& s1)
{
    delete str;
    size = s1.size;
    str = new char[size + 1];
    strcpy(str,s1.str);
    return *this;
```

```
    }

    String& String::operator+(const String &s1)
    {
        String *s2 = new String(strlen(str)+strlen(s1.str)+1);
        strcpy(s2->str, str);
        strcat(s2->str, s1.str);
        return *s2;
    }

    String String::operator += (String& s)
    {
        int newsize;
        char *tmp;

        newsize = size + s.size;
        tmp = new char[newsize];
        size = newsize;

        strcpy(tmp,str);
        delete str;
        str = tmp;
        strcat(str,s.str);

        return *this;
    }

    void String::StrInsert(int pos , char ch)
    {
        char *ptr = new char[strlen(str)+2];

        strncpy(ptr,str,pos);
        ptr[pos] = ch;

        for(int cnt = pos; cnt < strlen(str); cnt++)
            ptr[cnt+1] = str[cnt];
        ptr[cnt+1] = '\0';

        delete str;
        str = new char[cnt+1];
        strcpy(str,ptr);
        delete ptr;
    }
```

```
void String::StrInsert(int pos , String& s1)
{
    int slen = strlen(s1.str);
    char *ptr = new char[strlen(str)+slen+1];

    strncpy(ptr,str,pos);

    ptr[pos] = '\0';
    strcat(ptr,s1.str);
    int nlen = strlen(ptr);

    for(int cnt = pos; cnt < strlen(str); cnt++,nlen++)
        ptr[nlen] = str[cnt];
    ptr[nlen] = '\0';

    delete str;
    str = new char[nlen];
    strcpy(str,ptr);
    delete ptr;
}

char& String::operator [ ] (int pos)
{
    return str[pos];
}

void String::print(void) const
{
    cout << str;
}

String::~String(void)
{
    delete str;
}

main( )
{
    String s1("Oop in C++");
    s1.print( );

    String s2("Turbo ");
```

```
    s2.print( );

    s1.StrInsert(3,'s');
    s1.print( );

    s1.StrInsert(9,s2);
    s1.print( );
}
```

It's a lengthy program alright. But let's look at its essence and marvel at its simplicity.

We've got an overloaded function called *StrInsert( )*. To the function are passed two parameters. The first, a number that indicates the position at which you wish to insert the character or the *String*, and the other, the character or *String* you want to insert.

Whenever a *String* object is built, the pointer *str* is allocated enough memory to hold that string. If you want to insert one or more characters, therefore, the space you have reserved will not be enough. You have to make allowances for the extra characters. New memory thus has to be allocated. A good idea would be to deallocate the existing memory pointed to by *str* and have it point instead to the new chunk allocated.

In the program above, we're going to do both - insert a character *s*, and a string *Turbo*. So that the final string we get would be:

Oops in Turbo C++

Consider the overloaded method *StrInsert( )*. If you go through it line by careful line, it shouldn't be difficult to unravel. The logic is very very simple. So bore into it yourself and have some fun.

UnString

If you can insert a character/string, surely it's a logical step towards deleting a character/string. What can do it for you is the *StrDelete( )* method. Further, if you want to insert a row of similar characters into the string, you simply call the *StrFill( )* method. Let's see how:

PROGRAM 215

```cpp
#include <string.h>
#include <iostream.h>

class String
{
    private:
    int size;
    char *str;

    public:

    // constructors
    String(void);
    String(const char *ptr);
    String(String &s1);
    String(const int length);

    // create a character string from String method
    operator const char *( );

    // assignment operator
    String operator = (String &s1);

    // concatenation methods
    String& operator+(const String &s1);
    String operator += (String &);

    // to delete a substring
    void StrDelete(String &);

    // to fill up a string with certain character
    void StrFill(char ch , int count);

    char& operator [ ] (int pos);

    // print method
    void print(void) const;
```

```
        // destructor
        ~String(void);

};

String::String(void)
{
    size=0;
    str=0;
}

String::String(const char *ptr)
{
    size = strlen(ptr);
    str = new char[size + 1];
    strcpy(str,ptr);
}

String::String(String& s1)
{
    size = s1.size;
    str = new char[size + 1];
    strcpy(str,s1.str);
}

String::String(const int length)
{
    size = length;
    str = new char[size + 1];
    str[0] = '\0';
}


String String::operator = (String& s1)
{
    delete str;
    size = s1.size;
    str = new char[size + 1];
    strcpy(str,s1.str);
    return *this;
}

String& String::operator+(const String &s1)
```

```
{
    String *s2 = new String(strlen(str)+strlen(s1.str)+1);
    strcpy(s2->str, str);
    strcat(s2->str, s1.str);
    return *s2;
}

String String::operator += (String& s)
{
    int newsize;
    char *tmp;

    newsize = size + s.size;
    tmp = new char[newsize];
    size = newsize;

    strcpy(tmp,str);
    delete str;
    str = tmp;
    strcat(str,s.str);

    return *this;
}

void String::StrDelete(String& s1)
{
    char *tmp;
    int length , slen;

    slen = strlen(s1.str);
    length = strlen(str);
    tmp = new char[length-slen+1];
    tmp[0] = '\0';

    for(int count = 0 , cnt = 0 ; count < length ; count++ , cnt++)
    {
        if(strncmp(&str[count],s1.str,slen) == 0)
            count+=slen;
        *(tmp+cnt) = *(str+count);
    }
    tmp[cnt] = '\0';

    delete str;
```

```
    str = new char[cnt];
    strcpy(str,tmp);
    delete tmp;
}

void String::StrFill(char ch , int count)
{
    int length = strlen(str);

    if(count != length)
    {
        delete str;
        str = new char[count];
        memset(str,ch,count);
    }
    else
        memset(str,ch,count);
}

char& String::operator [ ] (int pos)
{
    return str[pos];
}

void String::print(void) const
{
    cout << str;
}

String::~String(void)
{
    delete str;
}

main( )
{
    String s1("Oop in C++");
    s1.print( );

    s1.StrDelete("in");
    s1.print( );

    s1.StrFill('z',10);
```

```
    s1.print( );
}
```

The output is where we'll start at:

```
Oop in C++
Oop  C++
ZZZZZZZZZ
```

And before you go into noddy-noddy land, we'd like to tell you this is the last program in building of that massive *String* class.

So wake up and do your bit. Concentrate on one subtle point. The *StrDelete( )* method has been defined to accept an object of type *String*. The call to *StrDelete( )*, however, is being made with a normal string pointer. Shouldn't that give you an error?

No. The C++ compiler is an intelligent cookie. It detects the differences between what it has been passed and what it is designed to accept. And goes about in its quiet way resolving the issue. It converts the string it was passed into a temporary object. And your program moves on without a hitch.

That clear, you can take on the rest of the program yourself. Most of its elements comprise the storeys you built in the earlier programs. You're ready now to build your own extensions on that skeleton.

Our attempt has been to mould a basic structure. Lay the first stones, so you have an enduring platform from which to take off. Our attempt has been to introduce a concept that takes the sting out of programming. Classes are definitely a step up the ladder of simplicity. An exciting world awaits you. So like Jack start climbing the beanstalk without a second thought. This is only the beginning - you can do a hundred things with this structure.

Advanced C++

If you've ever reminisced with old cronies about stealing neighbors' mangoes, playing truant, stealing a smoke behind the dormitory walls, midnight parties and dark rendezvous, treading forbidden paths and the joy it all gave, you'd have realized that everybody, but everybody, gets a kick from eating forbidden fruit. Let's recapture some of that old excitement, scale walls that have been built to keep trespassers away. It's always fun to hunt for little loopholes in the law and wriggle through them without getting caught. Right? So here's to a good hunt and a wonderful treasure.

What is the central theme in C++? Data encapsulation, right? Private members that are cached away from roving outsider functions. Let's look for those little cracks in the walls and wedge ourselves in without too many contortions.

Member Pointers

Member Pointers. That's going to be our tool.

Warm up with this tiny program:

```
PROGRAM 216
#include <stdio.h>

class Apples
{
    int color;
    int seeds;
    public:
    Apples(void)
    { seeds = 4; color = 'r'; }
};

main()
{
```

```
int Apples::*p, Apples::*q;
p = &Apples::color;
q = &Apples::seeds;

Apples Kashmir;
int i,j;

i = Kashmir.*p;
j = Kashmir.*q;

printf("color = %c ... seeds = %d\n",i,j);
}
```

We've defined a class here, *Apples*, with two private *ints, seeds* and *color*. And a constructor which initializes the two members.

Having said that, let's get the program on the road. There is a function in ANSI C - *offsetof( )*. It gives you the relative position of a member in the structure. But the process entails too many contortions and convolutions. C++, living up to its image of simplicity, of ironing out all kinds of unaesthetic wrinkles, provides a very useful shaft to lift the blocks out of the way. Let's understand its mechanism.

Take the statement *int Apples::*p*. Read in text, that would be: *p* is a pointer to an *int* member of the class *Apples*. Similarly, *q* is also a pointer to an *int* member of the same class. We then initialize *p* to store the relative position of the member *color* of *Apples*, and *q* to store the position of *seeds*.

We've then defined an object of class *Apples* called *Kashmir*. *Kashmir.*p* will thus access the data member *color*, and *Kashmir.*q*, the member *seeds*. The values of the members so accessed will be assigned to *i* and *j*, respectively. *printf( )* will then do the needful, and you'll receive the output:

color = r ... seeds = 4

Voila! You're inside.

Now that you're in, would you like to change anything while no one's looking. Quick. Do this:

PROGRAM 217

```c
#include <stdio.h>

class Apples
{
    int color;
    int seeds;
    public:
    Apples(void)
    { seeds = 4; color = 'r'; }
};

main( )
{
    int Apples::*p, Apples::*q;
    p = &Apples::color;
    q = &Apples::seeds;

    Apples Kashmir;
    int i,j;

    i = Kashmir.*p;
    j = Kashmir.*q;
    printf("color = %c ... seeds = %d\n",i,j);

    Kashmir.*p = 'g';
    Kashmir.*q = 6 ;

    i = Kashmir.*p;
    j = Kashmir.*q;
    printf("color = %c ... seeds = %d\n",i,j);
}
```

Simple? Through the pointer, you've achieved an alteration in the private data members of the class. *Kashmir.*p* is reinitialized to *g* and *Kashmir.*q* is reinitialized to 6. The values of *i* and *j* will now be changed to *g* and 6. And *printf( )* will print the relevant output:

```
color = r ... seeds = 4
color = g ... seeds = 6
```

Let's indulge our insane obsession with pointers, as true and traditional C programmers. So. Give in to temptation and change the syntax. Use a pointer to an object instead of an instance of an object to get us to the same spot:

PROGRAM 218

```
#include <stdio.h>

class Apples
{
    int color;
    int seeds;
    public:
    Apples(void)
    { seeds = 4; color = 'r'; }
};

main( )
{
    int Apples::*p, Apples::*q;

    p = &Apples::color;
    q = &Apples::seeds;

    Apples *Kashmir = new Apples;
    int i,j;

    i = Kashmir->*p;
    j = Kashmir->*q;
    printf("color = %c ... seeds = %d\n",i,j);

    Kashmir->*p = 'g';
    Kashmir->*q = 6 ;

    i = Kashmir->*p;
    j = Kashmir->*q;
    printf("color = %c ... seeds = %d\n",i,j);
}
```

With .*, you had the member pointer to the right of the operator, and an instance of the class to the left of that operator. When you have a pointer to an instance of the class to the left, however, you need to change the operator notation from .* to ->*. The output of this program will be no different:

```
color = r ... seeds = 4
color = g ... seeds = 6
```

Once you know how to get inside and pick a private data member, it's a small step to breaking the fences that guard private methods. Go ahead and savor some more fruits of mischief.

PROGRAM 219

```
#include <stdio.h>

class Apples
{
    int color;
    int seeds;
    void pm(void)
    { printf("Inside the core of Apples\n"); }
    public:
    Apples(void)
    { seeds = 4; color = 'r';}
};

main( )
{
    void (Apples::*ptom)( );

    ptom = &Apples::pm;

    Apples Kashmir;

    (Kashmir.*ptom)( );
}
```

Remember the concept of pointers to a function? A concept you must have thrashed out as part of your basic C tutorial? Well, methods are after all functions. So pointers to methods should not be any different. Pointers to the private members of a class is what we're dealing with here. Combine the two concepts - pointers to functions and member pointers, or pointers to private members of a class and you'll have a clear picture.

The statement *void (Apples::*ptom)( )* reads 'ptom' is a pointer to a method of the class 'Apples'. In *ptom* we've stored the position of the method in the class. So, saying *(Kashmir.*ptom)( )* invokes the method. And you've succeeded in jumping over that wall too.

Like normal pointers to functions which can be enlisted to pass parameters and accept return values, member pointers to methods too work similarly.

PROGRAM 220

```
#include <stdio.h>

class Apples
{
    int color;
    int seeds;
    int pm(int a,int b)
    {
        color = a; seeds = b;
        printf("Change in color = %c ... seeds = %d\n",color, seeds);
        return(1);
    }
    public:
    Apples(void)
    { seeds = 4; color = 'r'; }
};

main( )
{
    int (Apples::*ptom)(int, int);

    ptom = &Apples::pm;

    Apples Kashmir;
```

```
    int i = (Kashmir.*ptom)('y',8);

    printf("return value of ptom = %d\n",i);
}
```

We've succeeded in changing the values of *color* and *seeds* to *y* and 8, respectively, by invoking the method with the relevant parameters. *i* accepts the return value of the private method that has been invoked through the member pointer *ptom*.

The output stands testimony to this:

```
Change in color = y ... seeds = 8
return value of ptom = 1
```

Virtual Classes

Designing. That is the essence of classes in C++. Given a plethora of formats and rules, there are a hundred ways of stitching and trimming to give you a tailor-made class that is just right for you. The scope is tremendous. Inheritances, polymorphism, derivation of classes, they are all bases for such designing.

Let's bounce back into the realm of derived classes. And multiple inheritances. A class derived from another class contains all the attributes of that class, at least those which have been allowed to be passed on. A class derived from the combination of two base classes similarly contains qualities passed on from both. Each of these classes, as individual entities, could further have their own characteristics. Let's break that train of thought to make room for an example.

If you wanted to incorporate into your repertoire a multitasking operating system and a multiuser system, you'd need a basic operating system from which you could derive these. But what happens if you wanted a multitasking-multiuser operating system? A system that incorporated the features of both the multitasking and the multiuser systems and belonged in the final analysis to the larger governing body - the operating system? That is when your thinking cap gets to be worn.

Let's go on a voyage of discovery. Take this program:

PROGRAM 221

```
#include <stdio.h>

class os
{
    protected :
    int processid;
    public :
    os(int pr) { processid = pr; }
};

class multitasking:public os
{
    public:
    multitasking(int mu = 100) : os(mu) {}
};

class multiuser:public os
{
    public:
    multiuser(int ml = 200) : os(ml) {}
};

class idealos:public multitasking,multiuser
{
    public:
    idealos(int id) : os(id) {}
    void dispi(void)
    { printf("\nProcess ... %d\n",processid); }
};

void main( )
{
    idealos ouros(10);
    ouros.dispi( );
}
```

If the multitasking system inherited all the qualifying attributes of the operating system and the multiuser system inherited those same qualities, the combination of the two would result in a multitasking-multiuser system that comprises all the data inherited from the base. All the data is repeated twice.

Even the compiler recognizes this foolishness and will promptly register an error in such a situation. Two errors will be flagged: 'os' is not a base class of 'idealos' in function idealos::idealos(int), and Field 'processid' is ambiguous in 'idealos' in function idealos::dispi( ).

But what if you insist on a multitasking-multiuser operating system? What is the solution?

PROGRAM 222

```
#include <stdio.h>

class os
{
    protected :
    int processid;
    public :
    os(int pr) { processid = pr; }
};

class multitasking:virtual public os
{
    public:
    multitasking(int mu = 100) : os(mu) {}
};

class multiuser:virtual public os
{
    public:
    multiuser(int ml = 200) : os(ml) {}
};

class idealos:public multitasking,multiuser
{
    public:
    idealos(int id = 10) : os(id) {}
    void dispi(void)
    { printf("\nProcess ... %d\n",processid); }
};
```

```
void main( )
{
    idealos ouros;
    ouros.dispi( );
}
```

The word *virtual* prefixed to the base class name works like magic. To begin with, let's understand what it achieves. The two classes derived from the base class, simply act as intermediaries. The values of the base class are then transferred through the entire hierarchy - derivations from derivations - even to those classes that are not directly in the purview of the base class. That is, classes that have no umbilical connection to the base class. It is an abstract concept and it calls for immense patience and concentration.

Let's begin with *main( )*. *ouros* is the object we've defined of type *idealos*. *idealos* has been derived from the two classes *multitasking* and *multiuser*. These two classes are in turn derivations of the base class *os*. Since both these have been derived virtually from *os*, *idealos* can call the base class constructor *os* directly. Using the classes from which they were derived merely as vehicles.

Since the constructors of *multiuser* and *multitasking* have not been called by *idealos*, these constructors will be called with their default values, 100 and 200. The *idealos* constructor calls the *os* constructor on its own, giving *processid* the default value of the *idealos* constructor, 10. If *ouros* is called with a number, *processid* will take on the specified value and the default value will be overwritten normally.

The constructor values of the intermediate classes, thus have been ignored, and the data member of the base class was initialized through a class not directly derived from it. Could it be called a vicarious inheritance perhaps?

Consider the output of the program to give body to that abstraction:

Process ... 10

That was a very complex design, sure. A design where the onus of adjustment lies with the intermediary classes, rather than the class derived from them or their parent, the base class. It is up to the conscientious programmer, slogging in his ivory tower, to anticipate the kind of need that calls for a virtual base class.

Declaring a class as virtual brings its own package of advantages and disadvantages. We've just seen the plus point, let's talk briefly about the minus point. The fact is that when a class has been defined as virtual, you cannot have a reference or a pointer to the base class point to its derived classes. Keep those advantages and disadvantages in mind while you go ahead and build designer classes.

Put the virtual base classes at the back of your mind and let's get ahead with discovering more nuances about derivations, designing of classes and more ways to get choosy.

PROGRAM 223

```c
#include <stdio.h>

class Parent
{
    public:
    int val1;
    int val2;
    Parent(void)  { val1 = val2 = 0; }
    Parent(int a, int b) { val1 = a; val2 = b; }
};

class child : private Parent
{
    protected:
    int Parent::val1;
    public:
    void print(void)
    {
        val1 = 'A';
        val2 = 'Z';
```

```
        printf("Child can say %c ... %c\n",val1,val2);
    }
};

class doll : public child
{
    public:
    void print(void)
    {
        val1 = 'A';
        printf("This doll only says %c....\n",val1);
    }
};

main( )
{
    child Junior;
    Junior.print( );
    doll Barbie;
    Barbie.print( );
}
```

Consider a derivation where all the members of a base class are inherited by a derived class. If the access of the derivation has been specifically declared as *private*, all the *public* members derived will become *private* as the rule book states. But C++ allows you to make your own modifications to suit your own purposes.

By declaring the member *val1* as protected, we keep it open to the class derived from it, *doll*. Now consider the *main( )*. *Junior* is an object of the class *child*. *val1* and *val2* are both inherited by *child* from *Parent*. So *Junior.print( )* will output the statement:

Child can say A ... Z

Now look at the second output:

This doll only says A

Barbie of class *doll* can access *val1*, the member that was declared protected when it was derived from the base class in a private access. But *val2*, which remained private to *child* is out of the reach of *doll*.

C++ does exhibit a very lenient attitude of "Yours is but to pick and choose". If you just know how!

Here's some inside information on how the marketplace fares in terms of OOP compilers. There are compilers and compilers and compilers vying for a spot under the sun. Let's take our shopping bags and shop for some of these object oriented tools.

First there were three contenders: Smalltalk/V from DigitalkInc, Actor from the WhitewaterGroup and Zortech Inc's C++. A small band of programming classes that worked in fairly abstract environments. But as the rumors about the usefulness and elegance of these features spread, more and more enterprising groups picked up the winds and started producing their own versions. And incorporated them into more concrete and down-to-earth packages.

Borland's Turbo Pascal v 5.5 and Microsoft Corp's Quick Pascal v 1.0 were the next to enter the fray. Turbo C++, Comeau Computing's v 2.1, ImageSoft Inc's Glockenspiel v 2.0a ... were not far behind. In this flooded scenario, making a decision about which version to select, should be based on what you are comfortable working with and what the situation demands.

The various versions harbor very subtle differences. Different dialects of the same mother tongue. So, if the installation of a different version is required, you don't have to undergo a total attitude change. You've only got to pick up and understand those small differences. And you can have it running. As effortlessly as if you were reared on it.

C++. There are so many people singing its praises that it has become the programmer's anthem. It is being cheered vociferously around street corners of computing lanes. And, why not?

C++ has given structured programming a whole new meaning. If C was considered and raved about as a structured language, C++ is many notches ahead. Anchored in classes, C++ binds the loose body of C into a semblance of wholeness. It has given programming a cool and sensuous feel. Added a smooth and polished touch and tacked shoddy seams.

C++ is the language of the times. And if you're still hesitating after this perspective, you just need to sit through this recital again.

Perspectives 1991

The 70's gave way quietly to the 80's.

The last of the flower children were still roaming the cobbled streets. Radicalism, world peace, cults and nirvana ... the slogans were still breaking the winds. Flared trousers hadn't left, rock and roll still ruled. Amorphous, undefined, characterless, the 70's were the debris of the 60's. Lennon was dead, and C was no longer a giant attraction.

As the sun set on the decade and the world slipped unobtrusively into the 80's, electronic synthesizers and objects had completely usurped six-stringed guitars and functions. Structured programming had progressed from the idiosyncratic C to the hallowed C++.

Objects. That was the latest rallying point of the computer clan. Object Oriented language was the dialect that was slowly creeping into the programming mainstream. And it was attracting as many followers as the Pied Piper of Hamlin.

OOPs was the cry of the 80's.

But Object Oriented language was certainly no rabbit out of an 80's derby hat. It was a concept simmering silently under the surface, patiently waiting its turn. Before Bjarne Stroustrup harnessed it, there were other languages that had already embraced OOPs to their bosoms. There was SmallTalk, for instance, which floundered with its pigheaded dogmatism. A sound and reasonable idea without practical anchors, it remained in the realm of abstract reasoning. Admittedly though the power of object orientedness was acknowledged long before it was actually hauled on to the pedestal and the halo nailed around its coiffured head.

The honors of giving OOPs its rightful place, of course, goes to Bjarne Stroustrup, who recognized the potholes in C and conscientiously scooped lumps of solid material into them, mortaring objects into the viscous body of C and smoothening the bumps.

The light that he was seeking seems to have been efficiency. Channelizing the directionless blob into a definitive entity was the driving goal. Only Stroustrup saw the new formula he was developing merely as an unassuming extension to C. Hence, C++. He did not see fit to include a C++ compiler. What he wrote was basically a preprocessor that had to go through a C compiler to take shape.

Computer professionals, have, over the years attained the dubious reputation of being a dissatisfied lot. "The software does not work", that seems to be a regular and constant refrain. Whether it was structured programming, or concepts like 'CASE', even the most sophisticated software was not spared. The attitude was "Every silver lining has a cloud". In a world of hard-to-please people, C++ too was constantly poked and jibed to squeeze out and expose shortcomings.

The major drawback, the absence of a pure C++ compiler was set right by Zortech. They were the first to develop a self-reliant compiler that understood objects. They're incidentally, not the biggest name in C++ stories anymore. Borland'sTurbo C++ is the current leader of the swollen pack.

The who's who and what's what apart, C++ has emerged as an untainted, unsullied, pristine and beautiful being, absolutely blameless and blemish-free. Like snake oil, it's being touted as the cure for everything from hiccups to heartaches. A magic wand that can perform the most herculean of all tasks.

From the elfin users with their small needs to the giant corporations and their huge projects, the chant is the same. C++ is the most efficient tool, a productivity booster. A Quatro upgradation, from Version 1 to Version 5, with C++ for example, takes half the time it would have normally taken. Its spell has been so total, that traditional products like FoxPro and Lotus

1-2-3 spreadsheets are being rewritten in C++. In fact, imbibing LPL, Lotus' Programming Language, depends on how much OOPs you know.

In all fairness, though, the bright light of that halo is not all real. Some of it has been conjured by the feeble-minded afraid to touch the isms and logies of the language. To these, the gullible, cowering under the onslaught of a blitz that torched the ponderous terms, the light has been too blinding to approach. To them, we'd like to introduce Rudyard Kipling's pensive quartet:

"Woulds't thou," - so the helmsman
  answered,
"Know the secret of the sea?
 Only those who brave its dangers
 Comprehend its mystery."

Objects have been around for as long as you were this high in computers. What are fields in dBASE? What are forms in Accell? They're simply objects. C++, then, is merely just another presentation folder. It is more of the new, improved variety of a snake oil that has always been around.

An improvement, though, that has been a quantam leap in technology. As more and more people succumb to the lure of C++, it is obvious that this is the shuttle that's going to rocket you somewhere. As software grows, inundating markets with slicker versions every second, the need to keep pace becomes more urgent. As features escalate and documentation manuals begin to resemble mammoth tomes, survival becomes suspect. It is not enough anymore to be a weak and undernourished bystander. If you're not conversant with C++, you won't even catch the glimmer of the software streak that just swept past.

It's 1991. And if you're not into C++ yet, you'd better compere a comedy show.

Prologue

STAR WARS.....

The end approaches....The rebels are fighting a losing war. Attempts made to approach the Central Reactor have failed repeatedly. Luke Skywalker manages to enter the tunnel leading to the Central Reactor along with a few rebel spaceships. However luck doesn't seem to be on Luke's side as Darth Vader and his robots start getting better of the rebel crafts shielding Luke from Vader. Luke seems so near the reactor ...yet, so far. Vader attempts to lock on Luke's ship. He gets a lock. To Vader's surprise he is suddenly hit from behind! He loses control of the ship and rolls far away into infinity...It is none other than Han Solo to the rescue. With no one behind him, Luke can make it. Luke invokes the power hidden within him and locks on the target. He fires and hits home. As they move further away from the Death Star, behind them, fire annihilates the symbol of evil....

What in the name of Donald Duck is this in the middle of a C book ??!!? Nevertheless, if you have seen George Lucas' epic movie STAR WARS we are sure , for a moment you drifted away into the theatre where you, along with the audience, were spellbound with the special effects that movie had in store.

One question you might ask is 'How did they do all this ? ' Computers is indeed the answer. In a short documentary we saw once, they had shown how computers were used to create one of the finest special effects on that 70 mm screen. Special effects happen to be only one of the plethora of applications of Computer Graphics.

Graphics is a world where our imagination is the limit. But where in the world of beauty do we programmers fit in ? Well, as a matter of fact, everywhere . We today, can bring our dreams to life using C as our medium of expression. Armed with some functions and tools all we need to have is a fair amount of knowledge of the theoretical concepts upon which computer graphics is based. Instead of being awed by the sheer beauty of graphics if we try to understand and appreciate the concepts upon which these images have been created, we can get a step closer to generating them ourselves.

We will , in what follows , try to take you on a journey to where graphics dwells....... a kingdom of landscapes and Gremlins and......

Are we ready? Let's go.....

Getting Started

To begin with, when we start with graphics we need a HEADER FILE called GRAPHICS.H. This contains definitions and explanations of all the functions and constants we'll need. So we can consider this our starting point.

Now that we have the definitions of our functions, we can move on to our actual functions. These are kept in the graphics library file, GRAPHICS.LIB.

Both these files are provided as part of TURBO C.

So our minimum requirements to get started with graphics are:

1) the header file GRAPHICS.H

2) the graphics library file GRAPHICS.LIB

3) and a dream.

You will find some files with a BGI extension and some with a CHR extension. Be sure to transfer them to the directory in which you are currently working.

There is another point that must be kept in mind when you key in the programs that follow. You will notice that the *printf( )* function or any function associated with receiving a string as one of its parameters (*sprintf( )* for instance) typically appears as shown below :

```
printf(" AFTER GOING INTO GRAPHICS MODE. AND NOW
    QUITTING...\n" ) ;
```

Observe that the string between the opening and closing of inverted commas extends on the second line. This is erroneous and the Turbo C Compiler will flag an error. The entire string MUST be on a single line as shown below:

```
printf("AFTER GOING INTO GRAPHICS MODE.AND NOW
QUITTING...\n");
```

We are doing so because of space constraints on a single line. Most editors stretch across 255 columns, so you will not encounter any problems while making this change. Also note the fact that we've written our programs on the EGA and VGA monitors. For other monitors we expect you to make the necessary changes.

The Beginning : Switching To The Graphics Mode

We are currently in the text mode, with 25 rows and 80 columns. But now we'll switch to graphics by running this program:

PROGRAM 224

```
#include <graphics.h>

void main( )
{
    int gm , gd = DETECT ;

    printf(" BEFORE GOING INTO GRAPHICS MODE\n" ) ;
    getch( ) ;

    initgraph( &gd , &gm , "" ) ;

    printf(" AFTER GOING INTO GRAPHICS MODE. AND NOW"
        " QUITTING...\n" ) ;
    /* please reboot the machine */
}
```

This program takes you from the text mode to the graphics mode. What we have done in the program is:

-- defined 2 integers *gm* and *gd*, and then

-- called the function *initgraph( )*

Let's run this program.

The first *printf( )* will print in the text mode. The computer then waits for us to press a key. As soon as we press a key, the function *initgraph( )* will be called. And then the screen will be cleared, thus reflecting the switch from the text mode to the graphics mode.

Now the second *printf( )* will print in the graphics mode and the program will terminate. Now move the cursor to.....where's the cursor???!!!

Aha....remember, you're in the graphics mode, so the cursor will not be displayed. Graphics modes do not support the conventional cursor.

Now list the directory and see how slowly it scrolls compared to the text mode.

To return to the text mode you will have to reboot the machine. It is good practice to always go back to your starting point, in this case the text mode. This is what we'll do in the next program.

PROGRAM 225

```
#include <graphics.h>
void main( )
{
    int gm , gd = DETECT ;

    printf(" BEFORE GOING INTO GRAPHICS MODE\n" ) ;
    getch( ) ;

    initgraph( &gd , &gm , "" ) ;

    printf(" AFTER GOING INTO GRAPHICS MODE. AND NOW"
        " QUITTING...\n" ) ;
    getch( ) ;

    closegraph( ) ;

    printf(" AFTER GOING OUT OF GRAPHICS MODE "
```

```
            "INTO TEXT MODE\n" ) ;
}
```

Again, this program will print the first *printf( )* in text mode, wait for a key to be pressed, call *initgraph( )*, switch to graphics mode, print the next *printf( )* in graphics mode and then wait for you to press a key. As soon as you press a key, the function *closegraph( )* will be called. What does this function do? we hear you ask. It simply closes the graphics mode and restores the screen to its prior mode. Think of it as performing housekeeping chores.

Always use the *closegraph( )* function to leave the graphics mode.

Thus, *closegraph( )* negates *initgraph( )*.

About Graphic Modes And Drivers

Now that we've bothered you enough with how to get in and out of the graphics mode, let's look at some new concepts, introduced in the following program:

```
PROGRAM 226
#include <graphics.h>
void main( )
{
    int gm , gd = DETECT ;
    int mode ;
    char *name ;

    initgraph( &gd , &gm , "" ) ;

    printf(" GRAPHICS MODE : \n" ) ;

    mode = getgraphmode( ) ;

    name = getmodename( mode ) ;

    printf("Value of gm = %d\n" , gm ) ;
    printf("Current graphics mode number is : %d "
```

```
        "and mode name is %s\n " ,mode , name ) ;
    printf("Press a key\n" ) ;
    getch( ) ;

    closegraph( ) ;
}
```

Here, we have defined 3 integers, *gm, gd* and *mode*, and a pointer to a character. We will dwell for a while on *gm*, the second parameter passed to *initgraph( )*.

We know that when the DOS prompt is displayed, we are in the text mode. From here, we have seen how we can go to the graphics mode by calling the *initgraph( )*. All very straightforward. However, there are various modes within graphics, so we have to decide which graphics mode we require.

To understand this, we need to understand monitors and the concept of resolution. The number of dots or picture elements (pixels) available to us on the screen in the graphics mode, is known as the resolution. The greater the number of dots, the higher the resolution. Simply put, this means that the more dots available, the clearer our picture.

The function *initgraph( )* figures out the resolution and assigns it a number. This number is then put in the address of *gm*. Thus, *gm* is the current graphics mode and specifies the resolution. The *gm* number tells us which monitor we are using, and its resolution, the number of video pages it supports and the colors available.

The monitor we are using is the EGA, the maximum resolution of which is 640*350 (i.e. 640 pixels from left to right and 350 pixels from top to bottom).

The variables *gm* and *mode* are equivalent, the only difference being that *gm* is obtained by the function *initgraph( )* while *mode* is obtained by the function *getgraphmode( )*. The information regarding monitor and resolution, i.e. *gm*, is obtained by calling *getmodename( )* . The mode number is passed to this function. And *getmodename( )* accordingly returns a pointer to a string, where the required information is stored.

Let's proceed to the other two parameters, *gd* and "" (NULL).

To understand *gd*, we have to understand the concept of device drivers. Device drivers are small programs which talk directly to the hardware. Since we can't be machine-dependent at any time, we need programs we can communicate with in a standardized way. These will in turn communicate with the machine. These intermediary programs are known as device drivers.

Graphics drivers are a subset of device drivers and are applicable in the graphics mode. They work in the above fashion to execute whatever task we have assigned. Turbo C offers certain graphics drivers. These are the files with a BGI extension. Depending on what monitor is used, one of these drivers gets selected. Our programs have been developed on the EGA and, occasionally, the VGA monitors. Thus we need the EGAVGA.BGI file as our graphics driver.

So far, so good! Okay.....

In our program, *gd* has been assigned the value DETECT, thereby asking *initgraph( )* to figure out what BGI file is needed. This file is then loaded into memory.

Which is all very well, but WHERE is the BGI file stored? For this, *initgraph( )* requires the path to the driver files, which is specified in the third parameter. So everything fits in very neatly. Our program has assigned the value NULL ("") to this third parameter.

When *initgraph( )* sees a NULL, it assumes that the driver file lies in the current directory. To get the name of the driver file, we will call the function *getdrivername( )*, in the following program.

PROGRAM 227
```c
#include <graphics.h>
void main( )
{
    int gm , gd = DETECT ;
    int mode ;
    char *driver ;

    initgraph( &gd , &gm , "" ) ;
    printf(" GRAPHICS DRIVER : \n" ) ;

    driver = getdrivername( ) ;

    printf(" Current graphics driver name is %s\n " ,driver ) ;

    printf(" Press a key\n" ) ;
    getch( ) ;
    closegraph( ) ;
}
```

We have defined the variable *driver*, which is a pointer to a character and switched to the graphics mode by calling *initgraph( )* . The function *getdrivername( )* stores the driver name as a string and returns a pointer to this string. This pointer is assigned to the variable *driver*. The second *printf( )* simply prints the name of the driver. The driver name we got was EGAVGA.

So much for drivers. Let's go back to mode for a while. The next program shows how after switching to the graphics mode we can set the graphics mode of our choice :

PROGRAM 228
```c
#include <graphics.h>
void main( )
{
    int gm , gd = DETECT ;
    int mode ;

    initgraph( &gd , &gm , "" ) ;
    printf(" GRAPHICS MODE : \n" ) ;
```

```
        mode = getgraphmode( ) ;

        printf( " Graph mode number = %d \n " , mode ) ;
        printf("Press any key to change the graphics mode\n");
        getch( );

        setgraphmode( EGALO );

        mode = getgraphmode( ) ;

        printf( " New Graph mode number = %d \n " , mode ) ;
        printf(" Press a key\n" ) ;
        getch( ) ;
        closegraph( ) ;
    }
```

The function *getgraphmode( )* will give us the number of the graphics mode. Here it is 1, which corresponds to EGAHI (having a resolution of 640*350). If we change this value to 0, which corresponds to EGALO (having a resolution of 640*200), the display will change. Try it for yourself. The second display is much less sharp since the resolution is now lower.

What are the various modes available in Turbo C? Further, how many modes are you allowed?

To answer the first question, we have compiled the following list. The first column gives the name of the mode as defined in GRAPHICS.H. The numerical equivalents of the modes are listed in the second column. The third column gives details regarding each mode.

The Mode constant	Actual Values	Interpretation
CGAC0	0	320x200 palette 0; 1 page
CGAC1	1	320x200 palette 1; 1 page
CGAC2	2	320x200 palette 2; 1 page
CGAC3	3	320x200 palette 3; 1 page
CGAHI	4	640x200 1 page
MCGAC0	0	320x200 palette 0; 1 page
MCGAC1	1	320x200 palette 1; 1 page
MCGAC2	2	320x200 palette 2; 1 page
MCGAC3	3	320x200 palette 3; 1 page
MCGAMED	4	640x200 1 page
MCGAHI	5	640x480 1 page
EGALO	0	640x200 16 color 4 pages
EGAHI	1	640x350 16 color 2 pages
EGA64LO	0	640x200 16 color 1 page
EGA64HI	1	640x350 4 color 1 page
EGAMONOHI	0	640x350 64K,1 page /256K, 4 pages
HERCMONOHI	0	720x348 2 pages
ATT400C0	0	320x200 palette 0; 1 page
ATT400C1	1	320x200 palette 1; 1 page
ATT400C2	2	320x200 palette 2; 1 page
ATT400C3	3	320x200 palette 3; 1 page
ATT400MED	4	640x200 1 page
ATT400HI	5	640x400 1 page
VGALO	0	640x200 16 color 4 pages
VGAMED	1	640x350 16 color 2 pages
VGAHI	2	640x480 16 color 1 page
PC3270HI	0	720x350 1 page
IBM8514LO	0	640x480 256 colors
IBM8514HI	1	1024x768 256 colors

DIAGRAM 1.1

Now to deal with the second question: How many modes are we allowed?

Let's look at the following program.

PROGRAM 228

```c
#include <graphics.h>

void main( )
{
    int gm , gd = DETECT ;
    int mode , maxmode , lo , hi ;

    initgraph( &gd , &gm , "" ) ;
    printf(" GRAPHICS MODE : \n" ) ;

    mode = getgraphmode( ) ;

    printf(" Graph mode number = %d \n " , mode ) ;

    maxmode = getmaxmode( ) ;

    getmoderange(gd , &lo , &hi) ;

    printf(" Maximum Modes from GETMAXMODE = %d\n",
        maxmode ) ;
    printf(" Maximum Modes from GETMODERANGE = %d to %d\n",
        lo , hi ) ;

    printf(" Press a key\n" ) ;
    getch( ) ;
    closegraph( ) ;
}
```

We know that the function *getgraphmode( )* returns the number of the current mode. We have introduced two new functions: *getmaxmode( )* and *getmoderange( )* . Both these functions give us the maximum number of modes available on a particular driver. However there is a subtle difference between the two.

The function *getmaxmode( )* gives the maximum mode number available in the current graphics driver.It will work on any driver. The *getmoderange( )* , on the other hand, gives the range of valid mode numbers from low to high. It will work only on graphics drivers supplied by Borland. It therefore needs a parameter to indicate which driver is currently in use. This value is passed as the first parameter, viz. *gd*.

After running this program, we find that the value of maximum mode number was 1 and that the mode range was from 0 to 1, corresponding to EGALO and EGAHI, respectively.

Switching To And Fro, From Graphics To Text

Now, suppose you are in the graphics mode and want to switch to the text mode and then back to the graphics mode. Confused?? Don't be.....

PROGRAM 230

```c
#include <graphics.h>

void main( )
{
    int gm , gd = DETECT ;
    int mode ;

    /* assuming the drivers are in current subdirectory */

    initgraph( &gd , &gm , "" ) ;
    printf( " Press a key to enter TEXT Mode\n" ) ;
    getch( ) ;

    restorecrtmode( ) ;

    printf(" We are now in text mode. Press a key to get back.\n" ) ;
    getch( ) ;

    mode = getgraphmode( ) ;
    setgraphmode(mode) ;

    printf(" Back home and terminating...press a key...\n") ;
    getch( ) ;

    closegraph( ) ;
}
```

Here, as usual, we've initialized the graphics system. To switch to text, we call the function *restorecrtmode( )* . By doing so, we restore the mode that existed prior to calling *initgraph( )*.

In order to switch back to graphics, we'll need to call the function *getgraphmode( )*. The *getgraphmode( )* function will give us the current graphics mode and *setgraphmode( )* will set the graphics system to this mode.

We're sure you've had enough of graphics drivers and graphics modes for the moment. But don't leave now. It gets better, we promise.....

There is another way to initialize the graphics system. Here we use the function *detectgraph( )* . We have passed this function two parameters, viz. the addresses of *gd* and *gm*. Initially, *detectgraph( )* determines the graphics driver and the mode, and puts these values in *gd* and *gm*, respectively. The function *initgraph( )* is then called with the same values.

PROGRAM 231

```
#include <graphics.h>

void main( )
{
    int gm , gd ;

    detectgraph( &gd , &gm ) ;

    initgraph( &gd , &gm , "" ) ;
    printf(" GRAPHICS MODE : \n" ) ;
    printf( " Graphics Driver number from DETECTGRAPH %d "
           " name %s\n " ,gd , getdrivername( )) ;
    getch( ) ;
    closegraph( ) ;
}
```

The BGI Drivers And Your Application

At the beginning of our discussion we stressed the importance of BGI files to your graphics programs. The absence of these files renders your graphics programs redundant. These files are separately loaded onto memory. Now, it would simplify matters and significantly reduce the possibility of error if we could load the BGI files as part of the EXE files that you've created.

The BGI files first have to be converted to OBJ files. For this we need a program called BGIOBJ.EXE. We'll run it as follows:

First type in:

C> BGIOBJ   EGAVGA.BGI

Your C file will have a name. Let's assume that it is called GRAPH.C. Load a file called GRAPH.PRJ and enter the following into it:

```
GRAPH
EGAVGA.OBJ
```

Load your C file (GRAPH.C in this case) and choose the Project option. At Project name, give the name of the file you have just created, viz. GRAPH.PRJ. Now, in your C program, call the function *registerbgidriver( )* before calling *initgraph( )*. The parameter passed to *registerbgidriver( )* depends on the driver file. For example, if the driver file is EGAVGA.BGI, the parameter passed should be *EGAVGA_driver*.

The following list gives the driver files and the name to be used with *registerbgidriver( )* :

Driver File (.BGI)	Name when used in registerbgidriver( )
CGA	CGA_driver
EGAVGA	EGAVGA_driver
IBM8514	IBM8514_driver
HERC	Herc_driver
ATT	ATT_driver
PC3270	PC3270_driver

DIAGRAM 1.2

Now, if you need to load more than one driver, you may have a problem since more than one may not fit on a 64K segment. So we use *registerfarbgidriver( )* . The object file (OBJ file) should be created in the following manner:

C>BGIOBJ /F EGAVGA.BGI

The parameter passed to *registerfarbgidriver( )* will be *EGAVGA_driver_far.*

The following program demonstrates how the C file should be written:

PROGRAM 232

```
#include <graphics.h>
#include <stdio.h>

void main( )
{
    int gm , gd = DETECT ;

    registerbgidriver( EGAVGA_driver ) ;
```

```
    initgraph( &gd , &gm , NULL ) ;
    printf(" GRAPHICS MODE : \n" ) ;
    printf( " Graphics Driver number %d name %s\n " ,
            gd , getdrivername( )) ;
    getch( ) ;
    closegraph( ) ;
}
```

The function *registerbgidriver( )* tells *initgraph( )* not to load the BGI file since the driver is a part of the application (ie. the EXE file). Note that the path to the driver files is a NULL.

That brings us to the end of our discussion on all the modes and drivers supported by graphics. And with that out of the way, we can concentrate on what we're really here for. To work magic on the screen.

Ready when you are.

About Color....

At this point, endless options are open to us. Shall we start with color?

Whether we are in text or graphics mode, we have a set of foreground colors and a set of background colors. The next few programs play with color in graphics using the tools available to us in Turbo C.

The Color In The Foreground

Let's look at foreground color. We'll introduce two functions here, viz. *getcolor( )* and *setcolor( )*. The function *getcolor( )* gets the current foreground color and *setcolor( )* sets the color to what you specify.

PROGRAM 233

```
#include <graphics.h>

void main( )
{
    int gm , gd = DETECT ;
    int color ;

    initgraph( &gd , &gm , "" ) ;

    color = getcolor( ) ;

    printf("Color reported by GETCOLOR( ) = %d\n"
          "Press a key\n",color ) ;
    outtextxy( 200 , 100 , "->This is from outtextxy( ) before"
                          " color change" ) ;

    getch( ) ;

    setcolor( LIGHTRED ) ;

    outtextxy( 200 , 200 , "->This is from outtextxy( )"
```

```
                    " after color change" ) ;

              getch( ) ;
              closegraph( );
       }
```

After initializing the graphics system, we call the function *getcolor( )* and assign the value returned by this function to the variable *color*.

The function *printf( )* prints the number of the current foreground color, which is white by default.

The function *outtextxy( )* prints the text at the specified coordinates in the current foreground color -- white.

On pressing a key, the function *setcolor( )* is called. We have set the color to light red. Thus, *outtextxy( )* will now print the text in the new color.

The Color In The Background

Now let's play around with the background colors . The next program introduces the functions *getbkcolor( )* and *setbkcolor( )*.

PROGRAM 234

```c
#include <graphics.h>
void main( )
{
    int gm , gd = DETECT ;
    int bkcolor ;

    initgraph( &gd , &gm , "" ) ;

    bkcolor = getbkcolor( ) ;

    printf("Background color number = %d\n"
        "Press a key to change it\n" , bkcolor ) ;
    getch( ) ;
```

```
setbkcolor( LIGHTCYAN ) ;

getch( ) ;
closegraph( ) ;
}
```

This program differs from the previous one only in that it calls *getbkcolor( )* and *setbkcolor( )* instead of *getcolor( )* and *setcolor( )* . The background color reported by *getbkcolor( )* is black, and is the default. We change it to light cyan using the function *setbkcolor( )*.

Color ..Color ..Everywhere

How many colors are available to us? We can find out by checking the mode table given in our discussion of modes . (See the third column.) Another way is to call the function *getmaxcolor( )* , as shown here:

PROGRAM 235

```
/* gives all possible colors available */

#include <graphics.h>
#include <dos.h> /* delay ( ) */

void main( )
{
    int gm , gd = DETECT ;
    int maxcolor , i ;

    initgraph( &gd , &gm , "" ) ;

    maxcolor = getmaxcolor( ) ;

    for ( i = 0 ; i < maxcolor ; i++ )
    {
        setbkcolor( i ) ;
        delay( 500 ) ;
    }
    getch( ) ;
    closegraph( ) ;
```

}

After introducing *getmaxcolor( )* and storing the value returned in the variable *maxcolor*, we enter a loop. With this loop, we'll change the background color to all the available colors, one by one, at an interval of half a second. The function *delay( )*, defined in DOS.H, determines the interval. Incidentally , a constant defined in GRAPHICS.H also indicates the maximum number of colors available .This constant is MAXCOLORS. It reflects a value of 15 in our case implying that there are 16 colors available (0 through 15).

A Trifle On Palettes

Let's get back to basics. All the colors we see on the screen are combinations of the three primary colors, viz. red, green and blue. Different intensities of the three primaries give us all the colors we need, opening up our palette limitlessly. Did we say palette? That is an important concept in color. Let's see...

We know that the smallest element on the graphics monitor is a pixel (picture element) or a dot. Each pixel has a set of colors associated with it. The exact number of colors depends on the number of bits available for each pixel. On our monitor we've used the CGA color palette, each pixel has four bits, enabling it to hold 16 possible colors. In case of an EGA monitor 6 bits are available. A palette is a list of all these colors.

The next few programs demonstrate how to get palette information and how to change it.

PROGRAM 236

```
#include <graphics.h>

void main( )
{
    int gm , gd = DETECT ;
    struct palettetype far *pal ;
    struct palettetype cpal ;
    int i ;
```

```
initgraph( &gd , &gm , "" ) ;

pal = getdefaultpalette( ) ;
getpalette(&cpal) ;

printf(" total colors = %d and %d\n" ,
    pal->size , cpal.size ) ;

for( i = 0 ; i < MAXCOLORS+1 ; i++ )
{
    printf(" color[%d] = %d and %d\n" ,
        i,
        pal->colors[i] ,
        cpal.colors[i] ) ;
}
getch( ) ;
closegraph( ) ;
}
```

This program introduces two functions, viz. *getdefaultpalette( )*, which gives the structure of the palette at the time of initialization, and *getpalette( )*, which gives the current palette structure . The function *getdefaultpalette( )* returns a pointer (*pal*) to the palette structure while *getpalette( )* is passed the address of this palette structure (*cpal*), into which it puts the relevant information. The palette structure is defined in GRAPHICS.H as follows:

```
struct palettetype
{
    unsigned char size;
    signed char colors[MAXCOLORS+1];
};
```

size refers to the number of colors; *colors* is an array which gives the actual color values.

What if you wanted to change all the 16 colors to shades of one color? Today various graphics packages offer this feature. How do they do this? The functions *setallpalette( )* and *setpalette( )*

enable you to change the default palette to a palette of your choosing.

PROGRAM 237

```
#include <graphics.h>

void main( )
{
    int gm , gd = DETECT ;
    struct palettetype oldpal ,
    newpal[ ] = {16,5,4,3,2,1,0,20,7,56,57,58,59,60,61,62,63};

    initgraph( &gd , &gm , "" ) ;

    getpalette( &oldpal ) ;

    setbkcolor( EGA_CYAN ) ;
    setcolor( EGA_BLUE ) ;
    outtextxy( 10 , 10 , "This was according to old color map" ) ;
    outtextxy( 10 , 30 , "Now the new color map.Press a key ... " ) ;
    getch( ) ;

    setallpalette( newpal ) ;

    setbkcolor( EGA_CYAN ) ;
    setcolor( EGA_BLUE ) ;
    outtextxy( 10 , 50 ,"Notice the fore/back ground colors."
                        "Press a key to go back." ) ;
    getch( ) ;

    setallpalette( &oldpal ) ;

    setbkcolor( EGA_CYAN ) ;
    setcolor( EGA_BLUE ) ;
    outtextxy( 10 , 70 , "Notice the Switch back. Now lets change "
                        "RED to YELLOW using SETPALETTE( )." ) ;
    getch( ) ;

    setpalette( 4 , EGA_YELLOW ) ;

    setcolor( EGA_RED ) ;
    outtextxy( 10 , 90 , "This is your very own RED color, or is it ?"
```

```
                    " The end at a key press." ) ;
        getch( ) ;
        closegraph( ) ;
    }
```

Let's look at the variables *oldpal* and *newpal*. *oldpal* is a structure that represents *palettetype*, and *newpal* is an array of structures which represents *palettetype*. The first element in *newpal* is assigned the new palette structure.

We have initialized the graphics system and saved the current palette into *oldpal*. We have set the background color to cyan, and the foreground color to blue. Therefore, the text will be printed in blue.

Now we set a new palette using the function *setallpalette( )*. Again, we have kept the background color cyan, and the foreground color blue. However, since this is a new palette, notice the change....

The foreground and background colors are no longer blue and cyan. And when we restore the old palette, we go back to our original foreground and background colors, i.e. blue and cyan, respectively.

What if you wanted to change only one color to another? By using the function *setpalette( )* this can be done very easily. We have changed red to yellow in this manner. Now, yellow will appear on the screen wherever red is expected to appear.

Do you want to return to your original palette? You can do that using the function *graphdefaults( )*. Watch.....

PROGRAM 238

```
#include <graphics.h>

void main( )
{
    int gm , gd = DETECT ;

    initgraph( &gd , &gm , "" ) ;
```

```
        setcolor( RED ) ;
        setbkcolor( LIGHTCYAN ) ;
        outtextxy( 100, 100 , "Before calling graphdefaults( ) .Press a key.") ;
        getch( ) ;

        graphdefaults( ) ;

        outtextxy( 100 , 150 , "After graphdefaults( ) was called."
                                " Press a key to end");
        getch( ) ;

        closegraph( ) ;
}
```

So we're back to square one. Or, rather, palette one. That's all on color. And now you're on your own: have fun....

Lines And More

How good an artist are you? Well, stick around and find out for yourself. WHAT? "I can't draw a straight line...," did you say? Don't worry, we'll soon take care of that.

In the coordinate system we use, the x-axis goes horizontally across, and the y-axis goes vertically downward. The point(0,0) lies in the top left corner of the screen.

The basic tools we'll need for drawing images are lines and curves of various types. The following programs show functions which do this.

Starting With Lines

PROGRAM 239

```
#include <graphics.h>
#include <stdlib.h>
#include <conio.h>

void main( )
{
   int gm , gd = DETECT ;

   initgraph( &gd , &gm , "" ) ;

   line( 0 , 0 , 400 , 50 ) ;
   outtextxy( 10 , 60 , "see this line ... now lets freak out over them" ) ;
   getch( ) ;

   while( !kbhit( ) )
   {
      setcolor( random( MAXCOLORS )) ;
      line(320 , 240 , random( 640 ) , random( 480 )) ;
   }

   getch( ) ;
   closegraph( ) ;
```

}

This program draws a line from (0,0) to (400,50) using the function *line( )*. The *while* loop continues till a key is pressed.

We have randomly set the color to any color between 0 and 15. We want our line to start at (320,240) and end at any random location on the screen. We have assumed that this is a VGA monitor, having a resolution of 640*480.

DID I REALLY DO THIS???!!!

Yes you did.

If you want more details about the line you've drawn, you'll need the function *getlinesettings( )*, as shown in the next program:

PROGRAM 240

```
#include <graphics.h>

void main( )
{
    int gm , gd = DETECT ;
    struct linesettingstype lines ;
    char *style[ ] =
    {
        "SOLID_LINE" ,
        "DOTTED_LINE" ,
        "CENTER_LINE (alternate dash & dot)" ,
        "DASHED_LINE" ,
        "USERBIT_LINE (user-defined line style)"
    } ;
    char *thick[ ] =
    {
        "NOT DEFINED" ,
        "NORM_WIDTH (normal width) " ,
        "NOT DEFINED" ,
        "THICK_WIDTH"
    } ;

    initgraph( &gd , &gm , "" ) ;
```

```
    line( 300 , 200 , 600 , 250 ) ;

    getlinesettings( &lines ) ;

    printf( "Current line settings as reported by getlinesettings( ):\n" ) ;
    printf( " Line Style Number : %d ,Style : %s\n" ,
        lines.linestyle ,
        style[lines.linestyle] ) ;
    printf( " Thickness Number : %d ,Thickness : %s\n" ,
        lines.thickness ,
        thick[lines.thickness] ) ;
    getch( ) ;
    closegraph( ) ;
}
```

lines is a structure similar to *linesettingstype* defined in GRAPHICS.H as follows:

```
struct linesettingstype
{
    int linestyle;
    unsigned upattern;
    int thickness;
};
```

The member *linestyle* contains numbers which correspond to 5 types of lines:

0	solid line
1	dotted line
2	center line (alternating dashes and dots)
3	dashed line
4	user-defined line

The second member, viz. *upattern* is applicable only when the line style is 4, i.e. when the line is user-defined. We will return to this at a later point.

The third member, viz. *thickness* can assume the values 1 or 3. The former corresponds to a line thickness of one pixel (normal), the latter to a line thickness of three pixels (thick).

style and *thick* are arrays which hold strings corresponding to the style of the line and its thickness, respectively. For example, if the member *linestyle* is 1, we can get the name of that line style by accessing *style[1]*. This will give us a dotted line.

We have called *line( )*, which specifies the coordinates, and have passed the address of the structure *lines* to *getlinesettings( )*. This function determines the current line settings, i.e. style and width, and assigns these settings to the respective members of the structure *lines*.

Finally, we display the line style and thickness along with the corresponding names.

Lines, But With Style

Now if we want a different type of line, we simply specify the line settings and call the function *setlinestyle( )*.

```
PROGRAM 241
#include <graphics.h>

void main( )
{
    int gm , gd = DETECT ;

    int i ;
    char text[100] ;

    char *style[ ] =
    {
        "SOLID_LINE" ,
        "DOTTED_LINE" ,
        "CENTER_LINE" ,
        "DASHED_LINE" ,
        "USERBIT_LINE (user-defined line style)"
    } ;

    initgraph( &gd , &gm , "" ) ;
    printf( "setlinestyle( ) put to use :\n\n") ;
```

```
for( i = 0 ; i < 4 ; i++ )
{
    setlinestyle( i , 0 , NORM_WIDTH ) ;

    sprintf( text , "%d. style : %s ,normal width" , i+1 , style[i] ) ;
    outtextxy( 5 , 100+i*20 , text ) ;
    line( 300 , 100+i*20 , 600 , 100+i*20 ) ;
}

getch( ) ;

for( i = 0 ; i < 4 ; i++ )
{
    setlinestyle( i , 0 , THICK_WIDTH ) ;

    sprintf(text , "%d. style : %s ,thick width" ,i+1 , style[i] ) ;
    outtextxy( 5 , 200+i*20 , text ) ;
    line( 300 , 200+i*20 , 600 , 200+i*20 ) ;
}

getch( ) ;
closegraph( ) ;
}
```

Here, we'll see four types of lines, viz. the solid line, dotted line, center line and dashed line. The loop takes us through the four types, each of which will be printed one below the other. These will first be printed with a normal width (in the first *for* loop), and then with a thick width (in the second *for* loop).

Let's look at the first *for* loop:

In *setlinestyle( )*, the first parameter is the style of the line, which will range from 0 to 3. The next parameter is of no significance at present, since the line is not user- defined. The third parameter relates to the thickness, which we have specified as normal.

sprintf( ) and *outtextxy( )* print the description of the line alongside the line.

The second *for* loop is different only in that we have changed the width from normal to thick.

So far we have neatly avoided any discussion of user-defined lines. Now let's plunge into it head first.

To start at the beginning, a line segment is a set of 16 pixels. We have 16 bits available to us, each corresponding to a pixel. Further, when a bit has been set, it is at 1, and when it has been reset, it is at 0. Now, depending on whether a bit has been set or reset, the relevant pixel will or won't be displayed.

Thus, all 16 bits set (0xFFFF), would yield a solid line - since all the pixels would be displayed. Similarly, bits set and reset alternately (0x5555) would yield a dotted line.

Now, if we want a user-defined line, we would call the function *setlinestyle( )* , the first parameter being USERBIT_LINE and the second parameter being the particular bit pattern.

Now the member *upattern* is of significance. It holds the value of the bit pattern. The following program gives you 10 different user-defined lines.

PROGRAM 242

```
#include <graphics.h>

void main( )
{
    int gm , gd = DETECT ;

    int i ;
    char text[50] ;
    unsigned style[ ] =
    {
        0x0001,
        0xF000,
        0x1111,
        0x5555,
        0xCCCC,
        0x0F0F,
        0x0FF0,
        0x63C6,
        0x7FFE,
```

```
        0xFFFF
   } ;

   initgraph( &gd , &gm , "" ) ;

   printf( "setlinestyle( ) put to use with user defined styles:\n\n") ;

   for( i = 0 ; i < 10 ; i++ )
   {
       setlinestyle( USERBIT_LINE , style[i] , NORM_WIDTH ) ;

       setcolor( LIGHTCYAN ) ;
       sprintf(text,"user style :%d. value :%04X(hex)" ,i+1 , style[i] ) ;
       outtextxy( 1 , 100+i*20 , text ) ;
       line( 300 , 100+i*20 , 600 , 100+i*20 ) ;
   }

   getch( ) ;
   closegraph( ) ;
}
```

style is an array of unsigned integers which holds the 10 bit patterns. The *for* loop sets the style to each of these patterns and displays the corresponding lines, with descriptions.

More On Drawing Lines

So far we have specified both the coordinates of a line. If we want a line relative to a particular point on the screen, we first have to go to that particular point. Then, using the function *linerel( )*, we specify where we want the line to end, using the said point as our origin.

PROGRAM 243

```
#include <graphics.h>

void main( )
{
   int gm , gd = DETECT ;

   initgraph( &gd , &gm , "" ) ;
```

```
        printf(" Relative drawing of line using linerel( ) "
            "[ note:moveto( ) also used ]\n" ) ;
        setcolor( YELLOW ) ;
/* draw a line from 100 , 100 to 500 , 200 */

        moveto( 100 , 100 ) ; /* go to location 100,100 */

/* from 100,100 draw line up to a pt. 400 across and 100 down */

        linerel( 400 , 100 ) ;

        getch( ) ;
        closegraph( ) ;
}
```

We have reached our starting point (100,100) by calling the function *moveto( )*. From this point we want our line to extend 400 across and 100 down, RELATIVE TO our starting point. To do this, we call the function *linerel( )*. Thus, we have in effect terminated our line at the point (500,200).

The function *line( )* can be considered a combination of the two functions *moveto( )* and *lineto( )* . By specifying a point calling *moveto( )*, we can determine where we want to start the line. To determine where we want to terminate it, we call *lineto( )*, which is passed the destination of the line.

Note that both these points are with reference to the absolute origin, i.e. the top left corner of the screen.

PROGRAM 244

```
#include <graphics.h>
#include <dos.h> /* for delay( ) */

void main( )
{
    int gm , gd = DETECT ;

    initgraph( &gd , &gm , "" ) ;

    printf(" Drawing of lines using lineto( ) "
```

```
        "( note:moveto( ) also used ]\n" ) ;
    setcolor( YELLOW ) ;

    moveto( 125 , 100 ) ; /* go to location 125,100 */

    lineto( 500 , 200 ) ;

    delay( 700 ) ;
    lineto( 20 , 30 ) ;
    delay( 700 ) ;
    lineto( 200 , 400 ) ;
    delay( 700 ) ;
    lineto( 100 , 125 ) ;
    delay( 700 ) ;
    lineto( 400 , 400 ) ;
    delay( 700 ) ;
    lineto( 500 , 350 ) ;
    delay( 700 ) ;
    lineto( 125 , 100 ) ;

    getch( ) ;
    closegraph( ) ;
}
```

The end-result of this program is an arrow on the screen. A delay has been introduced to facilitate observation at each point. Note that this program has been designed on a VGA monitor. You will need to adjust the coordinates to suit your monitor. It may be helpful at this point, to keep in mind that you'll need to recalculate the coordinates if at any time the image extends beyond the screen.

Let's move from lines to *curves*. (Do we hear heavy breathing? OK, girls, let's wait till the guys get their breath back...!)

The Turning Point (Curves And Related Objects)

The First Arc

We'll start with arcs. The following program introduces the function *arc( )*. Within this function, we specify the center, the starting angle and the ending angle, and the radius.

PROGRAM 245

```
#include <graphics.h>
#include <stdlib.h> /* for random( ) */
#include <conio.h> /* for kbhit( ) */

void main( )
{
    int gm , gd = DETECT ;
    int rad , color ;
    initgraph( &gd , &gm , "" ) ;

    printf(" Noah's ARC ......" ) ;

    arc( 320 , 240 , 225 , 315 , 100 ) ;

    getch( ) ;
    printf( "And lots of 'em......\n\n" ) ;

    while( !kbhit( ) )
    {
        setcolor( random(MAXCOLORS) ) ;
        arc( 320 , 20 , 225 , 315 , random( 460 ) ) ;
    }

    getch( ) ;
    closegraph( ) ;
}
```

Try it. We're sure you'll like what you see.

After we've drawn the arcs, we can determine the coordinates of its endpoints by calling *getarccoords( )*. We'll pass it the address of a structure resembling the structure *arccoordstype* defined in GRAPHICS.H as follows:

```
struct arccoordstype
{
    int x, y;
    int xstart, ystart;
    int xend, yend;
};
```

Here *x* and *y* are the coordinates of the center. *xstart* and *ystart* are the coordinates of the arc's starting point, and *xend* and *yend* are the coordinates of the end point of the arc.

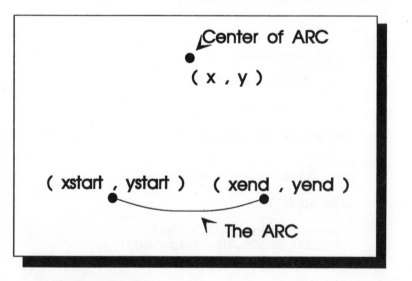

DIAGRAM 4.1 (The Arc)

The function *getarccoords( )* passes back the relevant coordinates of the arc drawn most recently.

```
PROGRAM 246
#include <graphics.h>

void main( )
{
    int gm , gd = DETECT ;
    struct arccoordstype thearc ;

    initgraph( &gd , &gm , "" ) ;

    setcolor( LIGHTCYAN ) ;
    arc( 320 , 240 , 225 , 315 , 100 ) ;

    getarccoords( &thearc ) ;

/* reads data into the structure thearc */

    printf("Using GETARCCOORDS( ) we found that...\n\n\n" ) ;
    printf( " Center is at %d , %d\n" , thearc.x , thearc.y ) ;
    printf( " Start is at %d , %d\n" , thearc.xstart , thearc.ystart ) ;
    printf( " End is at %d , %d\n" , thearc.xend , thearc.yend ) ;
    printf( "\n\nLets use these values to make a dish"
        " and a pie slice." ) ;
    printf(" Press a key....\n" ) ;
    getch( ) ;

    line( thearc.xstart , thearc.ystart , thearc.xend , thearc.yend ) ;
        /* dish */
    delay( 1500 ) ; /* 1.5 second delay */
    setcolor( BLACK ) ; /* remove horizontal line */
    line( thearc.xstart , thearc.ystart , thearc.xend , thearc.yend ) ;
        /* dish */
    setcolor( LIGHTCYAN ) ;
    line( thearc.x , thearc.y , thearc.xstart , thearc.ystart ) ; /* pie */
    line( thearc.x , thearc.y , thearc.xend , thearc.yend ) ;

    getch( ) ;
    closegraph( ) ;
}
```

After drawing the arc, we passed the address of the structure *thearc* to *getarccoords( )* . The series of *printf( )*s prints the center, the starting point and the end point of the arc.

Now, if we join the starting point and the end point, we get a dish. If we join the starting point and the end point to the center, we get a pie slice. Easy as pie, isn't it?

Moving In Colorful Circles

Let's move on to circles and ellipses.

The function *circle( )* is very straightforward. It asks for only the center and the radius. The function *ellipse( )* is much more demanding. It needs the center, the starting angle, the ending angle, the radius along the x-axis and the radius along the y-axis. To get a complete ellipse, the starting and ending angles should coincide (e.g. 0 and 360, or 45 and 405). You will get an incomplete ellipse, or an elliptical arc if these angles don't coincide (e.g. 110 and 390).

It is of interest to note that the function *getarccoords( )* is also applicable to an ellipse.

PROGRAM 247
```
/* circle and ellipse */
#include <graphics.h>
#include <conio.h>
#include <stdlib.h>

void main( )
{
    int gm , gd = DETECT ;

    initgraph( &gd , &gm , "" ) ;

    printf( "CIRCLE( ) and ELLIPSE( ) are quite similar."
            "Press a key for fun...\n" ) ;

    circle( 100 , 100 , 70 ) ;
```

```
ellipse( 300 , 100 , 0 , 360 , 100 , 50 ) ;
ellipse( 450 , 100 , 0 , 360 , 20 , 60 ) ;

/* now observe the fourth & third parameters */

ellipse( 560 , 100 , 110 , 390 , 40 , 20 ) ;

getch( ) ;

setcolor( LIGHTCYAN ) ;

line( 0 , 200 , 640 , 200 ) ;

while( !kbhit( ) )
{
   setcolor( random( MAXCOLORS ) ) ;
   ellipse( random(600) , 350+random(100) ,
      0 , 360 ,
      random(120), random(120) ) ;
}

closegraph( ) ;
}
```

Excuse us for getting carried away with *random( )*. Happens to the best of us....

Talking About Rectangles, Bars And 3d-Bars

We now move on to rectangles, bars and three-dimensional bars. The function *rectangle( )* and the function *bar( )* are very straightforward: they merely seek the coordinates of the left top corner and the right bottom corner. The function *bar( )* fills the figure so it appears solid, while *rectangle( )* gives the outline. The function *bar3d( )* seeks the coordinates of the top left corner, the bottom right corner, the depth and the top flag. The top flag serves a special purpose: it gives you the option of not displaying the top of the bar, and is achieved when the top flag is 0. It is useful when you want to stack bars.

PROGRAM 248

```
/* bar & bar3d */
#include <graphics.h>

void main( )
{
    int gm , gd = DETECT ;

    initgraph( &gd , &gm , "" ) ;

    printf( "rectangle( ) ,bar( ) and bar3d( ) are quite similar....\n" ) ;

    rectangle( 10 , 50 , 80 , 150 ) ;

    bar( 100 , 50 , 160 , 150 ) ;

    bar3d( 200 , 50 , 270 , 150 , 20 , 1 ) ;
/*
    observe the difference in the 2 BAR3D( )'s
    because of the last parameter being 1 and 0.
*/
    bar3d( 300 , 50 , 370 , 150 , 20 , 0 ) ;

    getch( ) ;
    closegraph( ) ;
}
```

The functions *rectangle( )* and *bar( )* are self-explanatory. Note that the top of the 3-D bar has been displayed, since we have assigned the last parameter the value 1. When we later change this parameter to 0, the top is not displayed.

Bar Graph !!

Everything we've done so far should have a practical application to be worthwhile. An obvious application of *bar( )* and *bar3d( )* is drawing a bar-graph.

This is a very simple operation. Anyone who has a grasp of the concept of bar-graphs can draw bar-graphs on the monitor using a few simple functions. The only thing you have to look out for is the coordinate system. Recall that in the coordinate system that we are using, the point(0,0) is at the top left corner. A bar graph necessarily needs the origin to be somewhere in the bottom left of the page since we need an x-axis which extends across the page and a y-axis which extends upward.

This is where your knowledge of mathematics is useful. You will need to adjust the coordinates within the functions called. Apart from that, drawing a bar-graph on the screen is simply a matter of calling the functions bar( ) and bar3d( ).

The next program demonstrates this:

PROGRAM 249

```
/* graphs using bar( ) & bar3d( )*/

#include <graphics.h>
#include <conio.h>
#include <stdlib.h>
#include <stdio.h>

void main( )
{
    int gm , gd=DETECT ;
    int i ;
    int y[100] , x1 , y1 , x2 , y2 , offset ;
    char temp[5] ;
    int maxy ;

    clrscr( ) ;
    printf(" BAR GRAPH demo using bar( ) and bar3d( ) \n\n\n" ) ;
    printf(" ENTER sequence of Numbers ( 0 to quit ) : \n" ) ;
    for( i = 0 ; i < 50 ; i++ )
    {
        printf("%d. : ",i+1 ) ;
        y[i] = atoi( gets( temp ) ) ;
        if( y[i] == 0 )
            break ;
    }

    initgraph( &gd , &gm , "" ) ;
```

```
/*
2 - D bar graph using bar( ) ,compare
the output with the next graph
*/

    maxy = getmaxy( ) ;
    setcolor( LIGHTRED ) ;
    line( 27 , 0 , 27 , maxy-10 ) ;
    line( 27 , maxy-10 , 600 , maxy-10 ) ;

    setcolor( LIGHTMAGENTA ) ;
    for( i = 0 ; i < 40 ; i+=2 )
    {
        sprintf(temp , "%3d-" , i*10 ) ;
        outtextxy( 0 , maxy-20-i*10 , temp ) ;
    }

    offset = 20 ;
    x1 = 10 ;
    x2 = x1+offset ;
    y2 = maxy-20 ;

    for( i = 0 ; i < 50 ; i++ )
    {
        if( y[i] == 0 )
            break ;
        x1 = x1+offset+5 ;
        x2 = x1+offset ;
        y1 = y2 - y[i]*4 ;

        setcolor( random( MAXCOLORS ) ) ;

        bar( x1 , y1 , x2 , y2 ) ;
        rectangle( x1 , y1 , x2 , y2 ) ;
    }

    outtextxy( 300 , 10 , "BAR GRAPH using bar( ).Press a key..." ) ;
    getch( ) ;

    /* 2 - D bar graph using bar3d .See the impact */

    cleardevice( ) ;
    setcolor( LIGHTRED ) ;
```

```
line( 27 , 0 , 27 , maxy-10 ) ;
line( 27 , maxy-10 , 640 , maxy-10) ;

setcolor( LIGHTMAGENTA ) ;
for( i = 0 ; i < 40 ; i+=2 )
{
    sprintf(temp , "%3d-" , i*10 ) ;
    outtextxy( 0 , maxy-20-i*10 , temp ) ;
}

offset = 20 ;
x1 = 10 ;
x2 = x1+offset ;
y2 = maxy-20 ;

for( i = 0 ; i < 50 ; i++ )
{
    if( y[i] == 0 )
        break ;
    x1 = x1+offset+15 ;
    x2 = x1+offset ;
    y1 = y2 - y[i]*4 ;

    setcolor( random( MAXCOLORS ) ) ;

    bar3d( x1 , y1 , x2 , y2 , 10 , 1 ) ;
}

outtextxy( 300 , 10 , "BAR GRAPH using bar3d( ).Press a key..." ) ;

getch( ) ;
closegraph( ) ;
}
```

We've just seen a program with 95 lines of code. At this point you could do one of two things. You could decide that it's too much of a bother, that it's all too technical to really be of any practical use, that it's not for you. Or you could, like we did, be drawn by the sheer beauty of graphics, by its inherent simplicity, by its smooth flow of logic.

Those of you who are still with us will encounter times when you wish you weren't. But wait. Get rid of whatever block you have towards what you're doing. Don't judge a program by the number of lines it contains. At the risk of sounding smug, may we say that the only difficult part is grasping how simple it all is.

As soon as you execute the program, you'll be asked to enter a sequence of numbers. Make sure that these numbers range from 1 to 100. After the last number, enter a 0, to indicate that you've terminated your list. Now you will see a bar-graph drawn which used the function *bar( )*.

The x-axis increases at a steady rate. The numbers you have entered will be reflected on the y-axis on a scale of 1:4. Thus, if you've entered 10, the bar will extend from 0 to 40 on the y- axis.

You will be asked to press a key while the graph is displayed. On doing so, the graph will be redrawn using the function *bar3d( )*.

Now let's use sample data and go through the program one line at a time.

clrscr( ) will clear the screen.

After the two *printf( )*s are executed, you enter a *for* loop, where *i* increases a step at a time from 0 to 50. You will enter numbers into an array called *y[i]*. Entering a 0 will get you out of the *for* loop. Let's enter 10, 20, 0. Thus *y[0]=10, y[1]=20, y[2]=0*.

Now we initialize the graphics system.

We call the function *getmaxy( )* , which returns the maximum possible value of y on the monitor and puts it in the variable *maxy*.

Now the color is set to light red.

Our origin will be at (27, maxy-10). From here we draw our x and y axes.

Now the color is set to light magenta.

We enter the second *for* loop, where *i* increases from 0 to 40, in increments of 2. This displays the units on the y-axis. When *i=0*, the array *temp* will contain *0-*. This gets printed at (0,maxy-20-0*10), i.e. 20 pixels above the bottom of the screen.

Now, with *i=2* (since *i* increases in increments of 2), the array temp will contain *20-*. This will be displayed 40 pixels above the bottom of the screen, at (0,maxy-20-2*10). Thus the completed y-axis is displayed.

At any point, *x1, y1* will correspond to the top left corner of the bar, *x2, y2* to the bottom right.

We initialize certain variables now. *offset* is the width of the bar; *y2* is the base of the bar. The initial value of *x1* is 10; that of *x2* is *x1+offset*, i.e. 30.

The next *for* loop actually draws the bar graph.

```
for( i = 0 ; i < 50 ; i++ )
{
    if( y[i] == 0 )
        break ;
    x1 = x1+offset+5 ;
    x2 = x1+offset ;
    y1 = y2 - y[i]*4 ;

    setcolor( random( MAXCOLORS ) ) ;

    bar( x1 , y1 , x2 , y2 ) ;
    rectangle( x1 , y1 , x2 , y2 ) ;
}
```

i increases from 0 to 50 in increments of 1. The initial value of *i* is 0. The *if* condition checks whether *y[0]=0*. Since it isn't, we proceed. *x1* is now increased by *(offset+5)*. Thus *x1=35*. Now *x2* is assigned the value of *x1+offset*, which is 55. *y1* is assigned the value of *y2-y[0]*4*, i.e. *y2- 40*. Thus we have the coordinates of the first bar. By calling *bar( )* with the above coordinates, we have our first bar.

Next, *i=1*. So *x1=35+20+5=60*. We want a distance of 5 pixels between bars. *x2=60+20=80. y1=y2-y[1]*4*, i.e. *y2-80*. We can call *bar( )* to draw the second bar.

Finally, with *i=2*, the value of *y[2]=0* and the *for* loop terminates. On our screen we now have two bars, the first extending from 0 to 40, and the second from 0 to 80.

As soon as you press a key , *cleardevice( )* will clear the screen.

The entire graph is now redrawn identically, except that the distance between the bars is increased to 15, and *bar3d( )* is called instead of *bar( )*.

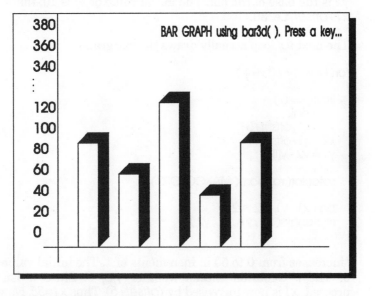

DIAGRAM 4.2(bar graph)

Did you survive that?!

On to polygons. A break may be in order now!!

Polygonally Yours...

In order to draw a polygon, we need an array to specify the x and y coordinates of all the points and the number of points on the polygon+1. The coordinates of the first point in the array will be repeated as the last point to ensure that we obtain a closed figure.

PROGRAM 250

/* polygons */

```c
#include <graphics.h>

void main( )
{
    int gm , gd=DETECT ;
    int i ;
    int polyarray[30] ;

    initgraph( &gd , &gm , "" ) ;

    printf(" The drawpoly( ) function used to draw polygons\n" ) ;

    setcolor( LIGHTCYAN ) ;
    polyarray[0] = 0 ;
    polyarray[1] = 200;

    polyarray[2] = 50;
    polyarray[3] = 300;

    polyarray[4] = 250;
    polyarray[5] = 300;

    polyarray[6] = 400;
    polyarray[7] = 250;

    polyarray[8] = 325;
    polyarray[9] = 225;

    polyarray[10] = 325;
```

```
polyarray[11] = 175;

polyarray[12] = 300;
polyarray[13] = 200;

polyarray[14] = 200;
polyarray[15] = 150;

polyarray[16] = 275;
polyarray[17] = 115;

polyarray[18] = 300;
polyarray[19] = 125;

polyarray[20] = 300;
polyarray[21] = 100;

polyarray[22] = 400;
polyarray[23] = 50;

polyarray[24] = 200;
polyarray[25] = 50;

polyarray[26] = 100;
polyarray[27] = 100;

polyarray[28] = 0;
polyarray[29] = 200;

setcolor(LIGHTCYAN) ;
drawpoly( 15 , polyarray ) ;

setcolor( LIGHTRED ) ;
ellipse( 200 , 100 , 90 , 270 , 20 , 10 ) ;
circle ( 200 , 100 , 10 ) ;

getch( ) ;
closegraph( ) ;
}
```

polyarray holds the coordinates of the points of the polygon. Note that the first and last points coincide (0,200). In all, we want a 14-sided figure, so 15 points will be plotted.

The *drawpoly( )* function is passed two parameters, the first being the number of points to be plotted, the second being the address of the array.

The circle and the ellipse are drawn to spice things up a bit. Careful -- it might byte!

Line Graphs !!

Earlier we saw that a practical application of *bar( )* and *bar3d( )* was the drawing of a bar graph. Similarly , *drawpoly( )* could be applied to get a line-graph on the screen. In fact, to draw a line graph we can use a number of functions, viz. *drawpoly( )*, *line( )*, *lineto( )* or *linerel( )*. In our program we have used *drawpoly( )*.

PROGRAM 251
/* line graph using drawpoly( ) */

```
#include <graphics.h>
#include <conio.h>
#include <stdlib.h>
#include <stdio.h>

void main( )
{
    int gm , gd=DETECT ;
    int i , j=0 , pts=0 ;
    int y[100] , x1 , y1 , y2 , offset ;
    int poly[200] ;
    char temp[5] ;
    int maxy ;

    clrscr( ) ;
    printf(" LINE GRAPH demo using drawpoly( ) \n\n\n" ) ;
    printf(" ENTER sequence of Numbers ( 0 to quit ) : \n" ) ;
    for( i = 0 ; i < 50 ; i++ )
    {
        printf("%d. : ",i+1 ) ;
        y[i] = atoi( gets( temp ) ) ;
        if( y[i] == 0 )
            break ;
```

```
        pts++ ;
    }

    initgraph( &gd , &gm , "" ) ;

    maxy = getmaxy( ) ;
    setcolor( LIGHTRED ) ;
    line( 27 , 0 , 27 , maxy-5 ) ;
    line( 27 , maxy-5 , 600 , maxy-5 ) ;

    setcolor( LIGHTMAGENTA ) ;
    for( i = 0 ; i < 10 ; i++ )
    {
        sprintf(temp , "%3d-" , i*5 ) ;
        outtextxy( 0 , maxy-5-i*40 , temp ) ;
    }

    offset = 20 ; x1 = 10 ; y2 = maxy-5 ;

    for( i = 0 ; i < 50 ; i++ )
    {
        if( y[i] == 0 )
            break ;
        x1 = x1+offset ;
        y1 = y2 - (y[i]*8) ;
        poly[j] = x1 ;
        j++ ;
        poly[j] = y1 ;
        j++ ;
    }

    setcolor( YELLOW ) ;
    drawpoly( pts , poly ) ;

    outtextxy( 300 , 10 , "LINE GRAPH using drawpoly( ).Press a key..." ) ;

    getch( ) ;
    closegraph( ) ;
}
```

As before you are first asked to enter a sequence of numbers ranging from 1 to 45. Enter a 0 to quit. On pressing 0, you will see a linegraph corresponding to the numbers entered. The x-axis increases at a steady rate of 20. The y-axis extends from 1 to 50, corresponding one to one with the range of numbers entered.

We need the x and y coordinates of all the points to be plotted and the total number of such points.

The first *for* loop requires the entry of numbers ranging from 1 to 45 . The variable *pts* maintains a count of the points entered.

When 0 is pressed, the *if* condition will break you out of the loop. For example, if we enter the values 10, 20 and 0, *y[0]* will be 10 (*pts=1*), *y[1]=20* (*pts=2*) and *y[2]=0*, respectively. The variable *pts* ignores the last value since we have broken out of the loop.

After initializing the graphics system, we call the function *getmaxy( )* to obtain the maximum possible value of y in the variable *maxy*. We have set the color to light red. Taking (27,maxy-5) as our point of origin we plot the x and y axes.

Next, we set the color to light magenta.

The next *for* loop starts at 0 and ends at 9. When i=0, the array *temp* will contain *0-*, which gets printed at (0, maxy-5-0*40), i.e. 5 pixels above the bottom of the screen. When i=1, the array will contain *5-* , which will be printed at (0, maxy-5-1*40), i.e. 45 pixels above the bottom of the screen. This continues till *I=9*, the last point plotted being *45-* . Thus, the completed y-axis is displayed.

The x-axis increases at a uniform rate of 20. Thus the *offset* is 20. The initial value of *x1* is 10, and that of *y2*, which is the base of the linegraph, is *maxy-5*.

The final *for* loop is the heart of the program.

```
for( i = 0 ; i < 50 ; i++ )
{
```

```
        if( y[i] == 0 )
            break ;
        x1 = x1+offset ;
        y1 = y2 - (y[i]*8) ;
        poly[j] = x1 ;
        j++ ;
        poly[j] = y1 ;
        j++ ;
    }
    setcolor( YELLOW ) ;
    drawpoly( pts , poly ) ;
```

When *i=0*, *y[i]=10*; *x1=x1+offset*, i.e. 10+20. *y1=y2- (y[i]*8)*, i.e. *maxy-5-(10*8)*. Here we introduce a new array *poly* which will hold the coordinates of all the points. Initially, when *j=0*, *poly[0]* is assigned the value of the first x- coordinate (*x1*); and when *j=1*, *poly[1]* is assigned the value of the first y- coordinate (*y1*). Now *j=2*.

With *i* now equal to 1, *y[i]=20* and *x1=30+offset*, i.e. 50. *y1=y2- (y[i]*8)*, i.e. *maxy-5-(20*8)*. Since *x1=50* and *j=2*, *poly[2]* is 50. *j* is now 3, and *poly[3]* is assigned the value of the second y-coordinate, being *y1*. *j* is now incremented to 4.

Now *i=2* and *y[i]=0*. The *if* condition is satisfied, and we leave the *for* loop.

poly[0] and *poly[1]* store the coordinates of the first point. *poly[2]* and *poly[3]* store the coordinates of the second point. the variable *pts* stores the total number of points to be plotted, which is 2.

After setting the color to yellow, we call *drawpoly( )* and pass it the variable *pts* and the address of the array *poly*.

Our linegraph is ready. (Whew!)

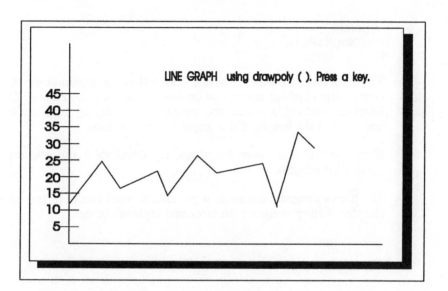

DIAGRAM 4.3 (line graph)

Yum Yum Pies...

Let us now proceed to pie slices and sectors. These are standard functions that yield a filled figure.

PROGRAM 252

```
#include <graphics.h>

void main( )
{
    int gm , gd = DETECT ;

    initgraph( &gd , &gm , "" ) ;

    printf(" pieslice( ) for circular pie & sector( ) for elliptical pie\n" ) ;

    pieslice( 100 , 200 , 30 , 100 , 150 ) ;
    sector ( 300 , 200 , 30 , 100 , 290 , 140 ) ;
```

```
    getch();
    closegraph();
}
```

The function *pieslice( )* seeks the following parameters: the center, the starting angle, the ending angle and the radius. The function *sector( )* seeks the center, the starting and ending angles, and the length of the major and minor axes.

If you notice ,the above functions, i.e. *pieslice( )* and *sector( )* yield filled images.

The above program comes as a prelude to what comes in the next chapter. Filling images with color and style of choice...

Drawing And Filling Images

Can we fill in the images which yield only an outline? Yes, by using the functions demonstrated in the next few programs.

Filling Ellipses

PROGRAM 253

```
#include <graphics.h>

void main( )
{
    int gm , gd = DETECT ;

    initgraph( &gd , &gm , "" ) ;

/* filling of images like the ellipse using fillellipse( ) */

    printf(" Initially an ellipse will be drawn\n" ) ;
    printf(" And then filled at the pressing of a key using "
        "the function fillellipse( ) \n" ) ;

    setcolor( LIGHTRED ) ;
    ellipse( 300 , 100 , 0 , 360 , 60 , 30 ) ;

    getch( ) ;

    fillellipse( 300 , 100 , 60 , 30 ) ;

    getch( ) ;
    closegraph( ) ;
}
```

The function *fillellipse( )* is very simple. It seeks the center and the major and minor axes.

Filling Polygons

The next program demonstrates how to fill a polygon. It calls the function *fillpoly( )*, and this function seeks parameters identical to those sought by *drawpoly( )*.

PROGRAM 254

```c
#include <graphics.h>

void main( )
{
    int gm , gd = DETECT ;
    int polyarray[30] ;

    initgraph( &gd , &gm , "" ) ;

/* filling of images like the polygon using fillpoly( ) */

    printf(" Initially a polygon will be drawn\n" ) ;
    printf(" And then filled at the pressing of a key "
           "using the function fillpoly( ) \n" ) ;

    setcolor( LIGHTRED ) ;

    polyarray[0] = 0 ;
    polyarray[1] = 200;

    polyarray[2] = 50;
    polyarray[3] = 300;

    polyarray[4] = 250;
    polyarray[5] = 300;

    polyarray[6] = 400;
    polyarray[7] = 250;

    polyarray[8] = 325;
    polyarray[9] = 225;

    polyarray[10] = 325;
    polyarray[11] = 175;
```

```
        polyarray[12] = 300;
        polyarray[13] = 200;

        polyarray[14] = 200;
        polyarray[15] = 150;

        polyarray[16] = 275;
        polyarray[17] = 115;

        polyarray[18] = 300;
        polyarray[19] = 125;

        polyarray[20] = 300;
        polyarray[21] = 100;

        polyarray[22] = 400;
        polyarray[23] = 50;

        polyarray[24] = 200;
        polyarray[25] = 50;

        polyarray[26] = 100;
        polyarray[27] = 100;

        polyarray[28] = 0;
        polyarray[29] = 200;

        drawpoly( 15 , polyarray );

        getch();

        fillpoly( 15 , polyarray );

        getch();
        closegraph();
    }
```

Flooding The Fill

The next program demonstrates the use of the function *floodfill( )*. This function needs 3 parameters: the x-coordinate of a point, the y-coordinate of the same point and a color. The function starts to fill the screen from the specified point till it encounters a closed boundary of the specified color. Make sure that you specify the right color, or else the function will seek a boundary you don't want:

PROGRAM 255

```
#include <graphics.h>

void main( )
{
    int gm , gd = DETECT ;

    initgraph( &gd , &gm , "" ) ;

/* filling of images using floodfill( ) */

    printf(" Initially a circle will be drawn\n" ) ;
    printf(" And then filled at the pressing of a key ");
    printf("\nusing the function floodfill( ) \n" ) ;

    setcolor( LIGHTRED ) ;
    circle( 100 , 200 , 50 ) ;

    getch( ) ;

    floodfill( 100 , 200 , LIGHTRED ) ;

/* now try floodfill( ) using the wrong color ie. parameter 3 */

    printf(" The last parameter is a color\n" ) ;
    printf(" floodfill( ) starts filling the screen from \n");
    printf(" the point specified by the first 2 parameters.\n");
    printf(" It searches for a closed boundary of a color\n");
    printf(" specified by the 3rd parameter.);
    printf(" In our case it is LIGHTRED.\n" ) ;
    printf(" floodfill( ) as a result fills the circle\n" ) ;
    printf(" Suppose we specify the wrong color......\n" ) ;
    getch( ) ;

    floodfill( 100 , 200 , BLUE ) ;

    getch( ) ;
```

```
    closegraph( ) ;
}
```

The first time we call *floodfill( )*, we specify the color correctly.
The next time, we specify the wrong color: note the output.

Upto this point all the figures we have generated have been
filled in the default color, i.e. white. How can we choose the color
and pattern in which our images should be displayed?

With What Do I Fill ?

For this purpose, we'll need to use the function *getfillsettings( )*
for information regarding the current filling color and pattern.
The structure *fillsettingstype* holds the relevant information. It is
defined in GRAPHICS.H as follows:

```
struct fillsettingstype
{
    int pattern;
    int color;
};
```

The function *getfillsettings( )* is passed the address of the
structure *fillsettingstype* and reports the current pattern and
color back to the structure.

PROGRAM 256

```
#include <graphics.h>

void main( )
{
    int gm , gd = DETECT ;
    struct fillsettingstype fst ;

    initgraph( &gd , &gm , "" ) ;

    printf(" Current fill settings as reported"
        "by getfillsettings( )\n" );

    getfillsettings( &fst ) ;
```

```
    printf("\the fill pattern : %d and"
        "the fill color : %d\n" ,
        fst.pattern ,
        fst.color ) ;
    getch( ) ;
    closegraph( ) ;
}
```

The pattern we obtain is 1, and the color is 15. 1 corresponds to a
solid fill. 15 corresponds to white. These form part of the 16 colors
and 12 patterns offered by Turbo C. How do we access the rest of
them? By using the function *setfillstyle( )* , the use of which is
shown in the next program.

PROGRAM 257

```
#include <graphics.h>

void main( )
{
    int gm , gd = DETECT ;
    int i ;
    char *fillstyle[ ] =
    {
     "fill with background pattern" ,
     "Solid fill" ,
     "horizontal line fill" ,
     "light slashes",
     "slashes" ,
     "back slashes" ,
     "light back slashes" ,
     "Hatch fill" ,
     "Cross hatch fill" ,
     "lines interleaved" ,
     "dots widely spaced" ,
     "dots closely placed" ,
    } ;


    initgraph( &gd , &gm , "" ) ;

    printf(" Setting the fill settings using"
```

```
      "setfillstyle( ).Press a key...\n" );

   ellipse( 100 , 100 , 0 , 360 , 50 , 50) ;

   getch( ) ;

   setfillstyle( SLASH_FILL , LIGHTRED ) ;

   fillellipse( 100 , 100 , 50 , 50 ) ;

   printf(" Press a key to see more patterns\n " ) ;
   getch( ) ;
   for( i = 0 ; i < 12 ; i++ )
   {
      cleardevice( ) ;

      setfillstyle( i , LIGHTCYAN ) ;

      fillellipse( 100 , 100 , 50 , 50 ) ;
      outtextxy( 50  , 200 , fillstyle[i] ) ;
      getch( );
   }
   closegraph( ) ;
}
```

The style SLASH_FILL covers the image with slashes in the specified color, i.e. light red. The function *fillellipse( )* displays the effect of the changes made.

Each pattern offered has a corresponding number ranging from 0 to 11. To see these various patterns we enter the *for* loop, where *i* corresponds to the pattern. Then, the function *outtextxy( )* specifies the name of the pattern.

In addition to the pre-defined patterns offered by Turbo C, we can specify our own user-defined patterns.

For user-defined patterns, we think in terms of pattern elements of 8 pixels * 8 pixels. Each pixel corresponds to a bit. A pixel is displayed when the bit corresponding to it is set. It is not displayed when the corresponding bit is reset. Thus, depending on the set and reset values of the bits, the corresponding pixels are activated and your user-defined image is generated on the screen.

PROGRAM 258

```c
#include <graphics.h>

void main( )
{
  int gm , gd = DETECT ;
  int i ;
  char user[2][8] =
    {
/* smiling face */
  0x3C,
  0x42,
  0xA5,
  0x81,
  0xBD,
  0x42,
  0x3C,
  0x00,
/* robot */
  0x3E,
  0x42,
  0x32,
  0x42,
  0xE2,
  0x22,
  0x3E,
  0x00,
    };

  struct fillsettingstype fst ;

  initgraph( &gd , &gm , "" ) ;

  printf(" Setting the fill settings using "
         "setfillpattern( ).Press a key...\n" );

  ellipse( 100 , 100 , 0 , 360 , 50 , 50) ;

  getch( ) ;
```

```
setfillpattern( user[0] , LIGHTRED ) ;

fillellipse( 100 , 100 , 50 , 50 ) ;

printf(" Press a key to see one more pattern" ) ;
getch( ) ;

setfillpattern( user[1] , LIGHTCYAN ) ;
fillellipse( 300 , 100 , 50 , 50 ) ;

printf("....that is all \n" ) ;

getfillsettings( &fst ) ;

printf(" from getfillsettings( ) : pattern # %d ,"
    "color # %d : " ,
    fst.pattern ,
    fst.color ) ;

if( fst.pattern == 12 )
    printf("pattern is user defined.\n" ) ;

getch( ) ;
closegraph( ) ;
}
```

We have presented two user-defined images: a smiling face and a robot. Each image is a character array of 8 bytes. The function *setfillpattern( )* is called once for each image. The parameter pattern is the address of the 8-byte array. The function *getfillsettings( )* informs us that the pattern is 12 (user-defined). The diagram below demonstrates the bit equivalent of the array members for the first image, i.e. the smiling face.

```
0x3C        00111100
0x42        10000010
0xA5        10100101
0x81        10000001
0xBD        10111101
0x42        01000010
0x3C        00111100
0x00        00000000
```

So we're left with two ellipses, the first filled with smiling faces, and the second with profiles.

Let's recapitulate for a minute: we've learnt how to draw lines and applied this knowledge to drawing linegraphs. Similarly, from bars we moved on to bar graphs. Then we drew sectors and pies and learnt how to fill images. Let's apply this to drawing pie graphs.

From Bar And Line Graphs To Pie Graphs

With a pie-graph we have 360 degrees at our disposal. Let's demonstrate with an example: suppose we want to display the % sales of a company's products. 100% sales would correspond to 360 degrees. We will use multiples of 5 to represent our data, up to a maximum of 100. We do not want to deal with the concept of floating point, so we'll reduce the above values to a minimum of 5% corresponding to 18 degrees. We'll use multiples of 5 to represent our data, up to a maximum of 100. This is done in the interest of simplicity. We can implement the floating point later.

PROGRAM 259

```c
#include <graphics.h>
#include <stdio.h>
#include <stdlib.h>
#include <dos.h>

main( )
{
    int gm , gd = DETECT ;
    char temp[5] ;
    char text[50] ;
    int coord[100] , num , tot ;
    int theta1 , theta2 , angle[25] ;
    int i , p , style = 1 , color = 1 ;

    printf(" Enter percentage not < 5 and the"
        " sum of the numbers must = 100\n" ) ;
    printf(" also multiples of 5\n ") ;
    i = 0 ;
    tot = 0 ;
```

```
printf( " Point #%d :", i+1 ) ;
while( ( num = atoi( gets( temp ) ) ) >= 5 )
{
    coord[i] = num ;
    i++ ;
    tot = tot + num ;
    if( tot > 100 ) /* error check */
    {
        printf("ERROR : Not permitted\n");
        exit(1) ;
    }
    if( tot == 100 )
        break ;
    printf( " Point #%d :", i+1 ) ;
}

theta1 = 0 ;
theta2 = 0 ;

/* calculation of the angles */

for( p = 0 ; p < i ; p++ )
{
    angle[p] = (coord[p]*18)/5 ;
}

initgraph( &gd , &gm , "" ) ;

for( p = 0 ; p < i ; p++ )
{
    theta2 = theta1 + angle[p] ;
    setfillstyle( style , color ) ;

    bar( 0 , p*15 , 20 , p*15+15 ) ;
    rectangle( 0 , p*15 , 20 , p*15+15 ) ;
    sprintf(text ,
        "Pie #%d : %d" ,
        p+1 , coord[p] ) ;
    outtextxy( 30 , p*15+3 , text ) ;

    pieslice( 400 , 200 , theta1 , theta2 , 100 ) ;

    delay( 500 ) ;
```

```
    theta1 = theta2 ;

    style++ ; color++ ;
    if( style == 11 )
        style = 1 ;
    if( color == 15 )
        color = 1 ;
    }

    getch( ) ;
    closegraph( ) ;
}
```

Let's go one step at a time. We've initialized two variables: *i* and *tot* to 0. The variable *i* will hold the total number of points entered +1. The variable *tot* will hold the running total of the values entered till the total reaches 100.

The first *while* loop keeps accepting numbers greater than 5, since this is the limitation we've imposed. These values are stored in the array *coord*. Any number entered is stored in *num* and then assigned to *coord[i]*. Initially the value of *i* is 0.

The first number we've entered is 10, therefore *coord[0]=10*. *i* is then incremented by 1. The total is 10. Since it isn't equal to or greater than 100, both the *if* conditions are ignored. Thus the first loop is complete. The next two numbers we've entered are 30 and 60. These go to *coord[1]* and *coord[2]*, respectively. *i* is now 3 and *tot=100*. The second *if* condition is then satisfied and we leave the loop.

The variables *theta1* and *theta2* are initialized to 0. *theta1* is the starting angle of the pie, and *theta2*, the ending angle. We have to calculate the angles corresponding to each value. The angle is calculated thus:

angle[p] = (coord[p]*18)/5 ;

p extends from 0 to 2. Thus *angle[0]=(10*18)/5=36* degrees. Similarly, *angle[1]=108* and *angle[2]* is 216 degrees.

After initializing the graphics system we enter the main *for* loop.

```
for( p = 0 ; p < i ; p++ )
{
    theta2 = theta1 + angle[p] ;

    setfillstyle( style , color ) ;
    bar( 0 , p*15 , 20 , p*15+15 ) ;

    rectangle( 0 , p*15 , 20 , p*15+15 ) ;

    sprintf(text , "Pie #%d : %d" , p+1 , coord[p] ) ;
    outtextxy( 30 , p*15+3 , text ) ;

    pieslice( 400 , 200 , theta1 , theta2 , 100 ) ;

    delay( 500 ) ;

    theta1 = theta2 ;

    style++ ; color++ ;
    if( style == 11 )
        style = 1 ;
    if( color == 15 )
        color = 1 ;
}
```

For *p=0, theta2=0+36.* So our first pie starts at 0 degrees and ends at 36 degrees. Each pie is displayed in a different style and color, both of which will be determined by *setfillstyle( )*. The color and style of each pie should be displayed in a key, which we build using the functions *bar( )* and *rectangle( )*.

Next, we draw the first pie slice. The delay is introduced so that we can observe each pie being built separately. The starting point of the second pie slice should be where the first pie slice ended. Thus, for the second pie slice, *theta1=theta2=36* degrees. To change the style and color of the second pie slice, we increment the parameters of *setfillstyle( )* by 1.

For *p=1*, *theta2=36+108=144*. The second pie slice and its key are drawn. *theta1* now becomes 144. For the last pie slice, *theta2=144+216=360*. And, voila, our piegraph is ready.

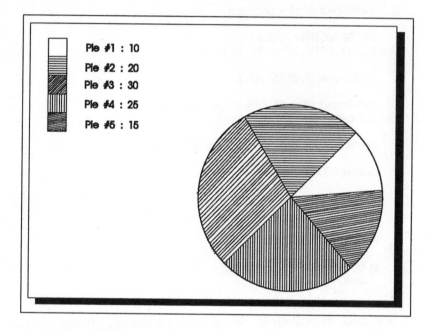

DIAGRAM 5.1(pie graphs)

Easy enough?

Yet Another Pie Graph

The next program also involves piegraphs, and follows a similar rationale as the preceding program. But it is a bit more complex. It involves two functions, *pie_graph( )* and *draw_pie_graphs( )*.

The *pie_graph( )* function is called by the function *draw_pie_graphs( )* four times, giving us four piegraphs. In turn, *draw_pie_graphs( )* is called by the main program.

PROGRAM 260

```c
# include <graphics.h>
# include <conio.h>

int maxcolors,maxx,maxy;
int accounts[4][9] =
{
    1985, 133,35,33,17,29,15,17,32,
    1986, 122,41,30,25,18,24,43,21,
    1987, 111,65,57,14,17,39,32,17,
    1988, 100,60,70,12,16,13,17,12
};

char * acctypes[9] =
{
    "   ",
    "Motor",
    "Acary",
    "Reprs",
    "Govmt",
    "Lease",
    "Tires",
    "Paint",
    "Misc"
};

void pie_graph(int dataset,int x,int y)
{
    int i, m = 135,r,s = 0, t = 0, hjust,vjust;
    int total = 0;
    int blank_line = 0x0000;
    int capcolor;
    struct arccoordstype arcrec;


    for(i = 1; i <= 8; i++)
    {
        total += accounts[dataset][i];
    }
    r = total/ 4;

    setlinestyle(USERBIT_LINE,blank_line,NORM_WIDTH);
    setfillstyle(0,0);
```

```
pieslice(x,y,m,m+1,r+10);

getarccoords(&arcrec);
if(maxcolors > 4)
    setcolor(WHITE);
settextstyle(SANS_SERIF_FONT,HORIZ_DIR,2);
settextjustify(RIGHT_TEXT,BOTTOM_TEXT);
settextstyle(DEFAULT_FONT,HORIZ_DIR,1);
if (maxcolors > 4)
    setcolor(EGA_YELLOW);
for(i =1; i<= 8;i++)
{
    setfillstyle(i,i);
    if( maxcolors > 4 )
        setcolor(WHITE);
    setlinestyle(SOLID_LINE,0,NORM_WIDTH);
    t += (int) (360 * (double) accounts[dataset][i] / (double) total+ 0.5);
    if (t > 360)
        t = 360;
    if ( i == 8)
        if (t < 360)
            t = 360;
    pieslice(x,y,s,t,r);
    setlinestyle(USERBIT_LINE,blank_line,NORM_WIDTH);
    setfillstyle(0,0);
    capcolor = i + 8;
    if (capcolor > 15)
        capcolor = 7;
    if (maxcolors > 4)
        setcolor(capcolor);
    m = (t - s) / 2 + s;
    pieslice(x,y,m,m+1,r+5);
    getarccoords(&arcrec);
    if(arcrec.xend > x)
        hjust = LEFT_TEXT;
    else
        hjust = RIGHT_TEXT;
    if(arcrec.yend > y)
        vjust = TOP_TEXT;
    else
        vjust = BOTTOM_TEXT;
    settextjustify(hjust,vjust);
    outtextxy(arcrec.xend,arcrec.yend,acctypes[i]);
```

```
      s = t;
    }
}

void draw_pie_graphs( )
{
    int y1 = getmaxy( ) * 0.275;
    int y2 = getmaxy( ) * 0.725;
    cleardevice( );
    graphdefaults( );
    rectangle(0,0,maxx,maxy);
    pie_graph(0,150,y1);
    pie_graph(1,450,y1);
    pie_graph(2,150,y2);
    pie_graph(3,450,y2);
}

void main( )
{

    int gm,gd = DETECT;

    initgraph(&gd,&gm,"");
    maxcolors = getmaxcolor( ) + 1;
    maxx = getmaxx( );
    maxy = getmaxy( );

    draw_pie_graphs( );

    getch( );
    closegraph( );
}
```

accounts is a 2-dimensional array holding information relating to the four piegraphs we want. *acctypes* is an array of pointers to characters. These strings will display the description of each pie in each pie graph.

The function *pie_graph( )* is passed 3 parameters: the index to *accounts* ranging from 0 to 3; the next two are the coordinates of the center.

s and *t* are the starting and ending angles. *r* is the radius. *m* is used to position the year label.

End of Greek lesson.

Text etc.

Out With Text !

How are we going to deal with all the text formatting introduced in the previous program? Let's look at the following text output and formatting programs.

The next program shows us how to go to a particular location on the screen and display something.

```
PROGRAM 261
include <graphics.h>

void main( )
{
    int gm,gd = DETECT;

    initgraph(&gd,&gm,"");
    printf( "Demo. for text output functions.\n" ) ;

    setcolor( YELLOW ) ;

    moveto( 10 , 100 ) ;
    outtext ("This is outtext( ).The 'T' of 'This' is at 10,100 "
            "because of moveto( )." ) ;

    getch( ) ;

    outtextxy( 10 , 150 , "This is outtextxy( ) which is a"
                " culmination of outtext( ) & moveto( )") ;

    getch( );
    closegraph( );
}
```

This is a very straightforward program. It moves us to a specific point using *moveto( )* and prints something at this point using *outtext( )*. Going a step further, *outtextxy( )* is a combination of the above two functions and displays the text at the specified position.

What if we wanted to print some more text below or adjacent to what we have already displayed. For this we'll need the functions *textheight( )* and *textwidth( )*, as demonstrated next:

PROGRAM 262

```
# include <graphics.h>

void main( )
{
    int gm,gd = DETECT;
    int height , width ;
    char text[100] ;

    initgraph(&gd , &gm , "");

    outtextxy( 10 , 20 , "textheight( ) and textwidth( ) " );

    setcolor( YELLOW ) ;

    outtextxy( 40 , 60 , "Flying High" ) ;

    height = textheight("Flying High" ) ;
    /* `height' used later in outtextxy( ) */

    width = textwidth ("Flying High" ) ;

    sprintf( text , "In PIXELs,height of 'Flying High' text = %d, "
                    "width of text = %d" ,height , width ) ;

    setcolor( LIGHTCYAN ) ;

    outtextxy( 40 , 60+height+10 , text ) ;

    getch( );
    closegraph( );
}
```

The height and width of the specified text are returned by the functions *textheight( )* and *textwidth( )*, respectively. Note the application of the variable height in the next call to *outtextxy( )*.

About The Type Of Text

Recall the use of the functions *getlinesettings( )* and *getfillsettings( )* : they supplied the type of line and type of image filling. Similarly, we can get information regarding the way in which our text can be displayed by calling the function *gettextsettings( )*. The relevant information is stored in a structure called *textsettingstype* which is defined in GRAPHICS.H.

```
struct textsettingstype
{
    int font;
    int direction;
    int charsize;
    int horiz;
    int vert;
};
```

The next program uses *gettextsettings( )* and reads the relevant information into the structure *textsettingstype*. The program supplies a table to interpret each value in the structure.

PROGRAM 263

```
# include <graphics.h>

void main( )
{

    int gm,gd = DETECT;
    char text[100] ;
    struct textsettingstype txt;

    initgraph(&gd , &gm , "");

    setcolor( LIGHTGREEN ) ;
    outtextxy( 10,10, "Lets get the settings of this text using"
```

```
                    " gettextsettings( )" ) ;

    gettextsettings( &txt ) ;

    setcolor( YELLOW ) ;

    sprintf( text , "FONT Number : %d" , txt.font ) ;
    outtextxy( 10 , 30 , text ) ;

    sprintf( text , "DIRECTION Number : %d" , txt.direction ) ;
    outtextxy( 10 , 40 , text ) ;

    sprintf( text , "Number giving size of characters : %d" , txt.charsize ) ;
    outtextxy( 10 , 50 , text ) ;

    sprintf( text , "Number telling horizontal justification of text: %d" ,
                    txt.horiz ) ;
    outtextxy( 10 , 60 , text ) ;

    sprintf( text , "Number telling vertical justification of text : %d" ,
                    txt.vert ) ;
    outtextxy( 10 , 70 , text ) ;

    setcolor( LIGHTMAGENTA ) ;

    outtextxy( 10 , 100 , "FONTS    DIRECTION  CHARACTER SIZE "
                    " HORIZ. JUSTIFN. VERT. JUSTIFN" ) ;
    line( 10 , 110 , getmaxx( ) , 110 ) ;
    outtextxy( 10 , 120 , "Default - 0  horiz. - 0  8 by 8 bits - 1"
                    " left - 0   bottom - 0" ) ;
    outtextxy( 10 , 140 , "triplex - 1  vert . - 1  16 by 16bits - 2"
                    " center-1    center - 1" ) ;
    outtextxy( 10 , 160 , "small - 2       :      right- 2  top - 2" ) ;
    outtextxy( 10 , 180 , "sans serif-3     :" ) ;
    outtextxy( 10 , 200 , "gothic - 4       80 by 80 bits-10 ") ;

    getch( ) ;
    closegraph( ) ;
}
```

The *outtextxy( )* displays a string. We have a structure *txt* similar to *textsettingstype*. We call *gettextsettings( )* and pass it the address of this structure. The subsequent *outtextxy( )*s print the values assigned to the members of the structure.

The table gives a detailed interpretation of the values of the members. For our string, the font was 0, which is the default. The direction was 0, which is horizontal. The character size was 1, implying that each character occupies a block of 8 by 8 pixels. The justification was left top.

We saw how we could receive the information in the default settings. The function *settextstyle( )* enables us to change the font, direction and character size.

At this point it is important to note that we have four fonts in addition to the default font. These are triplex, small, sans serif and Gothic. They are contained in files having a CHR extension. Thus, it is mandatory to load the said files.

The next program specifies the changes desired after printing the text in the default settings. We want the font to be triplex, the direction to be vertical and the size to be 32 by 32 pixels.

PROGRAM 264

```
# include <graphics.h>

void main( )
{
    int gm,gd = DETECT;

    initgraph(&gd,&gm,"");

    setcolor( LIGHTCYAN ) ;
    outtextxy(10 , 10 , "This is the default format of outputting text." ) ;
    outtextxy(10 , 20 , "settextstyle( ) can change it.Lets make"
                        " it vertical and larger");
    outtextxy(10 , 30 , "and change the fonts too...press a key") ;

    getch( ) ;

    settextstyle( TRIPLEX_FONT , VERT_DIR , 4 ) ;
```

```
    setcolor( LIGHTGREEN ) ;
    outtextxy( 10 , 40 , "OOPS ! Slipped.." ) ;

    getch( );
    closegraph( );
}
```

A detailed explanation of the fonts and sizes available follows.

PROGRAM 265

```
# include <graphics.h>

void main( )
{
    int gm,gd = DETECT;
    int font[ ] = { 0 , 1 , 2 , 3 , 4 } ;
    char *fonttext[ ] =
    {
        "default fonts" ,
        "triplex fonts" ,
        "small fonts" ,
        "sans serif fonts" ,
        "gothic fonts"
    } ;

    int i ;

    initgraph(&gd,&gm,"");

    setcolor( LIGHTCYAN ) ;
    outtextxy(10 , 20 , "settextstyle( ) explained fully") ;
    outtextxy(10 , 30 , "press a key...") ;
    getch( ) ;

    for( i = 0 ; i < 5 ; i++ )
    {
        cleardevice( ) ;

        settextstyle( font[i] , HORIZ_DIR , 4 ) ;

        outtextxy(0 , 0 ,"Fonts available :" ) ;
        outtextxy( 10 , 100 , fonttext[i] ) ;
```

```
    getch( ) ;
}
for( i = 1 ; i < 11 ; i++ )
{
    cleardevice( ) ;

    settextstyle( TRIPLEX_FONT , HORIZ_DIR , i ) ;

    outtextxy( 100 , 100 , "Sizing" ) ;
    getch( ) ;
}
cleardevice( ) ;

settextstyle( TRIPLEX_FONT , HORIZ_DIR , 5 ) ;
outtextxy(10 , 200 , "HORIZONTAL." ) ;

settextstyle( TRIPLEX_FONT , VERT_DIR , 5 ) ;
outtextxy(400 , 10 , "VERTICAL." ) ;

getch( );
closegraph( );
}
```

Two arrays are defined: the first contains numbers corresponding to the fonts, and the second is an array of strings containing the corresponding names of the fonts. For example, *font[0]=0*, and *fonttext[0]* is default fonts.

In the first *for* loop we called *settextstyle( )* to change the font. The direction and size are kept constant at horizontal and 4, respectively. The *outtextxy( )*s are displayed in the specified style.

In the next *for* loop, *settextstyle( )* changes the size from 1 to 10, i.e. from 8*8 pixels to 80*80 pixels.

The function *cleardevice( )* is the graphics equivalent of *clrscr( )* and clears the screen after each value of *i* appears on screen.

Lastly, we call *settextstyle( )* twice: once to display the text in a horizontal direction, a second time to display it in a vertical direction.

What could be simpler?!

Text Justification

Justification of text simply means positioning it with reference to a particular point. Remember that each character occupies a block of pixels. Thus, the terms right, left, top and bottom refer to the corners of the block. Similarly, a string would occupy a series of blocks and the above terms would apply to the entire series, treating it as a whole. We call the function *settextjustify( )* just for this purpose.

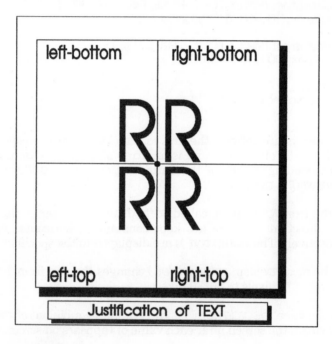

DIAGRAM 6.1

PROGRAM 266

include <graphics.h>

```
void main( )
{
    int gm,gd = DETECT;
    int x , y ;

    initgraph(&gd,&gm,"");

    x = getmaxx( )/2 ;
    y = getmaxy( )/2 ;

    printf(" JUSTIFICATION OF TEXT WITH RESPECT \n" ) ;
    printf(" TO THE PT. WHERE THE CROSS MEETS.\n" ) ;

    settextstyle( TRIPLEX_FONT , HORIZ_DIR , 4 ) ;

    setcolor( LIGHTCYAN ) ;
    line( x-250 , y , x+250 , y ) ;
    line( x, y-100 , x , y+100 ) ;

    settextjustify( LEFT_TEXT , BOTTOM_TEXT ) ;

    setcolor( YELLOW ) ;
    outtextxy( x , y , "1. left-bottom" ) ;

    settextjustify( LEFT_TEXT , TOP_TEXT ) ;

    setcolor( YELLOW ) ;
    outtextxy( x , y , "2. left-top" ) ;

    settextjustify( RIGHT_TEXT , BOTTOM_TEXT ) ;

    setcolor( YELLOW ) ;
    outtextxy( x , y , "3. right-bottom" ) ;

    settextjustify( RIGHT_TEXT , TOP_TEXT ) ;

    setcolor( YELLOW ) ;
    outtextxy( x , y , "4. right-top" ) ;

    printf("Press a key...\n" ) ;
    getch( ) ;
```

```
cleardevice( ) ;
line( x-250 , y , x+250 , y ) ;
line( x, y-100 , x , y+100 ) ;
settextjustify( CENTER_TEXT , CENTER_TEXT ) ;

setcolor( LIGHTCYAN ) ;
outtextxy( x , y , "1. center-center" ) ;

getch( );
closegraph( );
}
```

x and *y* are the coordinates of the center of the screen. *settextstyle( )* specifies the font, direction and size. Then two lines are drawn passing through the center(x,y), which is our reference point.

The function *settextjustify( )* is then called and the justification specified as left bottom. Now, left bottom corresponds to the left bottom corner of the text 1. left- bottom taken as a whole. So, our reference point (x,y) corresponds to the left bottom of the text.

We have similarly demonstrated justifying at the left top, right bottom, right top and center.

Text - Big And Small

By default we have sizes ranging from 1 to 10. However, we need not be limited by this. We can have our own user-defined sizes. The *setusercharsize( )* function is the required function. Note that in *settextstyle( )* we should specify the last parameter as USER_CHAR_SIZE.

This is defined as 0 in GRAPHICS.H.

PROGRAM 267

```c
# include <graphics.h>
# include <dos.h>

void main( )
{
    int gm,gd = DETECT;
    int i ;

    initgraph(&gd,&gm,"");

    setusercharsize( 20 , 1 , 10 , 1 ) ;

    settextstyle( TRIPLEX_FONT , HORIZ_DIR , USER_CHAR_SIZE ) ;
    outtextxy( 0,0 ,"B" ) ;

    getch( ) ;
    setcolor( YELLOW ) ;
    i = 0 ;

    while(!kbhit( ))
    {
        i++ ;
        cleardevice( ) ;

        setusercharsize( i*2 , 1 , i , 1 ) ;

        settextstyle(TRIPLEX_FONT , HORIZ_DIR ,USER_CHAR_SIZE ) ;
        outtextxy( 0,0 , "B" ) ;

        delay(500) ;
    }

    getch( );
    closegraph( );
}
```

The *setusercharsize( )* function has four parameters. The way they work is best demonstrated with an example. In the program, the four parameters we have passed are 20, 1, 10, 1.

Take the first two parameters. Dividing the first by the second, we get the width we want -- in this case, 20 times as wide as the default. Similarly, the last two parameters give us the height we want -- in this case 10 times as high as the default. Thus, in general, the quotient of the first two parameters gives us the width we want and the quotient of the last two parameters gives us the height we want.

The *while* loop increments the size of the character till a key is pressed. So, do you want your text to be big and bold, or small and discreet? The choice, as always, is yours.

The Fonts And Your Application

We noted earlier that in order to use fonts, we would need files with a CHR extension. Four files are available to us, one for each font: TRIP.CHR, LITT.CHR, SANS.CHR and GOTH.CHR. It is possible to convert these CHR files to OBJ files and link them to our application. For example, if our program is called GRAPH.C, and we want to include the CHR files in our program, we would do the following:

1. Run the BGIOBJ.EXE program as follows:

```
C>BGIOBJ TRIP
```

Thus the file TRIP.OBJ is created. Similarly create GOTH.OBJ, LITT.OBJ and SANS.OBJ.

2. Create a file called GRAPH.PRJ which should contain the following:

```
GRAPH
TRIP.OBJ
GOTH.OBJ
SANS.OBJ
LITT.OBJ
```

3. In your GRAPH.C file, go to the project option. Specify the name of the project file as GRAPH.PRJ.

4. Key in the C program and compile the application.

The function *settextstyle( )* needs to be informed that the fonts are now part of the program, and hence don't need to be loaded externally. For this purpose we call the function *registerbgifont( )* and pass the font name. This is done in a specific way. See the following list:

FONT file (.CHR)	Name to be used with registerbgifont( )
TRIP	triplex_font
LITT	small_font
SANS	sansserif_font
GOTH	gothic_font

DIAGRAM 6.2

Each of these names is a pointer to a function which returns a void. Henceforth, when we speak of fonts, the graphics system will use these function pointers to refer to the respective fonts. Note that *registerbgifont( )* has to be called before calling *initgraph( )*.

Normally, we use the small model to compile programs. Here the code cannot extend beyond 64K. Obviously, the more fonts we register, the less space we have. So we convert our function pointers to far function pointers. For this we need to run the BGIOBJ.EXE program in a slightly different way, i.e.

C>BGIOBJ /F TRIP

Also, when we pass a parameter to *registerbgifont( )*, we do not merely say, for example, *triplex_font*. Instead we say *triplex_font_far*.

This entire process is analogous to what we had done earlier for registering BGI drivers.

PROGRAM 268

```
# include <graphics.h>

void main( )
{
    int gm,gd = DETECT;

    registerbgifont( gothic_font ) ;
    registerbgifont( sansserif_font ) ;
    registerbgifont( triplex_font ) ;
    registerbgifont( small_font ) ;

    initgraph(&gd,&gm,"");

    settextstyle( TRIPLEX_FONT , HORIZ_DIR , 4 ) ;
    outtextxy( 10 ,110 , "boo!" ) ;

    getch( );
    closegraph( );
}
```

This program illustrates what we have discussed above.

Receiving Input In Graphics Mode

So far we've learnt how to output graphics information. How do we receive input in the graphics mode? There is no function available to us which does this, which is justifiable since it is not easy to adjust coordinates for strings. We have written a function called *intextxy( )* which receives input from the screen, which in its present avatar is not very refined. We have included it as a starting point for you so you can write a more generic function.

PROGRAM 269

```
#include <graphics.h>
```

```c
#include <bios.h>
#include <stdio.h>

void main( )
{
    int gm ;
    int gd = DETECT ;
    char str[100] ;

    initgraph( &gd , &gm , "" ) ;

    settextstyle( TRIPLEX_FONT , HORIZ_DIR , 2 ) ;

    setcolor( LIGHTRED ) ;
    outtextxy( 10 , 100 , "ENTER:" ) ;

    setcolor( LIGHTCYAN ) ;
    intextxy( 100 , 100 , str , 20 , LIGHTCYAN ) ;

    outtextxy( 200 , 300 , str ) ;

    getch( ) ;
    closegraph( ) ;
}

int intextxy( int x , int y , char *str , int len , int color )
{
    int i ;
    char *temp ;
    unsigned int ch ;

    temp = str ;
    i = -1 ;
    setcolor( color ) ;
    ch = 65 ;
    while(1)
    {
        /* increment i iff key is normal ascii or left arrow */
        if( (ch & 0x00FF) | | (ch>>8) == 75 )
        i++ ;
        ch = bioskey(0) ;
        /* if the ENTER has been pressed */
        if( (ch & 0x00FF) == 13 ) /* enter */
```

```
    {
       temp[i] = 0 ;
       break ;
    }
    /* If The LEFT ARROW has been pressed */
    else if( (ch>>8) == 75 && (ch & 0x00ff) == 0 )
    {
       if( i > 1 )
       {
          i = i - 2 ;
          temp[i+1] = 0 ;
       }
       else
       {
          i = -1 ;
          temp[i+1] = 0 ;
          putchar( 7 ) ;
       }
       setfillstyle(SOLID_FILL , BLACK) ;
       bar(x+1 , y+1 , x+16*len-1 , y+25-1 ) ;
       setcolor( color ) ;
       outtextxy( x , y , temp ) ;
    }
/* buffer full */
    else if (( i > len - 2 ) && ( (ch & 0x00FF)!=0 ))
    {
       putchar( 7 ) ;
       return 0 ;
    }
    /* normal character */
    else if ( (ch & 0x00FF) != 0 )
    {
       temp[i] = ch & 0x00FF ;
       temp[i+1] = 0 ;
       outtextxy( x , y , temp ) ;
    }
  }
  return 0 ;
}
```

Before writing the function *intextxy( )* we had to keep a few basics
in mind.

Firstly, we need the starting coordinates of where the text is to be entered. We also need an array for the string and the maximum length of the array.

This is important because when we're in text mode each character is the same size. In graphics, this is not so. For instance, the character m is much wider than the character l. Consequently, a large number of ms will not fit on one line, while the same number of ls will. It is important, therefore, to be careful about the length of the string. For this purpose, we may use the functions *textheight( )* and *textwidth( )*.

To get a character, we can call *getch( )*, put each character into an array, and exit when the enter key is pressed. Further, the left and right arrow keys are used for editing. The *getch( )* function can't process these keys. So we've used *bioskey( )* to manually process each key pressed.

When we use the left arrow key to delete a character to the left, we have to make sure that we stop at the first character of the line. To display what is entered, we call *outtextxy( )* after clearing the previous contents of the line.

Let's look at the program....

In the main program we have an array called *str* which is 100 bytes long. The function *intextxy( )* is called with five parameters: the coordinates, the address of the array, the maximum length of the string and the color. (100, 100, str, 20, LIGHTCYAN).

We have equated *temp*, which is a pointer to a character, with the array. So *temp* points to the start of the array. An integer *i* has been initialized at -1. There is also an unsigned integer *ch*, which gives a character when a key is pressed.

After setting the color, we enter an infinite loop. If, and only if, the key pressed is the left arrow key or a normal ASCII character, *i* is incremented. The function *bioskey( )* is then called (the command being 0) implying that we are waiting for a key to be pressed, which value will be stored in the variable *ch*. In this variable, the high byte contains the scan code, and the low byte contains the ASCII code. If a special character has been entered -- in this case the left arrow key -- the low byte will contain a 0.

The second *if* condition checks whether the key pressed was the enter key and quits the loop if this is the case. We then return to the calling program.

Let's assume that the first key pressed is T. Then the second, third and fourth *if* conditions fail. The fifth *if* condition, however, is satisfied since the key pressed is a normal ASCII character. Therefore, *temp[i]*, i.e. *temp[0]='T'*, and *temp[1]=0*. The *outtextxy( )* function displays the null terminated string in the array *temp*.

We then return to the beginning of the loop and *i* is incremented to 1. C is entered on the keyboard, and the entire chain of events is repeated. Finally, *temp[0] ='T'*, *temp[1]='C'* and *temp[2]=0*. The function *outtextxy( )* displays TC.

With *i=2*, we press the left arrow key. The third *if* condition i.e.

else if((ch>>8) == 75 && (ch & 0x00ff) == 0) /*left*/

is satisfied. As soon as the left arrow key is pressed, there are two conditions possible: either there may be no characters to be deleted, i.e. at the beginning of the array, or there may be.

At this point, we satisfy the second condition, since *i>1*. Thus *i* is decremented by 2 (so *i=0*) and *temp[1]=0*. We overwrite the previous string with a black bar and write the new string, which is T.

If the left arrow key is pressed, the same *if* condition is satisfied. Within this *if* condition, there is another *if* and *else* condition. Since *i=0*, the *else* is satisfied. Consequently, *i=-1* and *temp[0]=0*. Further, a beep is heard, indicating that we are on the first character. Thus, any subsequent entering of the left arrow key satisfies the *else* condition, which restricts the user from deleting further.

If more than 18 characters are entered we are forced to return to the calling function due to

else if (((i > len - 2) && ((ch & 0x00FF) != 0))

Any other special key, eg. the up arrow, F1, etc, is not processed because of the restrictions put by the four *if* conditions.

You might have noticed the operations AND and right shifting being applied to *ch*. *ch>>8* shifts *ch* to the right by 8 bits. This operation gives us the high byte of the integer *ch*. Similarly, *ch & 0x00FF* yields the low byte. All of this serves to inform us whether the key entered is a special key or an ASCII character.

The subsequent *outtextxy( )* in the main program displays the string. We don't know about you, but we're taking a break now.

We're BACK!!!!!!!

The following program applies the function *intextxy( )* to create an user interface to receive names and telephone numbers.

PROGRAM 270

```c
#include <graphics.h>
#include <bios.h>
#include <stdio.h>
#include <string.h>

void main( )
{
    int gm ;
    int gd = DETECT ;
    char name[40],number[8],ans[3] ;
    int p ;

    initgraph( &gd , &gm , "" ) ;

    setcolor( LIGHTBLUE ) ;
    rectangle( 1 , 1 , getmaxx( )-1 , getmaxy( )-1 ) ;

    while(1)
```

```
        {
            settextstyle( TRIPLEX_FONT , HORIZ_DIR , 4 ) ;
            settextjustify( CENTER_TEXT , CENTER_TEXT ) ;

            setcolor( YELLOW ) ;
            outtextxy( getmaxx( )/2 , 20 , "T E L E P H O N E S" ) ;

            settextstyle( TRIPLEX_FONT , HORIZ_DIR , 2 ) ;
            settextjustify( LEFT_TEXT , TOP_TEXT ) ;

            setcolor( LIGHTGREEN ) ;
            outtextxy( 5 , 60 , "Name :" ) ;
            outtextxy( 5 , 100 , "Number :" ) ;

            setcolor( LIGHTCYAN ) ;
            intextxy1( 100 , 60 , name , 30 ) ;
            intextxy1 ( 100 , 100 , number , 8 ) ;

            setcolor( LIGHTMAGENTA ) ;
            outtextxy( 10 , 300 , "Any More To Come ?(Y/N) :" ) ;
            intextxy1( 500 , 300 , ans , 3 ) ;
            p = strcmp( "N" , ans ) ;
            if( p == 0 )
            {
                break ;
            }
            p = strcmp( "n" , ans ) ;
            if( p == 0 )
            {
                break ;
            }
            else
            {
                setfillstyle ( SOLID_FILL , BLACK ) ;
                bar( 2 , 2 , getmaxx( ) - 2 , getmaxy( ) - 2 ) ;
            }
        }
        getch( ) ;
        closegraph( ) ;
    }

    int intextxy1( int x , int y , char *str , int len )
    {
```

```
int i ;
char *temp ;
unsigned int ch ;

temp = str ;
i = -1 ;
settextjustify( LEFT_TEXT , TOP_TEXT ) ;
while(1)
{
    if( (ch & 0x00FF) I I (ch>>8) == 75 )
        i++ ;
    rectangle( x , y , x+16*len , y+25 ) ;
    ch = bioskey(0) ;
    if( (ch & 0x00FF) == 13 )
    {
        temp[i] = 0 ;
        break ;
    }
/* if LEFT ARROW or BACK SPACE Pressed */
    else if( ( (ch>>8) == 75 && (ch & 0x00ff) == 0 ) I I
            (ch & 0x00FF) == 8 )
    {
        if( i > 1 )
        {
            i = i - 2 ;
            temp[i+1] = 0 ;
        }
        else
        {
            i = -1 ;
            temp[i+1] = 0 ;
            putchar( 7 ) ;
        }
        setfillstyle(SOLID_FILL , BLACK) ;
        bar(x+1 , y , x+16*len-1, y+25 ) ;
        outtextxy( x , y , temp ) ;
    }
    else if (( i > len - 2 ) && ( (ch & 0x00FF) != 0 ))
    {
        putchar( 7 ) ;
        return 0 ;
    }
    else if ( (ch & 0x00FF) != 0 )
```

```
    {
        temp[i] = ch & 0x00FF ;
        temp[i+1] = 0 ;
        outtextxy( x , y , temp ) ;
    }
}
    return 0 ;
}
```

The calling of the function *rectangle( )* in *intextxy1( )* is the only difference between this and the previous *intextxy( )*.

You are asked to enter a name. By way of example, enter a row of ls the first time, and a row of ms the second time. Recall our discussion on the size of characters in graphics.

Fun With Text

One last program on text, and then you're ready for anything.

```
PROGRAM 271

#include <graphics.h>
#include <conio.h>
#include <bios.h>

#define ESC   27
#define UP   372
#define DOWN  380
#define PGUP  373
#define PGDN  381

unsigned int getonech( ) ;

main( )
{
    int gd = DETECT;
    int gm;
    int ch=0 ;
    int x = 2 , y = 2 , dim ;

    initgraph(&gd,&gm,"");
```

```
        setusercharsize( 2 , 10 , 2 , 10 ) ;
        settextstyle( TRIPLEX_FONT , HORIZ_DIR , USER_CHAR_SIZE ) ;
        outtextxy( 10 , 10 , "Food" ) ;
        dirn = HORIZ_DIR ;

        while(1)
        {
           ch = getonech( ) ;
           cleardevice( ) ;
           setcolor( LIGHTCYAN ) ;
           if( ch == ESC )
           {
              break ;
           }
           if( ch == UP )
           {
              x++ ; y++ ;
              if( x == 200 ) x = x-1 , y = y-1;
           }
           if( ch == DOWN )
           {
              x-- ; y-- ;
              if( x == 1 ) x = 2 , y = 2;
           }
           if( ch == PGDN )
           {
              dirn = HORIZ_DIR ;
           }
           if( ch == PGUP )
           {
              dirn = VERT_DIR ;
           }
           setusercharsize( x , 10 , y , 10 ) ;
           settextstyle(TRIPLEX_FONT,dirn,USER_CHAR_SIZE ) ;
           outtextxy( 10 , 10 , "Food" ) ;
        }
        closegraph( );
    }

    unsigned int getonech( )
    {
        unsigned int ch ;
        int hi , lo ;
```

```
ch = bioskey(0) ;
hi = ch >> 8 ;
lo = ch & 0x00ff ;
if( lo == 0 )
{
    ch = 300 + hi ;
    return ch ;
}
else
{
    ch = lo ;
    return ch ;
}
}
```

Before getting into the program proper, let's see what *getonech( )* does. The function *bioskey( )* waits for a key to be pressed and returns it to *ch. ch* is shifted to the right by 8 bits. Consequently, the high byte of *ch* is isolated and stored in the variable *hi.*

Similarly, *ch & 0x00FF* yields the low byte, which is stored in *lo.* If *lo* =0, it implies that a special key has been pressed. The scan code of this key is in *hi.* Thus, *hi* is incremented by 300 and returned to the calling function. Lastly, if *lo* is not 0, it implies that a normal key was pressed, and its ASCII code is returned to the calling function.

In the main program, the size of the character is set at two-tenths of the default by calling *setusercharsize( ).* The function *settextstyle( )* is passed the relevant parameters, and *outtextxy( )* prints Food in the style specified. The variables *x, y* and *dirn* are initialized at 2, 2 and HORIZ_DIR, respectively.

In the *while* loop, we wait for a key to be pressed. The code is returned in *ch.* After clearing the screen, we ascertain the key pressed. If it was the ESCape key, we quit the program. If instead, we entered an up arrow key, the variables *x* and *y* are incremented by 1, and the *if* condition checks whether *x=200.*

If this is so, *x* and *y* are decremented by 1. *x* should have a maximum value of 200 since we've decided that the size should not exceed 20 times the default size. Similarly, pressing the down arrow key decrements *x* and *y* by 1. When *x* attains a value of 1, both *x* and *y* are assigned the value 2. By doing this, we ensure that our character size will not, at any point, be less than two-tenths the default size.

The following two *if* conditions deal with the direction of the text. If we press the page-down key, the variable *dirn* is assigned the HORIZ_DIR. Likewise, pressing the page up key assigns the value VERT_DIR to the variable *dirn*.

The next three lines specify the way in which the text is to be displayed, and then print it. The *setusercharsize( )* function changes the size of the text according to the values of *x* and *y*. The function *settextstyle( )* determines the font (TRIPLEX_FONT), the direction (as specified by the variable *dirn*) and also reiterates that the size is user-defined. The *outtextxy( )* function prints the text *Food* at the specified coordinates.

You now have at your disposal various tools which enable you to display and receive text in the graphics mode. We saw, especially in the last program, how inherently simple it is to control the keyboard and make the keys function any way you want .

Down to the nitty-gritty now: pixel level graphics.

Of Pixels And Dots And Lots

Pause for a moment and reflect on how all these things that we've done boil down to the playing around of pixels. They are the basic units, the atomic level, so to speak. For example, a line element is a row of 16 pixels. User-defined fillstyles implement pixels in the manner specified. The list continues. The following discussion on pixel level graphics elaborates further.

A New 'Point' Of View

The two functions *getpixel( )* and *putpixel( )* constitute the backbone of pixel level graphics.

PROGRAM 272

```
/* getpixel( ) --- putpixel( ) */

#include <graphics.h>
#include <stdlib.h>
#include <conio.h>

void main( )
{
    int gm , gd = DETECT ;
    char text[60] ;
    int col ;

    initgraph( &gd , &gm , "" ) ;

    printf("demo 'for' PUTPIXEL( )\n" ) ;

    putpixel( 200 , 202 , )

    outtextxy( 203 , 200 , "<- see the pixel ! .... " ) ;
    outtextxy( 203 , 210 , "lets get some info 'bout the"
                           " pixel using GETPIXEL( )" ) ;

    getch( ) ;
```

```
col = getpixel( 203 , 200 ) ;

sprintf( text, "Color number of pixel = %d.
        Press a key 'for' some fun.." , col ) ;
outtextxy( 203 , 220 , text ) ;
getch( ) ;
cleardevice( ) ;
while( !kbhit( ) )
{
    putpixel( random( getmaxx( ) ) ,
    random( getmaxy( ) ) ,
    random( MAXCOLORS ) ) ;
}
closegraph( ) ;
}
```

We have called the function *putpixel( )* to place a yellow pixel at the given coordinates. The function *getpixel( )* returns the color of the pixel. In this case the number it returns is 14, corresponding to yellow, the color of our pixel. We now clear the screen by calling *cleardevice( )*. The positions of the pixels are random, as are the colors. Now, till a key is pressed, we will see a beautiful sprinkling of color flood the screen.

Drawing And Interacting

We can literally draw an image on the screen as we would manually, by using the left, right, up and down arrow keys to position the pixels. Pressing the *i* key, to insert, we can generate a continuous flow of pixels. The *q* key lets you overwrite, for example, if you want to begin redrawing at another point.

Picasso should have been around now!

PROGRAM 273

```
/* getpixel( ) --- putpixel( ) */
/* draw mode - 'i' ; no draw - 'q' */

#include <graphics.h>
#include <stdlib.h>
#include <conio.h>
```

```c
#define YES      1
#define NO       0
#define UP       372
#define DOWN     380
#define LEFT     375
#define RIGHT    377

unsigned int getonech( ) ;

void main( )
{
    int gm , gd = DETECT ;
    unsigned int ch ;
    int x=1 , y=1 , draw = NO ;

    initgraph( &gd , &gm , "" ) ;

    while(1)
    {
        ch = getonech( ) ;
        if( ch == 27 )
            break ;
        if( ch == UP )
        {
            if( draw == NO )
                putpixel( x , y , getbkcolor( )) ;
            y – ;
            if( y == 0 ) y = 1 ;
            putpixel( x , y , YELLOW ) ;
        }
        if( ch == DOWN )
        {
            if( draw == NO )
                putpixel( x , y , getbkcolor( )) ;
            y ++ ;
            if( y == getmaxy( ) ) y = getmaxy( )-1 ;
            putpixel( x , y , YELLOW ) ;
        }
        if( ch == LEFT )
        {
            if( draw == NO )
                putpixel( x , y , getbkcolor( )) ;
```

```
            x -- ;
            if( x == 0 ) x = 1 ;
            putpixel( x , y , YELLOW ) ;
        }
        if( ch == RIGHT )
        {
            if( draw == NO )
                putpixel( x , y , getbkcolor( )) ;
            x ++ ;
            if( x == getmaxx( ) ) x = getmaxx( )-1 ;
            putpixel( x , y , YELLOW ) ;
        }
        if( ch == 'i' )
            draw = YES ;
        if( ch == 'q' )
            draw = NO ;
    }
    closegraph( ) ;
}


unsigned int getonech( )
{
    unsigned int ch ;
    int hi , lo ;

    ch = bioskey(0) ;
    hi = ch >> 8 ;
    lo = ch & 0x00ff ;
    if( lo == 0 )
    {
        ch = 300 + hi ;
        return ch ;
    }
    else
    {
        ch = lo ;
        return ch ;
    }
}
```

The function *getonech( )* returns the code of the key. Initially, the variables *x* and *y* are 1. These coordinates specify the pixel's position. The variable *draw* is initialized at NO, implying that we're in the overwrite mode.

We then enter an infinite *while* loop and wait for a key to be pressed. If the key pressed is the ESCape key, we break out of the *while* loop. Now, if we press the up arrow key, we have to satisfy an *if* condition. If the variable *draw* is set at NO, which it is in this case, we call *putpixel( )* to put a pixel at the specified coordinates.

We have specified the color as the background color, so effectively we see nothing. This is as it should be, since we don't want to draw as yet. *y* is decremented by 1. We don't want *y* to have a value of 0 since that would exceed the limits of the screen. So when that happens, we assign a value of 1 to *y*. At that point, we place a yellow pixel.

If we press the down arrow key, we have to satisfy a similar *if* condition. A similar procedure is followed for the left and right arrow keys, except that now we change the values of the x-coordinate.

From now on, if we press the key *i* for insert, the variable *draw* will be set at YES. Thus the condition

if(draw==NO)

fails, ensuring that the previous pixel is not overwritten. If the *q* key is pressed, the value of *draw* is set to NO. So we're back to the overwrite mode.

By setting another key, we can change the color of the pixel. The mouse can be used in a similar way. Thus, a lot of avenues are now open to us.

Approaching Bit-Mapped Graphics

We'll look at bit-mapped graphics now. If a bit is set, the corresponding pixel is displayed, and vice versa. Using this logic, we can generate our own user-defined fonts.

In the following program we generate some letters of the Hindi alphabet. Although the program is in a raw state, it serves to explain the rationale.

Each character is represented in a block made up of bits. If instead, we had a block made up of bytes, it would serve to magnify the bit block. Each byte can be set (1), or reset (0). We have a 25*25 byte block, with each byte either set or reset, depending on the image desired. On the screen, this corresponds to a 25*25 pixel block. For the matras (vowel appendages), we need a smaller byte block since these do not occupy as much space as an alphabet. Thus they have byte blocks of 10*13 and 25*7.

We simply trap keys to get the predefined alphabets or matras. The tricky part is positioning the symbols on the screen.

Get ready for a whopper of a program....

PROGRAM 274
/* A few letters of the HINDI alphabet */

```
#include <graphics.h>
#include <ctype.h>
#include <bios.h>

char arr[25][25] , marr[25][7] ;
char aearr[10][13] ;

void mhind(int x , int y)
{

    int i ; int j ;

    for( i = 0 ; i < 25 ; i++ )
```

```
    {
      for( j = 0 ; j < 25 ; j++ )
        arr[i][j] = 0 ;
      arr[0][i] = 1 ;
      arr[i][20] = 1 ;
    }

    for( i = 0 ; i < 20 ; i++ )
      arr[11][i] = 1 ;
    for( i = 0 ; i < 17 ; i++ )
      arr[i][7] = 1 ;
    for( i = 11 ; i < 17 ; i++ )
      for( j = 0 ; j < 7 ; j++ )
        if( i-11 == j ) arr[i][j] = 1 ;

    for( i = 0 ; i < 25 ; i++ )
      for( j = 0 ; j < 25 ; j++ )
        if( arr[i][j] == 1 )
          putpixel( x+j , y+i , YELLOW ) ;
}


void ghind(int x , int y)
{

    int i ; int j ;

    for( i = 0 ; i < 25 ; i++ )
    {
      for( j = 0 ; j < 25 ; j++ )
        arr[i][j] = 0 ;
      arr[0][i] = 1 ;
      arr[i][20] = 1 ;
    }

    for( i = 0 ; i < 5 ; i++ )
      arr[11][i] = 1 ;
    for( i = 0 ; i < 17 ; i++ )
      arr[i][7] = 1 ;
    for( i = 11 ; i < 17 ; i++ )
      for( j = 0 ; j < 7 ; j++ )
        if( i-11 == j ) arr[i][j] = 1 ;
```

```
        for( i = 0 ; i < 25 ; i++ )
          for( j = 0 ; j < 25 ; j++ )
            if( arr[i][j] == 1 )
              putpixel( x+j , y+i , YELLOW ) ;
}

void nhind(int x , int y)
{

    int i ; int j ;

    for( i = 0 ; i < 25 ; i++ )
    {
      for( j = 0 ; j < 25 ; j++ )
        arr[i][j] = 0 ;
      arr[0][i] = 1 ;
      arr[i][20] = 1 ;
    }

    for( i = 0 ; i < 20 ; i++ )
      arr[11][i] = 1 ;
    for( i = 11 ; i < 17 ; i++ )
      arr[i][7] = 1 ;
    for( i = 11 ; i < 17 ; i++ )
      for( j = 0 ; j < 7 ; j++ )
        if( i-11 == j ) arr[i][j] = 1 ;

    for( i = 0 ; i < 25 ; i++ )
      for( j = 0 ; j < 25 ; j++ )
        if( arr[i][j] == 1 )
          putpixel( x+j , y+i , YELLOW ) ;
}

void rhind( int x , int y )
{

    int i ; int j ;

    for( i = 0 ; i < 25 ; i++ )
    {
      for( j = 0 ; j < 25 ; j++ )
        arr[i][j] = 0 ;
      arr[0][i] = 1 ;
```

```
        }
        for( i = 10 ; i < 25 ; i++ )
            for( j = 0 ; j < 15 ; j++ )
                if( i-10 == j ) arr[i][j] = 1 ;
        j = 14 ;
        for( i = 0 ; i < 15 ; i++ )
        {
            arr[i][j] = 1 ;
            j-- ;
        }

        for( i = 10 ; i < 15 ; i++ )
            arr[i][0] = 1 ;

        for( i = 0 ; i < 25 ; i++ )
            for( j = 0 ; j < 25 ; j++ )
                if( arr[i][j] == 1 )
                    putpixel( x+j , y+i , YELLOW ) ;
}

void shind( int x , int y )
{

    int i ; int j ;

    for( i = 0 ; i < 25 ; i++ )
    {
        for( j = 0 ; j < 25 ; j++ )
            arr[i][j] = 0 ;
        arr[0][i] = 1 ;
        arr[i][20] = 1 ;
    }

    for( i = 10 ; i < 25 ; i++ )
        for( j = 0 ; j < 15 ; j++ )
            if( i-10 == j ) arr[i][j] = 1 ;
    j = 14 ;
    for( i = 0 ; i < 15 ; i++ )
    {
        arr[i][j] = 1 ;
        j-- ;
    }
```

```
        for( i = 10 ; i < 15 ; i++ )
            arr[i][0] = 1 ;

        for( i = 4 ; i < 21 ; i++ )
            arr[13][i] = 1 ;

        for( i = 0 ; i < 25 ; i++ )
            for( j = 0 ; j < 25 ; j++ )
                if( arr[i][j] == 1 )
                    putpixel( x+j , y+i , YELLOW ) ;
    }

    void amatra( int x , int y )
    {

        int i ;
        int j ;

        for( i = 0 ; i < 25 ; i++ )
            for( j = 0 ; j < 7 ; j++ )
                marr[i][j] = 0 ;

        for( i = 0 ; i < 7 ; i++ )
            marr[0][i] = 1 ;
        for( i = 0 ; i < 25 ; i++ )
            marr[i][3] = 1 ;
        for( i = 0 ; i < 25 ; i++ )
            for( j = 0 ; j < 7 ; j++ )
                if( marr[i][j] == 1 )
                    putpixel( x+j , y+i , YELLOW ) ;
    }

    void aeomatra( int x , int y , int type )
    {
        int i ; int j ;

        for( i = 0 ; i < 13 ; i++ )
            for( j = 0 ; j < 10 ; j++ )
                aearr[j][i] = 0 ;

        for( i = 2 ; i < 13 ; i++ )
            for( j = 0 ; j < 10 ; j++ )
```

```
          if( i - 2 == j ) aearr[j][i] = 1 ;

      for( i = 0 ; i < 6 ; i++ )
         aearr[3][i] = 1;
      aearr[2][0] = 1 ;
      aearr[1][1] = 1 ;
      aearr[0][2] = 1 ;

      if( type == 2 )
      {
         for( i = 0 ; i < 10 ; i++ )
            for( j = 0 ; j < 13 ; j++ )
               if( aearr[i][j] == 1 )
                  putpixel( x-13+j , y-10+i , YELLOW ) ;
      }
      if( type == 3 )
      {
         for( i = 0 ; i < 10 ; i++ )
            for( j = 0 ; j < 13 ; j++ )
               if( aearr[i][j] == 1 )
                  putpixel( x-5+j ,
                     y+25+i ,
                     YELLOW ) ;
      }

}

unsigned int getonech( )
{
   unsigned int ch ;
   int hi , lo ;

   ch = bioskey(0) ;
   hi = ch >> 8 ;
   lo = ch & 0x00ff ;
   if( lo == 0 )
   {
      ch = 300 + hi ;
      return ch ;
   }
   else
   {
      ch = lo ;
```

```
        return ch ;
    }
}


main( )
{
    int gd = DETECT;
    int gm;
    int ch ;
    int cpos=0 , rpos=0 ;

    initgraph(&gd,&gm,"");

    cleardevice( ) ;
    while(1)
    {
        ch = toupper(getonech( )) ;

        if( ch == 27 )
        {
            break ;
        }

        if( ch == 13 )
        {
            rpos = 0 ;
            cpos = cpos + 46 ;
            if( cpos >= getmaxy( )-46 )
            {
                cpos = 0 ;
                cleardevice( ) ;
            }
        }

        if( ch == 'R' )
        {
            rhind( rpos , cpos ) ;
            rpos = rpos + 26 ;

            if( rpos >= getmaxx( )-26 )
            {
                rpos = 0 ;
```

```
            cpos = cpos + 46 ;
            if( cpos >= getmaxy( )-46 )
            {
                cpos = 0 ;
                cleardevice( ) ;
            }
        }
    }

    if( ch == 'G' )
    {
        ghind( rpos , cpos ) ;
        rpos = rpos + 26 ;

        if( rpos >= getmaxx( )-26 )
        {
            rpos = 0 ;
            cpos = cpos + 46 ;
            if( cpos >= getmaxy( )-46 )
            {
                cpos = 0 ;
                cleardevice( ) ;
            }
        }
    }

    if( ch == 'N' )
    {
        nhind( rpos , cpos ) ;
        rpos = rpos + 26 ;

        if( rpos >= getmaxx( )-26 )
        {
            rpos = 0 ;
            cpos = cpos + 46 ;
            if( cpos >= getmaxy( )-46 )
            {
                cpos = 0 ;
                cleardevice( ) ;
            }
        }
    }
```

```
if( ch == 'S' )
{
    shind( rpos , cpos ) ;
    rpos = rpos + 26 ;

    if( rpos >= getmaxx( )-26 )
    {
        rpos = 0 ;
        cpos = cpos + 46 ;
        if( cpos >= getmaxy( )-46 )
        {
            cpos = 0 ;
            cleardevice( ) ;
        }
    }
}

if( ch == 'M' )
{
    mhind( rpos , cpos ) ;
    rpos = rpos + 26 ;
    if( rpos >= getmaxx( )-26 )
    {
        rpos = 0 ;
        cpos = cpos + 46 ;
        if( cpos >= getmaxy( )-46 )
        {
            cpos = 0 ;
            cleardevice( ) ;
        }
    }
}

if( ch == '1' )
{
    amatra( rpos , cpos ) ;
    rpos = rpos + 8 ;
    if( rpos >= getmaxx( )-8 )
    {
        rpos = 0 ;
        cpos = cpos + 46 ;
        if( cpos >= getmaxy( )-46 )
        {
```

```
                    cpos = 0 ;
                    cleardevice( ) ;
                }
            }
        }

        if( ch == '2' )
        {
            aeomatra( rpos , cpos , 2 ) ;
        }

        if( ch == '3' )
        {
            aeomatra( rpos , cpos , 3 ) ;
        }

        if( ch == ' ' )
        {
            rpos = rpos + 8 ;
            if( rpos >= getmaxx( )-8 )
            {
                rpos = 0 ;
                cpos = cpos + 46 ;
                if( cpos >= getmaxy( )-46 )
                {
                    cpos = 0 ;
                    cleardevice( ) ;
                }
            }
        }
    }
    closegraph( );
}
```

DON'T GO AWAY!!!!!!!!! THINGS CAN ONLY GET BETTER!

There are three 2-dimensional arrays, *arr*, *marr* and *aearr*. The first stores the alphabets, the second and third store the matras. The keys associated with the alphabets and the matras are given in the list that follows.

Hindi Alphabet or Matra	Character Eqt.
	M
	N
	G
	R
	S
	1
	2
	3

DIAGRAM 7.1

Let's take a look at how these alphabets were created. We'll need to discuss the function *mhind( )*. It takes two parameters: the coordinates of the position of :

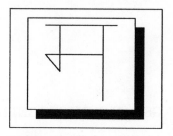

DIAGRAM 7.2

justified left top. The first *for* loop fills the array with zeros. Whenever a pixel in the block needs to be displayed, the corresponding element of *arr* is set. The following diagram demonstrates the byte equivalent:

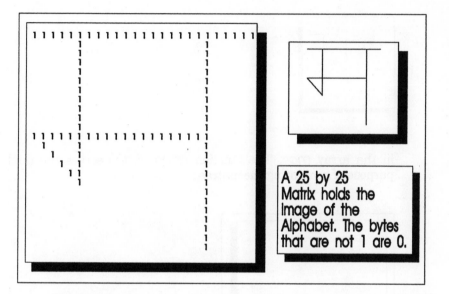

DIAGRAM 7.3

Similarly, the functions *ghind( )*, *nhind( )*, *rhind( )* and *shind( )* yield :

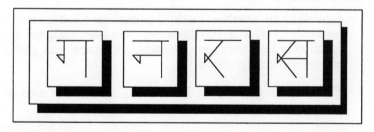

DIAGRAM 7.4

, respectively.

Moving on to the matras, the function *amatra( )* generates :

DIAGRAM 7.5

in tha array *marr*. The function *aeomatra( )* serves the dual purpose of generating the matras :

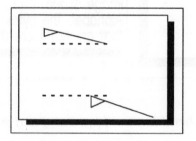

DIAGRAM 7.6

depending on whether the third parameter *type* is equal to 2 or 3, respectively. The reason these two have been assigned to only one function is that they are structurally identical and gain meaning only by virtue of position.

The function *getonech( )*, as usual, returns the code of the key pressed.

In the main program, we have to look out for many loopholes. The ESCape key is used to quit the program. The enter key takes you to the next line. The question is, where is the next line situated? 46 pixels below the previous one. Let's see how...

25 pixels are allocated to the height of each alphabet. 10 pixels are allocated to a matra appearing ABOVE AN ALPHABET, and 10 to a matra appearing BELOW AN ALPHABET. Thus, in effect, the total height of each alphabet, taking into account two matras, is 45 pixels. The next line starts two pixel rows below this.

The width of the alphabets chosen is 25. That of the :

DIAGRAM 7.7

matra ,is 7. Thus it is crucial to correctly specify the coordinates. At the end of each line, we have to go to the next line. This is not as facetious as it sounds. We must simulate the enter key at the end of every line and readjust the coordinates. Finally, the space bar separates two adjoining characters by 7 pixels. When the end of the page is reached, the screen is cleared.

Let's take an example: to get :

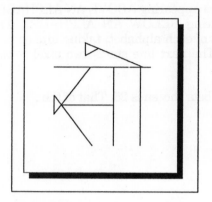

DIAGRAM 7.8

we would enter,

S--1--2

In the main program, the variables *cpos* and *rpos* hold the x and y coordinates of the subsequent position of the alphabet or matra.

We enter an infinite *while* loop, wherein we get a character by calling the function *getonech( )*. This character is converted to its upper case by calling the function *toupper( )*. The value is thereafter assigned to the variable *ch*.

Next, we are faced with a series of *if* conditions. The first one makes us quit the program if the ESCape key is pressed. The second one ensures that the subsequent character appears 46 rows below. Also, if the bottom of the page is reached, we start on a new page after clearing the screen. The subsequent *ifs* display the relevant characters. And also perform an end of line check and an end of page check.

Proceeding along these lines, bit-mapped graphics make it possible to compile an editor for any script. The broader rationale is to demonstrate the inherent simplicity and power of bit-mapped graphics. It may be rewarding to supplement these basics with your own contribution, thereby further tapping the power of this logic.

A Tryst With Animation

At a higher level we have animated images. Here, the image is simply moved to predetermined subsequent locations, giving the illusion of movement. The applicable functions are *getimage( )* and *putimage( )*. The former picks up any specified image, and the latter positions it at any specified point.

PROGRAM 275

```
/* imagesize , getimage and putimage */


#include <graphics.h>

void main( )
{
    int gm , gd = DETECT ;
    unsigned int size ;
    void *buffer ;
    char text[100] ;

    initgraph( &gd , &gm , "") ;

    circle( 100 , 100 , 10 ) ;  /* the image */
    floodfill( 100 , 100 , WHITE ) ;

    size = imagesize( 90 , 90 , 110 , 110 ) ;
      /* getting size of image */

    sprintf( text ,
        "Size of image  using IMAGESIZE( ) = %u" , size ) ;
    outtextxy( 1,1 , text ) ;
    getch( ) ;

    buffer = (void *)malloc( size ) ;

    outtextxy( 1 , 10 , "Allocated memory 'for' BUFFER") ;
```

```
getimage( 90 , 90 , 110 , 110 , (void *)buffer ) ;

outtextxy( 1 , 20 , "Saved the image using GETIMAGE( )."
                    "Press a key to clip it." ) ;

getch( ) ;

putimage( 90 , 90 , (void *) buffer , XOR_PUT ) ;

outtextxy( 120 , 100 , "<-the image made to disappear "
                       " using XOR_PUT.Press a key to copy." ) ;

getch( ) ;

putimage( 200 , 200 , (void *) buffer , COPY_PUT ) ;

outtextxy( 230 , 210 ,
           "<- the image pasted here using PUTIMAGE( ) " ) ;

getch( ) ;
closegraph( ) ;
}
```

We want to move a circle across the screen.

After drawing a filled circle, we store it in memory. After removing the image from the screen, we pick it up from memory and place it wherever we want it to be positioned.

We have drawn a circle at (100, 100) and filled it with white. Now we want to store it in memory. For this we need to know the size of the circle. We get this by calling *imagesize( )* -- which gets us the size of the block in bytes -- so that we can determine how much space needs to be allocated in memory. The parameters passed to *imagesize( )* are the top and bottom corners of the block. The value is returned in the variable *size*. The next step is to allocate memory, which is done by calling the function *malloc( )*. The pointer returned by *malloc( )* is stored in the variable *buffer*.

The function *getimage( )* requires five parameters, the first four being the coordinates of the top left and bottom right of the block, and the last being the address of the memory location from where *getimage( )* will start storing the image.

The function *putimage( )* requires four parameters: the first two are the coordinates of the top left corner of the block, the third is the address of the block from where the image is to be retrieved, and the fourth specifies how the image should be displayed. In this case the 4th parameter is XOR_PUT. We want to remove the image from the screen. So we XOR the image with itself. Since we want to copy the image at another point, we pass the parameter COPY_PUT to *putimage( )*. Thus any previous image at the same point will be overwritten.

PACMAN!!!

Animation is simply an application of the above two functions. We've demonstrated this with the ubiquitous Pacman.

PROGRAM 276

```c
#include <graphics.h>
#include <stdio.h>
#include <dos.h>
#include <alloc.h>

main( )
{
    void *pacman1 ;
    void *pacman2 ;
    int x1 = 50 , y1 = 50 , x2 = 100 , y2 = 100 , i ;
    int gm , gd = DETECT ;
    unsigned size ;

    initgraph( &gd , &gm , "" ) ;

    setcolor( YELLOW ) ;

    setfillstyle( SOLID_FILL , LIGHTRED ) ;
    bar( x1 , y1 , x1+25 , y1+10 ) ;
    bar( x2 , y2 , x2+25 , y2+10 ) ;
```

```
setfillstyle( SOLID_FILL , YELLOW ) ;
pieslice( x1 , y1 , 45 , 315 , 20 ) ;
pieslice( x2 , y2 , 20 , 340 , 20 ) ;

setfillstyle( SOLID_FILL , RED  ) ;

pieslice( x1+7 , y1-10 , 0 , 360 , 5 ) ;
pieslice( x2+7 , y2-10 , 0 , 360 , 5 ) ;

size = imagesize( 0 , 0 , 50 , 50 ) ;
   /* slightly larger than the pie */

pacman1 = (void  *) malloc( size ) ;
if( pacman1 == NULL )
{
    outtextxy( 200 , 200 , "ERROR: Malloc failed 'for' pacman1" ) ;
    delay( 1000 ) ;
    closegraph( ) ;
    exit(1) ;
}
pacman2 = (void *) malloc( size ) ;
if( pacman2 == NULL )
{
    outtextxy( 200 , 200 , "ERROR: Malloc failed 'for' pacman2" ) ;
    delay( 1000 ) ;
    closegraph( ) ;
    exit(1) ;
}

getimage( x1-25 , y1-25 , x1+25 , y1+25 , pacman1) ;
getimage( x2-25 , y2-25 , x2+25 , y2+25 , pacman2) ;

getch( ) ;
cleardevice( ) ;
setfillstyle( SOLID_FILL , LIGHTRED ) ;
bar( 0 , getmaxy( )/2 , getmaxx( )-20 , getmaxy( )/2+10 ) ;

x1 = 0 ;
y1 = getmaxy( )/2 ;

while(1)
{
```

```
        putimage(x1-10 , y1-25 , pacman1 , COPY_PUT ) ;
        delay( 200 ) ;
        putimage(x1-10 , y1-25 , pacman1 , XOR_PUT ) ;

        putimage(x1 , y1-25 , pacman2 , COPY_PUT ) ;
        delay( 200 ) ;
        putimage(x1 , y1-25 , pacman2 , XOR_PUT ) ;

        x1 += 20 ;
        if( x1 > getmaxx( ) )  break ;
    }

    free( pacman1 ) ;
    free( pacman2 ) ;

    settextstyle( TRIPLEX_FONT , HORIZ_DIR , 5 ) ;
    outtextxy( 100 , 100 , "B U R P !" ) ;
    sound( 100 ) ;
    delay( 2000 ) ;
    nosound( ) ;
    getch( ) ;
    closegraph( ) ;
}
```

Here we generate two Pacman images. The second image will
have a mouth wider than that of the first. First we draw two red
bars. The reason for this will be obvious while viewing the
output. Next, we draw two yellow pie slices and fill in the eyes.
We have taken the size as slightly larger than the original. Then
we allocate memory for both the images. The images are stored
in *pacman1* and *pacman2*, respectively.

After clearing the screen, we draw a red bar horizontally across
the screen. We have initialized the starting point of the two
figures. Now we enter a *while* loop. The series of events is as
follows: *pacman1* is displayed at a specified location and made
to disappear by displaying it again at the same position while
simultaneously XORing it with itself.

There is a delay of 200 milliseconds so that the image can be
perceived. At a point slightly to the right of *pacman1*, we

display *pacman2*, and follow the same procedure, i.e. erase the figure by XORing it with itself -- after displaying it for 200 milliseconds. This pattern continues till we reach the extreme right of the screen. Finally, we deallocate the memory by calling *free( )*. Note that it is always good practice to do so.

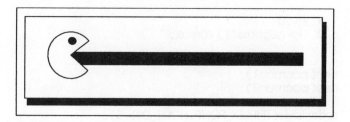

DIAGRAM 7.9

Yet Another P A C M A N !!!

To make the program more attractive, we've introduced sound to accompany the text for two seconds. Pacman begs your pardon.

And now that we're on a roll, let's stick with Pacman in the next program.

PROGRAM 277

```
#include <graphics.h>
#include <stdio.h>
#include <dos.h>
#include <alloc.h>

#define BIG        1
#define SMALL      2
#define UP         372
#define DOWN       380
#define LEFT       375
#define RIGHT      377
#define ESC        27
```

```
unsigned int getonech( )
{
    unsigned int ch ;
    int hi , lo ;

    ch = bioskey(0) ;
    hi = ch >> 8 ;
    lo = ch & 0x00ff ;
    if( lo == 0 )
    {
        ch = 300 + hi ;
        return ch ;
    }
    else
    {
        ch = lo ;
        return  ch ;
    }
}


main( )
{
    void *cover ;
    void *pacleft1 ;
    void *pacleft2 ;
    void *pacright1 ;
    void *pacright2 ;
    void *pacup1 ;
    void *pacup2 ;
    void *pacdown1 ;
    void *pacdown2 ;

    int mouth = BIG ;
    int ch ;
    int x1 = 50 , y1 = 50 ;
    int x2 = 50 , y2 = 100 ;
    int ox = 0 , oy = 0 , i ;

    int gm , gd = DETECT ;
    unsigned size ;

    initgraph( &gd , &gm , "" ) ;
```

```
setcolor( YELLOW );

setfillstyle( SOLID_FILL , YELLOW );
pieslice( x1 , y1 , 315 , 45 , 20 ); /* right */
pieslice( x2 , y2 , 340 , 20 , 20 );

pieslice( x1+50 , y1 , 0 , 360 , 20 );  /* left */
pieslice( x2+50 , y2 , 0 , 360 , 20 );

pieslice( x1+100 , y1 , 0 , 360 , 20 ); /* up */
pieslice( x2+100 , y2 , 0 , 360 , 20 );

pieslice( x1+150 , y1 , 0 , 360 , 20 ); /* down */
pieslice( x2+150 , y2 , 0 , 360 , 20 );

setfillstyle( SOLID_FILL , BLACK );
setcolor( BLACK );
pieslice( x1+50 , y1 , 200 , 160 , 20 );
  /* left mask*/

pieslice( x2+50 , y2 , 225 , 135 , 20 );

pieslice( x1+100 , y1 , 110 , 70 , 20 ); /* up mask*/
pieslice( x2+100 , y2 , 135 , 45 , 20 );

pieslice( x1+150 , y1 , 250 , 290 , 20 );
  /* down mask*/

pieslice( x2+150 , y2 , 225 , 315 , 20 );

setfillstyle( SOLID_FILL , RED );
setcolor( YELLOW );
pieslice( x1+7 , y1-10 , 0 , 360 , 5 );
pieslice( x2+7 , y2-10 , 0 , 360 , 5 );

pieslice( x1+50-7 , y1-10 , 0 , 360 , 5 );
pieslice( x2+50-7 , y2-10 , 0 , 360 , 5 );

pieslice( x1+100+7 , y1 , 0 , 360 , 5 );
pieslice( x2+100+7 , y2 , 0 , 360 , 5 );

pieslice( x1+150+7 , y1 , 0 , 360 , 5 );
```

```
pieslice( x2+150+7 , y2 , 0 , 360 , 5 ) ;

size = imagesize( 0 , 0 , 50 , 50 ) ;
    /* size slightly larger than the pie */

cover = (void *) malloc( size ) ;
if( cover == NULL )
{
    outtextxy( 200 , 200 , "ERROR: Malloc failed 'for' cover" ) ;
    delay( 1000 ) ;
    closegraph( ) ;
    exit(1) ;
}

getimage( getmaxx( )- 50 ,
    getmaxy( ) - 50 ,
    getmaxx( ) ,
    getmaxy( ) ,
    cover ) ;

pacright1 = (void *) malloc( size ) ;
if( pacright1 == NULL )
{
    outtextxy( 200 , 200 , "ERROR: Malloc failed 'for' pacright1" ) ;
    delay( 1000 ) ;
    closegraph( ) ;
    exit(1) ;
}

pacright2 = (void *) malloc( size ) ;
if( pacright2 == NULL )
{
    outtextxy( 200 , 200 , "ERROR: Malloc failed 'for' pacright2" ) ;
    delay( 1000 ) ;
    closegraph( ) ;
    exit(1) ;
}

pacleft1 = (void *) malloc( size ) ;
if( pacleft1 == NULL )
{
    outtextxy( 200 , 200 , "ERROR: Malloc failed 'for' pacleft1" ) ;
    delay( 1000 ) ;
```

```
        closegraph( ) ;
        exit(1) ;
}

pacleft2 = (void *) malloc( size ) ;
if( pacleft2 == NULL )
{
    outtextxy( 200 , 200 , "ERROR: Malloc failed 'for' pacleft2" ) ;
    delay( 1000 ) ;
    closegraph( ) ;
    exit(1) ;
}

pacup1 = (void *) malloc( size ) ;
if( pacup1 == NULL )
{
    outtextxy( 200 , 200 , "ERROR: Malloc failed 'for' pacup1" ) ;
    delay( 1000 ) ;
    closegraph( ) ;
    exit(1) ;
}

pacup2 = (void *) malloc( size ) ;
if( pacup2 == NULL )
{
    outtextxy( 200 , 200 , "ERROR: Malloc failed 'for' pacup2" ) ;
    delay( 1000 ) ;
    closegraph( ) ;
    exit(1) ;
}

pacdown1 = (void *) malloc( size ) ;
if( pacdown1 == NULL )
{
    outtextxy( 200 , 200 , "ERROR: Malloc failed 'for' pacdown1" ) ;
    delay( 1000 ) ;
    closegraph( ) ;
    exit(1) ;
}

pacdown2 = (void *) malloc( size ) ;
if( pacdown2 == NULL )
{
```

```
      outtextxy( 200 , 200 , "ERROR: Malloc failed 'for' pacdown2" ) ;
      delay( 1000 ) ;
      closegraph( ) ;
      exit(1) ;
}


getimage( x1-25 , y1-25 ,
        x1+25 , y1+25 , pacright1 ) ;
getimage( x2-25 , y2-25 ,
        x2+25 , y2+25 , pacright2 ) ;
getimage( x1-25+50, y1-25 ,
        x1+25+50 , y1+25 , pacleft1 ) ;
getimage( x2-25+50, y2-25 ,
        x2+25+50 , y2+25 , pacleft2 ) ;
getimage( x1-25+100 , y1-25 ,
        x1+25+100 , y1+25 , pacup1 ) ;
getimage( x2-25+100 , y2-25 ,
        x2+25+100, y2+25 , pacup2 ) ;
getimage( x1-25+150 , y1-25 ,
        x1+25+150 , y1+25 , pacdown1 ) ;
getimage( x2-25+150 , y2-25 ,
        x2+25+150 , y2+25 , pacdown2 ) ;

getch( ) ;
cleardevice( ) ;

x1 = 0 ; y1 = 100 ;

while(1)
{
   ch = getonech( ) ;

   if( ch == ESC )
   {
      break ;
   }

   putimage( ox , oy , cover , COPY_PUT ) ;

   if( ch == RIGHT )
   {
      switch( mouth )
```

```
        {
            case BIG :
            putimage(x1 , y1 , pacright1 ,COPY_PUT ) ;
            mouth = SMALL ;
            sound( 1000 ) ;
            break ;

            case SMALL :
            putimage(x1 , y1 , pacright2 , COPY_PUT ) ;
            mouth = BIG ;
            sound( 2000 ) ;
            break ;
        }
        ox = x1 ;
        oy = y1 ;
        x1 += 10 ;
        if( x1 > getmaxx( ) )
        {
            cleardevice( ) ;
            x1 = 0 ;
        }
    }

    if( ch == LEFT )
    {
        switch( mouth )
        {
            case BIG :
            putimage(x1 , y1 , pacleft1 , COPY_PUT ) ;
            mouth = SMALL ;
            sound( 2300 ) ;
            break ;

            case SMALL :
            putimage(x1 , y1 , pacleft2 , COPY_PUT ) ;
            mouth = BIG ;
            sound( 800 ) ;
            break ;
        }
        ox = x1 ;
        oy = y1 ;
        x1 -= 10 ;
        if( x1 < 0 )
```

```
   {
      cleardevice( ) ;
      x1 = getmaxx( ) ;
   }
}

if( ch == UP )
{
   switch( mouth )
   {
      case BIG :
      putimage(x1 , y1 , pacup1 , COPY_PUT ) ;
      mouth = SMALL ;
      sound( 1500 ) ;
      break ;

      case SMALL :
      putimage(x1 , y1 , pacup2 , COPY_PUT ) ;
      mouth = BIG ;
      sound( 2500 ) ;
      break ;
   }
   ox = x1 ;
   oy = y1 ;
   y1 -= 10 ;
   if( y1 < 0 )
   {
      cleardevice( ) ;
      y1 = getmaxy( ) ;
   }
}

if( ch == DOWN )
{
   switch( mouth )
   {
      case BIG :
      putimage(x1 , y1 , pacdown1 , COPY_PUT ) ;
      mouth = SMALL ;
      sound( 500 ) ;
      break ;

      case SMALL :
```

```
            putimage(x1 , y1 , pacdown2 , COPY_PUT ) ;
            mouth = BIG ;
            sound( 1500 ) ;
            break ;
        }
        ox = x1 ;
        oy = y1 ;
        y1 += 10 ;
        if( y1 > getmaxy() )
        {
            cleardevice( ) ;
            y1 = 0 ;
        }
    }
}

    nosound( ) ;

    free( cover ) ;
    free( pacright1 ) ;
    free( pacright2 ) ;
    free( pacleft1 ) ;
    free( pacleft2 ) ;
    free( pacup1 ) ;
    free( pacup2 ) ;
    free( pacdown1 ) ;
    free( pacdown2 ) ;

    closegraph( ) ;
    exit(1) ;
}
```

This program generates a series of Pacman figures whose movements can be controlled using the four arrow keys.

Initially, we defined some constants. Then we checked *getonech( )* for the code of the key pressed. After this, in the main program, we listed pointers to voids. In the previous program, we needed two Pacman figures which moved in one direction. Now we want the Pacman figures to move in four directions, viz. upward, downward, left and right. Thus, we'll need eight Pacman figures. For these figures, we have eight pointers. The pointer *cover* points to a blank block.

Subsequently, we enumerated some variables. The variables *x1* and *y1* hold the next position of the figure at any given point. The variables *ox* and *oy* hold the previous position of the figure at any given point. The value of the variable *mouth* decides the position of the mouth, i.e. BIG or SMALL. At first, it is set at BIG.

The foreground is set at yellow, and the fill style fills the figure with a solid yellow color. Next, we have a series of pie slices which generate the eight required Pacman figures.

Here we encounter a problem. When the pie slices created on the default settings, we are not allowed to orient the figures in the way we want. Recall that we want the figures facing four different directions, and moving in the four corresponding directions. To circumvent this problem we'll have to approach it in a roundabout fashion. The illustrations given below demonstrate this.

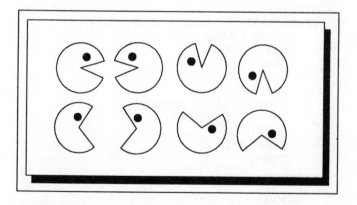

DIAGRAM 7.10

imagesize( ) determines the size of the figure and passes the value to the variable *size*. Each Pacman figure will be the same size. A series of *malloc( )s* allocates memory first to the pointer *cover*, where a blank block is stored. Now, there will be a blank area wherever the pointer *cover* appears. Then, the subsequent *malloc( )s* allocate memory to *pacright1* and *pacright2*, *pacleft1* and *pacleft2*, *pacup1* and *pacup2*, and *pacdown1* and *pacdown2*.

Next, there is a series of *getimage( )s* which picks up the images and stores them in the corresponding memory blocks specified by the pointers.

After clearing the screen, we initialize *x1* to 0 and *y1* to 100. Next, we enter a *while* loop where we wait for a key to be pressed. If the ESCape key is pressed, we break out of the program. Before pressing any other key, we use *cover* to blank the area in which the previous figure appeared.

Now the right arrow key is pressed.

```
if( ch == RIGHT )
{
    switch( mouth )
    {
        case BIG :
        putimage(x1 , y1 , pacright1 ,COPY_PUT ) ;
            mouth = SMALL ;
            sound( 1000 ) ;
            break ;

        case SMALL :
        putimage(x1 , y1 , pacright2 ,
                COPY_PUT ) ;
            mouth = BIG ;
            sound( 2000 ) ;
            break ;
    }
    ox = x1 ;
    oy = y1 ;
    x1 += 10 ;
    if( x1 > getmaxx( ) )
    {
```

```
        cleardevice();
        x1 = 0 ;
    }
}
```

We first check the previous value of *mouth*. If it is BIG, we display *pacright1* and change the value of *mouth* to SMALL. Then a sound of 1000Hz is generated and we break out of the case statement.

If the value of *mouth* is SMALL, *pacright2* is displayed. We change the value of *mouth* to BIG and generate a sound of 2000Hz, and then break.

Now the current value of *x1* is assigned to *ox*, and that of *y1* is assigned to *oy*. When the value of *x1* is changed, it is necessary to check whether *x1* has reached the right end of the screen. If so, the screen is cleared and *x1* is given the value of 0. Thus we start at the left side of the page.

Pressing the up arrow, down arrow or left arrow keys yield correspondingly similar results. The only difference is that with the up arrow key, we use the images stored in the memory blocks pointed to by *pacup1* and *pacup2* and check whether we have reached the top of the screen. Similarly, with the down arrow key, *pacdown1* and *pacdown2* are used and we check whether we have reached the bottom of the screen. With the left arrow key, we use *pacleft1* and *pacleft2* and check whether we have reached the left end of the screen.

That takes care of everything, and you're on your way to creating your own computer game.

More About Clipping Images

You may have noticed that while clipping images, we clip the entire block in which the image is contained. Thus, if we were to clip the image of a circle, the remaining area of the block which is not occupied by the circle is also clipped. This does not allow us to show a circular object moving across a solid object since what moves across would be the entire block.

Further, when we call *putimage( )*, we do so with the last parameter being COPY_PUT or XOR_PUT. There are other ways of calling this function. For example, the image could be ANDed or ORed or NOTed with itself.

The following program gives the illusion of a circular object moving over a solid object.

PROGRAM 278

```
/* imagesize , getimage and putimage */
/* movement using XOR_PUT & COPY_PUT & AND_PUT*/

#include <graphics.h>
#include <dos.h>
#include <alloc.h>

void *xormask , *andmask , *covered;

main( )
{
    int gm,gd = DETECT;

    initgraph(&gd,&gm,"");

    drawball( );

    getch( );

    moveball( );

    getch( );
    closegraph( );
}

drawball( )
{
    covered = malloc(imagesize(35,85,65,115));
    xormask = malloc(imagesize(35,85,65,115));
    andmask = malloc(imagesize(35,85,65,115));
```

```
getimage(35,85,65,115,covered); /*getback ground image */
printf("Covered ...");
getch();
setfillstyle(SOLID_FILL,getmaxcolor( )-1);
bar(35,85,65,115);     /* white colored bar */

setcolor(0);
setfillstyle(SOLID_FILL,0);
pieslice(50,100,0,360,12);
/* black pie slice in white bar bk.*/

getimage(35,85,65,115,andmask);
printf("AND mask ...");
getch();

putimage(35,85,covered,COPY_PUT); /* remove image */
printf("put Covered ...");
getch();

setcolor(getmaxcolor( ));
setfillstyle(SOLID_FILL,getmaxcolor( )-1);
pieslice(50,100,0,360,12);
/* white colored pieslice-black bk. */

getimage(35,85,65,115,xormask); /* clip image */
printf("XOR mask ...");
getch()

putimage(35,85,covered,COPY_PUT);
/* remove from screen */

printf("Put COVERED ...");

setfillstyle(HATCH_FILL,LIGHTRED);

bar3d(100,10,150,199,0,0);

putimage(35,85,andmask,AND_PUT);
/*black pie white bar */

printf("put ANDed ...");
getch();
```

```
        putimage(35,85,xormask,XOR_PUT);
/*white pie black bar */

    printf("put XORed ");

}

moveball( )
{
    int i;
    for(i = 0; i < 150; i+=2)
    {
        putimage(35+i,85,covered,COPY_PUT);
/* replace previous ball by image prior to drawing of ball */
        getimage(35+2+i,85,65+2+i,115,covered);
/*
'covered' now has clip of next image to be over written by ball
*/
        putimage(35+i+2,85,andmask,AND_PUT);
/* black pie white bar ANDed */
        putimage(35+i,85,xormask,XOR_PUT);
/* white pie black bar XORed */
        delay(50);
    }
}
```

The principle behind this is as follows. When we XOR an image (I1) with an image existing in the background (I2), if the bit of the background image is set, the new image (I1) will have changed color. If we want this new image to appear in its original color, we'll have to create another slightly different image (I3) and AND it with the background image (I2). The result of this will be XORed with our image (I1).

Thus, the final image we obtain is only the object, and not the entire block containing the object. To restore the background image, we would have to save it prior to ANDing and XORing.

To recap, we first save the screen (I2), AND the screen with a particular image (I3), XOR the screen with another image (I1), and restore the screen, with its original background image.

The *drawball( )* function creates the AND mask and the XOR mask. The function *moveball( )* moves the figure across the background image.

drawball( ) allocates memory for the three pointers *covered*, *xormask* and *andmask*. The variable *covered* holds the background image. The variables *xormask* and *andmask* are ANDed and XORed with the background image. At each stage, the series of *printf( )*s gives information about the masks.

The *bar3d( )* function is called to draw the background image. Then, *putimage( )* is called twice to place the AND mask and the XOR mask at the left of the background image. Now, when we return from *drawball( )*, the figure is displayed on the screen.

In *moveball( )*, we enter a *for* loop.

```
moveball( )
{
    int i;
    for(i = 0; i < 150; i+=2)
    {
        putimage(35+i,85,covered,COPY_PUT);
/* replace previous ball by image prior to drawing of ball */
        getimage(35+2+i,85,65+2+i,115,covered);
/*
'covered' now has clip of next image to be over written by ball
*/
        putimage(35+i+2,85,andmask,AND_PUT);
/* black pie white bar ANDed */
        putimage(35+i,85,xormask,XOR_PUT);
/* white pie black bar XORed */
        delay(50);
    }
}
```

This accomplishes a number of things: the background image is put on the screen using *covered*. The *getimage( )* function is called to save the image which appears to the immediate right. The AND mask and the XOR mask are placed here. There is a delay of 50 milliseconds, and the process is repeated 75 times.

Note that the above method is not practical when the images are large due to time constraints. This is not a problem, however, with small images.

Going For A Ride On A Bicycle

Using *line( )* and *circle( )*, the next program creates a bicycle. To move this bicycle, we'll call *getimage( )* and *putimage( )* . It's easy to take the computer for a ride, if you only know how....

```
PROGRAM 279
#include <graphics.h>
#include <alloc.h>
#include <conio.h>

#define STEP 5
void *bike;

main( )
{
    int gmode,gdriver = DETECT;
    initgraph(&gdriver,&gmode,"");
    drawbike( );
    movebike( );
    getch( );
    closegraph( );
}

drawbike( )
{
    circle(50,100,25);
    circle(150,100,25);
    line(50,100,80,85);
    line(80,85,134,85);
    line(77,82,95,100);
    line(130,80,150,100);
    line(128,80,113,82);
    line(128,80,116,78);
    line(72,81,89,81);
    line(73,82,90,82);
    circle(95,100,5);
    line(92,105,98,95);
```

```
line(91,105,93,105);
line(97,95,99,95);
line(95,100,136,87);

bike = malloc(imagesize(25,75,175,125));
if(bike == NULL)
{
    closegraph( );
    printf("Not enough memory to draw bike ");
    exit(1);
}

getimage(25,75,175,125,bike);
}

movebike( )
{
    int i ;
    for( i = 0 ; i < getmaxx( )-180; i+=STEP)
    {
        putimage(25+i,75,bike,XOR_PUT);
        putimage(25+STEP+i,75,bike,XOR_PUT);
    }
}
```

In this program, there are two functions: *drawbike( )* and *movebike( )*. The function *drawbike( )*, with a series of calls to *circle( )* and *line( )*, generates the image of a bicycle. The *malloc( )* function assigns memory to store this image and assigns the address to the global variable *bike*. The image is then saved by *getimage( )*.

In *movebike( )*, we enter a *for* loop which removes the current image and repositions it immediately to the right. This gives the illusion of movement.

In the main program, we simply call *drawbike( )* and *movebike( )*, which function as described above.

Yet Another Ride Across The River

Let's incorporate moving pedals into the previous program. Recall our Pacman program: we had generated the image of Pacman eating his way across the screen by simply placing two images with different mouth positions alongside each other. Using the same principle, we can generate the image of revolving pedals. •

PROGRAM 280

```
#include <graphics.h>
#include <alloc.h>
#include <conio.h>

#define STEP 5
void *bike1,*bike2,*bike3,*bike4;

main( )
{
    int gmode,gdriver = DETECT;

    initgraph(&gdriver,&gmode,"");
    drawbike( );
    movebikeandpedals( );

    getch( );
    closegraph( );
}

drawbike( )
{
    void *pedals;

    circle(50,100,25);
    circle(150,100,25);
    line(50,100,80,85);
    line(80,85,134,85);
    line(77,82,95,100);
    line(130,80,150,100);
    line(128,80,113,82);
    line(128,80,116,78);
    line(72,81,89,81);
    line(73,82,90,82);
```

```
bike1 = malloc(imagesize(25,75,175,125));
bike2 = malloc(imagesize(25,75,175,125));
bike3 = malloc(imagesize(25,75,175,125));
bike4 = malloc(imagesize(25,75,175,125));
pedals = malloc(imagesize(85,90,110,110));

circle(95,100,5);
line(95,100,136,87);
getimage(85,90,110,110,pedals);

line(86,100,104,100);
line(85,100,87,100);
line(103,100,105,100);
getimage(25,75,175,125,bike1);

putimage(85,90,pedals,COPY_PUT);
line(88,96,102,104);
line(87,96,89,96);
line(101,104,103,104);
getimage(25,75,175,125,bike2);

putimage(85,90,pedals,COPY_PUT);
line(95,95,95,105);
line(94,95,96,95);
line(94,105,96,105);
getimage(25,75,175,125,bike3);

putimage(85,90,pedals,COPY_PUT);
line(102,96,88,104);
line(101,96,103,96);
line(87,104,89,104);
getimage(25,75,175,125,bike4);

free(pedals);
}

movebikeandpedals()
{
    int i,c ;
    for( i = 0 ,c=0; i < getmaxx( )-150; i+=STEP,c++)
    {
        switch(c % 4)
```

```
        {
            case 0 :
            putimage(25+i,75,bike4,XOR_PUT);
            putimage(25+STEP+i,75,bike1,XOR_PUT);
            break;

            case 1 :
            putimage(25+i,75,bike1,XOR_PUT);
            putimage(25+STEP+i,75,bike2,XOR_PUT);
            break;


            case 2 :
            putimage(25+i,75,bike2,XOR_PUT);
            putimage(25+STEP+i,75,bike3,XOR_PUT);
            break;

            case 3:
            putimage(25+i,75,bike3,XOR_PUT);
            putimage(25+STEP+i,75,bike4,XOR_PUT);
            break;

        }
        delay(10);
    }
}
```

In *drawbike( )*, memory is allocated to the four variables *bike1*, *bike2*, *bike3* and *bike4*. These will hold four similar images of the bike, with different pedal positions. The variable *pedals* will hold a temporary image of the pedals.

The function *movebikeandpedals( )* performs a switch statement in the *for* loop. A series of the four bikes with different pedal positions is executed repeatedly, i.e. *bike1*, *bike2*, *bike3*, *bike4*, *bike1*, *bike2*, *bike3*, *bike4*, and so on. This renders a moving bike, with pedals revolving, across the screen.

Thus our discussion of computerised animation has simply applied the methods of conventional animation, wherein a series of consecutively changing images ,is displayed in quick succession.

A Little More On Animation

ASPECTfully Yours..

The aspect ratio is an important concept in graphics. It is simply the ratio of a pixel's width to its height. In the EGA monitor, the aspect ratio is 0.775. Thus there are more pixels horizontally than vertically, and the resolution is 640*350. In the VGA monitor, the aspect ratio is 1, i.e. the pixels are square, unlike the rectangular pixels in the EGA monitor. The VGA has a resolution of 640*480, and thus has a resolution higher than that of the EGA.

The functions *circle( )*, *arc( )* and *pieslice( )* use the aspect ratio. If we call *getaspectratio( )*, we get two numbers -- the x- aspect and the y- aspect. The aspect ratio is the ratio of these two numbers. In the EGA monitor, the x- aspect is 7750 and the y- aspect is 10000, and yields an aspect ratio of 0.775. Thus, each pixel is roughly a third taller than it is wide. The VGA monitor has equivalent x and y aspects, i.e. 10000; thus, each pixel is square.

By changing the aspect ratio, we can change the way in which a figure is drawn. For example, by decreasing the x-aspect, the pixels get thinner . Thus, we can trick *circle( )* into drawing an ellipse.

PROGRAM 281

```
/* demo for get/setaspectratio */
#include <graphics.h>
#include <conio.h>

main( )
{
    int gm , gd = DETECT ;
    char text[100] ;
    int xa , ya , temp ;
```

```
initgraph( &gd , &gm , "" ) ;

outtextxy( 1 , 1 , "Use and significance of get/setaspectratio( )" ) ;

getaspectratio( &xa , &ya ) ;


sprintf( text , "Aspect Ratio : x - %u , y - %u" , xa , ya ) ;
outtextxy( 1 , 12, text ) ;

temp = xa ;

circle( 50 , 150 , 16 ) ;
circle( 150 , 150 , 16 ) ;

arc( 75 , 175 , 30 , 180+40 , 7 ) ;
arc( 125 , 175 , 320 , 150 , 7 ) ;
arc( 100 , 200 , 270-60 , 270+60 , 10 ) ;
arc( 10 , 150 , 45 , 97 , 50) ;
arc( 200-10 , 150 , 90-7 , 135 , 50 ) ;
arc( 100-50 , 113 , 180 , 180+45 , 50 ) ;
arc( 100+50 , 113 , 360-45 , 0 , 50 ) ;

while(!kbhit( ))
{
     xa = temp ;
     setcolor( LIGHTCYAN ) ;
     while(1)
     {

        setaspectratio(xa,ya ) ;

        circle( 50 , 150 , 15) ;
        putpixel( 50,150 ,YELLOW) ;
        circle( 150 , 150 , 15) ;
        putpixel( 150,150 ,YELLOW) ;
        xa -= 20;
        if( xa <= 1 ) break ;
     }
     setcolor(BLACK) ;
     while(1)
     {
```

```
        setaspectratio(xa,ya) ;

        circle( 50 , 150 , 15) ;
        putpixel( 50,150 ,YELLOW) ;
        circle( 150 , 150 , 15) ;
        putpixel( 150,150 ,YELLOW) ;
        xa += 20;
        if( xa >= temp-50 ) break ;
    }

    setcolor( WHITE ) ;
    circle( 50 , 150 , 15 ) ;
    circle( 150 , 150 , 15 ) ;
}

getch( ) ;
closegraph( ) ;
}
```

The function *getaspectratio( )* is passed two parameters, the addresses of *xa* and *ya. xa* is assigned the value of the x - aspect and *ya* is assigned the value of the y - aspect. Then the value of *xa* is assigned to *temp*. By calling the functions *circle( )* and *arc( )* , we generate the image of the character Mogwai from Steven Spielberg's film 'Gremlins'.

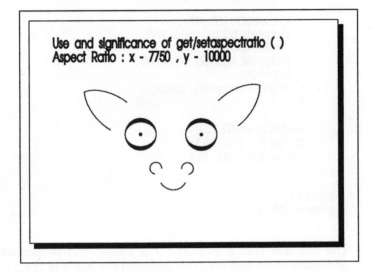

Use and significance of get/setaspectratio ( )
Aspect Ratio : x - 7750 , y - 10000

DIAGRAM 8.1

Now we enter a loop which will terminate only when a key is pressed. *xa* is reassigned the value of *temp*. We set the color to light cyan and enter an infinite loop. The function

setaspectratio( ) is called, and we pass it the aspect ratio, i.e. *xa* and *ya*. The aspect ratio is thus changed.

We draw two circles of radius 15, the first at (50,150) and the second at (150,150). These will be the eyes. *xa* is now reduced by 20, and when it reaches 1, we quit the loop. If not, *xa* is set to the new value and the same circles are drawn again. With the *xa* decreasing, we get circles which are flattened at every decreased value. This continues till the circles disappear and we break out of the loop.

Now we change the color to black and enter another *while* loop. Here we keep increasing the value of *xa* and draw the circles till the original value of *xa* is reached. Another two circles are drawn as an outline to the eyes. Thus, we get to open and close the eyes, and this continues till a key is pressed. Note that the circles are drawn at the same point, with the same radius. Only the aspect ratio is changed.

Remember, the 3 rules:

1) Don't feed Mogwai after midnight.

2) Keep him away from water and light.

3) And run this program only on an EGA or a VGA monitor.

Recall that the values returned by *getmoderange( )* indicated that the modes extended from 0 to 1. 0 corresponds to EGALO, which has four pages of 640*200; 1 corresponds to EGAHI, which has two pages of 640*350. These pages are analogous to those in the text mode. We can switch between these pages at will.

Leafing Through Those Pages In Memory....

Turbo C offers two functions: *setactivepage( )* and *setvisualpage( )*. The active page is the screen on which all the outputs from the functions are directed. This is transparent to the user. For displaying the result of the active page, the corresponding visual page is called. This is what we see on the screen. Note that it is not necessary that when we are on a particular active page, the corresponding visual page should be displayed. We can think of the active page as the backstage worker, while the visual page occupies centerstage.

In the next program, we are in the EGALO mode, where we have four pages. We call *setactivepage( )* to draw four images, one on each page. Then we enter a loop which calls *setvisualpage( )* and displays a series of the four images, thus animating them.

PROGRAM 282

```
/* for EGA( 4 pages ) only */
/* setactive/visualpage */
```

```
#include <graphics.h>
#include <conio.h>
#include <dos.h>

int xmid , ymid ;

image1()
{
    xmid = getmaxx( )/2 -50;
    ymid = getmaxy( )/2;
    moveto( xmid , ymid-100 ) ;
    lineto( xmid+15 , ymid-100+25 ) ;
    lineto( xmid+15 , ymid-100+55 ) ;
    lineto( xmid+23 , ymid-100+55 ) ;
    lineto( xmid+23 , ymid-100+53 ) ;
    moveto( xmid , ymid-100 ) ;
    lineto( xmid-10 , ymid-100+25 ) ;
    lineto( xmid-30 , ymid-100+50 ) ;
    lineto( xmid-25 , ymid-100+55 ) ;
}

image2()
{
    xmid = getmaxx( )/2 ;
    ymid = getmaxy( )/2;
    moveto( xmid , ymid-100 ) ;
    lineto( xmid+5 , ymid-100+30 ) ;
    lineto( xmid+7 , ymid-100+53 ) ;
    lineto( xmid+14 , ymid-100+51 ) ;
    moveto( xmid , ymid-100 ) ;
    lineto( xmid+8 , ymid-100+27 ) ;
    lineto( xmid-5 , ymid-100+55 ) ;
    lineto( xmid+2 , ymid-100+55 ) ;
    lineto( getx( ) , gety( )-3 ) ;
}

image3()
{
    xmid = getmaxx( )/2 +50;
    ymid = getmaxy( )/2;
    moveto( xmid , ymid-100 ) ;
    lineto( xmid+15 , ymid-100+25 ) ;
    lineto( xmid+15 , ymid-100+55 ) ;
```

```
        lineto( xmid+23 , ymid-100+55 ) ;
        moveto( xmid , ymid-100 ) ;
        lineto( xmid-10 , ymid-100+25 ) ;
        lineto( xmid-30 , ymid-100+50 ) ;
        lineto( xmid-25 , ymid-100+55 ) ;
        lineto( getx( )+4 , gety( )-3 ) ;
}

image4( )
{
        xmid = getmaxx( )/2 +100;
        ymid = getmaxy( )/2;
        moveto( xmid , ymid-100 ) ;
        lineto( xmid+5 , ymid-100+30 ) ;
        lineto( xmid+7 , ymid-100+53 ) ;
        lineto( xmid+14 , ymid-100+51 ) ;
        lineto( getx( ) , gety( )-4 ) ;
        moveto( xmid , ymid-100 ) ;
        lineto( xmid+8 , ymid-100+27 ) ;
        lineto( xmid-5 , ymid-100+55 ) ;
        lineto( xmid+2 , ymid-100+55 ) ;
}

main( )
{
        int gm , gd = DETECT ;
        int i ;

        initgraph( &gd , &gm , "" ) ;

        setgraphmode( EGALO ) ;

        setactivepage( 0 ) ;
        cleardevice( ) ;
        outtextxy( 0 , 0 , "page 0" ) ;
        image1( ) ;
        setactivepage( 1 ) ;
        cleardevice( ) ;
        outtextxy( 0 , 0 , "page 1" ) ;
        image2( ) ;
        setactivepage( 2 ) ;
        cleardevice( ) ;
        outtextxy( 0 , 0 , "page 2" ) ;
```

```
    image3( ) ;
    setactivepage( 3 ) ;
    cleardevice( );
    outtextxy( 0 , 0 , "page 3" ) ;
    image4( ) ;
    i = 0 ;
    while( !kbhit( ) )
    {
        setvisualpage(i) ;
        i++ ;
        delay( 800 ) ;
        if( i == 4 ) i = 0 ;
    }
    closegraph( ) ;
}
```

The four functions *image1( )*, *image2( )*, *image3( )* and *image4( )* generate the images of 4 pairs of legs, in different walking positions. In the main program, we set the active page to 0, clear it and draw the first image by calling *image1( )*.

Similarly, we set the active page to 1, 2 and 3, and draw the second, third and fourth images by calling *image2( )*, *image3( )* and *image4( )* respectively. Now we enter a *while* loop, which terminates when a key is pressed. We use *setvisualpage( )* to set the visual page from 0 to 3 and back again from 0 to 3....

Now we go to the next program.

A Window To Eternity...

When we look out of a window, the view is limited by the window's boundaries. Similarly, generating a window on the screen demarcates our working area. We are, in effect, creating a screen within a screen. If we create a window extending between the coordinates (20,20) and (100,100), this area is now a "virtual screen" with coordinates starting from (0,0). Thus, this is now our new frame of reference.

In the next program, we call *setviewport( )* to generate a window.

PROGRAM 283

```c
#include <graphics.h>
#include <dos.h>

void plane( int x , int y )
{
    line( x , y , x+10 , y-3 ) ;
    line( x+10 , y-3 , x+25 , y-2 ) ;
    line( x+25 , y-2 , x+29 , y-7 ) ;
    line( x+29 , y-7 , x+27 , y ) ;
    line( x+27 , y , x , y ) ;
    line( x+11 , y-1 , x+15 , y-1 ) ;
}

main( )
{
    int gm , gd = DETECT ;
    int i , w ;

    initgraph( &gd , &gm , "" ) ;

    setviewport( 300 , 100 , 500 , 200 ,1) ;

    setbkcolor(WHITE) ;
    setfillstyle( SOLID_FILL , RED ) ;
    bar( 0 , 0 , 200 , 100 ) ;
    for( i = 100 ; i+200 > 0 ; i-=5 )
    {
        delay(100) ;
        setfillstyle( SOLID_FILL , RED ) ;
        bar( 0 , 0 , 200 , 100 ) ;
        setfillstyle( SOLID_FILL , YELLOW ) ;/* the sun */
        fillellipse( 88 , 3 , 12 , 9 ) ;
        plane( i , 10 ) ;
        plane( i+15 , 30 ) ;
        plane( i+50 , 13 ) ;
        plane( i+70 , 70 ) ;
        outtextxy( i , 50 , "Let them be birds and not war planes..." ) ;
    }

    getch( ) ;
    closegraph( ) ;
}
```

The function *setviewport( )* is the graphics equivalent of the text function *window( )*. It generates a window on the screen.

The parameters passed to *setviewport( )* are the coordinates of the left top and right bottom corners, and a parameter called the *clipflag*. If the *clipflag* has a non-zero value, display will be limited to the area demarcated by the window. If *clipflag* is set at zero, display may extend beyond the perimeters of the window.

The *setviewport( )* function cannot impose limitations on the functions *getimage( )* or *putimage( )*. These functions can still display images anywhere on the screen, oblivious to window perimeters and regardless of the *clipflag* setting.

In the program, we call *setviewport( )* and generate a window from (300,100) to (500,200). The *clipflag* is also set. Next, we draw a red bar from (0,0) to (200,100). Note that the reference frame for our coordinates is now the window. Thus, since the coordinates of the bar coincide with those of the window, the bar fully occupies the window.

We then enter a *for* loop, in which *i*, the starting point, decreases from 100 to -200 in steps of 5. We have generated a series of images of an aircraft, which appears to move across the window. The aircraft are generated using the function *plane( )*.

The diagram that follows shows how the display will look at an instant. The rest of the screen is white. Remove the white background and you will see the text coming 'out' of the end of the window or 'viewport'.

DIAGRAM 8.2

An Encounter With The Third Dimension

We now enter the realm of the third dimension and generate images which appear to have depth. Thus we render a flat, 2-dimensional object having only length and breadth, as a 3-dimensional object with the added dimension of depth.

Bar Graphs In The 3rd

We are already familiar with the function *bar3d( )*. To fully tap the utility of this function, the placement of the 3-d bars is important. The skill lies in getting our coordinates right. We assume an imaginary axis (the z-axis) for the depth dimension. By creating bars using *bar3d( )*, and positioning them at specific locations on the z-axis, we can generate 3-dimensional bar graphs, one of the most powerful applications of business graphics.

PROGRAM 284

```
#include <graphics.h>
#include <conio.h>
#include <dos.h>

main( )
{
    int gmode , gdriver = DETECT;
    int maxy ;

    int march1=145 ,march2=130, march3=148 ;
    int april1=128 ,april2=125, april3=132 ;
    int may1=110 ,may2=112, may3=115 ;
    int june1=120 ,june2=16, june3=117 ;

    char title[ ] = "THE THIRD DIMENSION :Animated Bar Graph Demo";

    initgraph(&gdriver,&gmode,"");
```

```
        maxy = getmaxy( ) ;
        outtextxy(1,0,title);

        yahobar( 215 , 195 , 625 , 210 , LIGHTGRAY , WHITE , 10 ) ;

        yahobar( 113 , 10 , 530-7 , 299 , LIGHTGRAY, WHITE ,100 ) ;
        setfillstyle( SOLID_FILL , WHITE ) ;
        floodfill( 163 , 285 , WHITE ) ;

        yahobar( 101 , 197 , 112 , 287 , LIGHTGRAY ,WHITE ,100 ) ;

        getch( ) ;

        yahobar(200+30 , march1 , 200+50+30 , 235 ,
                LIGHTCYAN , CYAN , 15);
        yahobar(350+30 , march2 , 350+50+30 , 235 ,
                LIGHTCYAN , CYAN , 15);
        yahobar(500+30 , march3 , 500+50+30 , 235 ,
                LIGHTCYAN , CYAN , 15);

        yahobar(200 , april1 , 200+50 , 235+15 , LIGHTRED , RED , 15);
        yahobar(350 , april2 , 350+50 , 235+15 , LIGHTRED , RED , 15);
        yahobar(500 , april3 , 500+50 , 235+15 , LIGHTRED , RED , 15);

        yahobar(200-30 , may1 , 200+50-30 ,235+30 ,
                LIGHTGREEN , GREEN , 15);
        yahobar(350-30 , may2 , 350+50-30 ,235+30 ,
                LIGHTGREEN , GREEN , 15);
        yahobar(500-30 , may3 , 500+50-30 ,235+30 ,
                LIGHTGREEN , GREEN , 15);

        yahobar(200-60 , june1 , 200+50-60 ,235+45 , LIGHTBLUE , BLUE , 15);
        yahobar(350-60 , june2 , 350+50-60 ,235+45 , LIGHTBLUE , BLUE , 15);
        yahobar(500-60 , june3 , 500+50-60 ,235+45 , LIGHTBLUE , BLUE , 15);

        getch( );
        closegraph( );
}

yahobar(int left, int top, int right, int bottom, int color,
        int bkcolor ,int depth)
{
    int i ;
```

```
for( i = 0 ; i <= top ; i++ )
{
    setfillstyle( SOLID_FILL , color ) ;
    setcolor( bkcolor ) ;
    bar3d( left , bottom-i , right , bottom , depth , 1 ) ;
}
}
```

The core of the program is the function *yahobar( )*. The parameters passed to it are the x - coordinate of the left top, the height, the coordinates of the right bottom, the color of the bar, the outline color of the bar and the bar's depth.

We initialize a counter and enter a *for* loop. In this loop we generate a 3-d bar which is animated such that it appears to grow in height. We do this by drawing a series of overlapping bars, with each subsequent bar being slightly taller than the preceding one. This is repeated till we reach the top of the bar.

The reason we generate so many bars for a single solid bar entity is twofold: firstly, to give a dynamic representation of growth, and secondly, to give a further impression of depth using the concept of light and shade. This is done by selecting a darker tone for the outline. When these outlines are closely stacked, they give the impression of solid color.

The rest is done by the main program where *yahobar( )* is called with the appropriate points and colors.

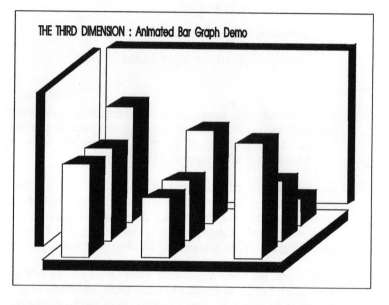

THE THIRD DIMENSION : Animated Bar Graph Demo

DIAGRAM 9.1 (3-D bar graph)

A Bar Graph Again !!

The program to generate a cylindrical bar graph (which follows), shares many features with the previous program. The only difference is that the function *yahobar( )* is altered. Instead of *yahobar( )*, we have a function called *yahoel( )*. In *yahobar( )*, we called *bar3d( )*, whereas in *yahoel( )* we'll call *fillellipse( )* and change the coordinates. The rest of the code remains the same.

PROGRAM 285

```
#include <graphics.h>
#include <conio.h>
#include <dos.h>

main( )
{
```

```
int gmode , gdriver = DETECT;

int march1=145 ,march2=130, march3=148 ;
int april1=128 ,april2=125, april3=132 ;
int may1=110 ,may2=112, may3=115 ;
int june1=120 ,june2=16, june3=117 ;

char title[ ] = "THE THIRD DIMENSION :Animated Bar Graph Demo";

initgraph(&gdriver,&gmode,"");

outtextxy(1,0,title);

yahobar( 215 , 195 , 625 , 210 , LIGHTGRAY , WHITE , 10 ) ;

yahobar( 113 , 10 , 530-7 , 299 , LIGHTGRAY, WHITE ,100 ) ;
setfillstyle( SOLID_FILL , WHITE ) ;
floodfill( 163 , 285 , WHITE ) ;

yahobar( 101 , 197 , 112 , 287 , LIGHTGRAY ,WHITE ,100 ) ;

getch( ) ;

yahoel(200+30 , march1 , 200+50+30 , 235 , LIGHTCYAN , CYAN );
yahoel(350+30 , march2 , 350+50+30 , 235 , LIGHTCYAN , CYAN );
yahoel(500+30 , march3 , 500+50+30 , 235 , LIGHTCYAN , CYAN );

yahoel(200 , april1 , 200+50 , 235+15 ,LIGHTRED , RED );
yahoel(350 , april2 , 350+50 , 235+15 , LIGHTRED , RED );
yahoel(500 , april3 , 500+50 , 235+15 , LIGHTRED , RED );

yahoel(200-30 , may1 , 200+50-30 ,235+30 , LIGHTGREEN , GREEN );
yahoel(350-30 , may2 , 350+50-30 ,235+30 , LIGHTGREEN , GREEN );
yahoel(500-30 , may3 , 500+50-30 ,235+30 , LIGHTGREEN , GREEN );

yahoel(200-60 , june1 , 200+50-60 ,235+45 , LIGHTBLUE , BLUE );
yahoel(350-60 , june2 , 350+50-60 ,235+45 , LIGHTBLUE , BLUE );
yahoel(500-60 , june3 , 500+50-60 ,235+45 , LIGHTBLUE , BLUE );

getch( );
closegraph( );
}
```

```
yahobar(int left, int top, int right, int bottom, int color,
           int bkcolor ,int depth)
{
    int i ;

    for( i = 0 ; i <= top ; i++ )
    {
        setfillstyle( SOLID_FILL , color ) ;
        setcolor( bkcolor ) ;
        bar3d( left , bottom-i , right , bottom , depth , 1 ) ;
    }
}

yahoel( int left, int top, int right, int bottom, int color,
          int bkcolor )
{
    int i ;

    for( i = 0 ; i <= top ; i++ )
    {
        setfillstyle( SOLID_FILL , bkcolor ) ;
        setcolor( color ) ;
        fillellipse( (left+right)/2 , bottom-i , 30,5) ;
    }
}
```

In the main program , we call a series of *yahoel( )*s and pass these coordinates : the x - coordinate of the top left , the height and the coordinates of the right bottom. The coordinates of the center have to be specified when we call *fillellipse( )*. This is done by dividing the left and right x coordinates by 2. The y coordinate follows the same principle as in the previous program. The last two parameters are the x and y radii of the ellipse.

The preceding programs incorporated the functions *line( )* , *pieslice( )* , *bar( )* and *bar3d( )* . These serve a wide variety of applications in business graphics. Although we have hard-coded the parameters, thus making the programs less generic, it is possible to tailor the programs to suit your own specific needs.

In this way you can now generate visually appealing displays to render business applications more comprehensible and lucid.

MATHing Away...

We are approaching the end of our tryst with graphics. Before signing off let's go a step beyond merely calling functions, and delve into the mathematical core. Sophisticated wave forms and curves, such as sine and cosine waves, tangential and parabolic curves. Let's implement equations and transform them into their graphic representations. The ensuing discussion desires you to possess some knowledge about these waveforms and curves.

Plotting Sine , Cos And Tan Waveforms

The next program introduces sine waves, cosine waves and tangential curves.

PROGRAM 286

```c
#include <math.h>
#include <graphics.h>
#include <stdlib.h>

double x=0 , sinx , cosx , tanx ;
double multi ;
int ay , ax , newx=0 , ox , oy ;
int maxx , maxy , midy ;

void sinewave(int , int ) ;
void cosinewave(int , int ) ;
void tanwave(int , int ) ;

main( int argc , char *argv[ ] )
{
    int gd = DETECT , gm ;

    clrscr( ) ;

    if( argc < 4 )
    {
        printf("Usage: %s <X-MULTIPLE> <Y-MULTIPLE> "
            "<TYPE (1/2/3 for sin/cos/tan)>\n" , argv[0] ) ;
```

```
        exit(1);
    }

    initgraph( &gd , &gm , "" );

    maxx = getmaxx( );
    maxy = getmaxy( );

    midy = maxy/2;

    setlinestyle( SOLID_LINE , 0 , THICK_WIDTH );
    setcolor( LIGHTRED );

    rectangle( 0 , 0 , maxx , maxy );

    setcolor( YELLOW );

    line( 1 , 0 , 1 , maxy );
    line( 1 , midy , maxx , midy );

    switch( atoi( argv[3] ) )
    {
        case 1:
            sinewave(atoi(argv[1]), atoi(argv[2]) );
            setcolor( YELLOW );
            outtextxy( 10 , 10 , "S I N E W A V E" );
            break;

        case 2:
            cosinewave(atoi(argv[1]),atoi(argv[2]));
            setcolor( YELLOW );
            outtextxy( 10 , 10 , "C O S I N E W A V E" );
            break;

        case 3:
            tanwave(atoi(argv[1]) , atoi(argv[2]) );
            setcolor( YELLOW );
            outtextxy( 10 , 10 , "T A N G E N T I A L" );
            break;
    }

    getch( );
    closegraph( );
```

```
}

void sinewave(int xmult , int ymult )
{
    x = 0 ;
    newx = 0 ;
    ox = oy = 0 ;

    maxx = getmaxx( ) ;
    midy = getmaxy( )/2 ;

    setlinestyle( SOLID_LINE , 0 , NORM_WIDTH ) ;

    while( newx < maxx )
    {
        while(1)
        {
            if( x > 3.142000 )
                    break ;
            sinx = sin( x ) ;
            multi = sinx*ymult ;
            ay = multi ;
            ax = newx + x*xmult ;
            setcolor( random( MAXCOLORS+1 ) ) ;
            moveto( ox , midy-oy ) ;
            lineto( ax , midy-ay ) ;
            x = x+0.01 ;
            ox = ax ;
            oy = ay ;
        }

        newx = ax ;
        x = 0 ;

        while( 1 )
        {
            if( x > 3.142 )
                    break ;
            sinx = sin( x ) ;
            multi = sinx*ymult ;
            ay = multi ;
            ax = newx+x*xmult ;
            setcolor( random( MAXCOLORS+1 ) ) ;
```

```
            moveto( ox , midy+oy ) ;
            lineto( ax , midy+ay ) ;
            x = x+0.01 ;
            ox = ax ;
            oy = ay ;
        }
        newx = ax ;
        x = 0 ;
    }

}

void cosinewave(int xmult , int ymult )
{
    x = 0.01 ;
    ox = oy = 0 ;
    newx = 0 ;
    maxx = getmaxx( ) ;
    midy = getmaxy( )/2 ;

    setlinestyle( SOLID_LINE , 0 , NORM_WIDTH ) ;

    while( newx < maxx )
    {
        while(1)
        {
            if( x > 3.14000 )
                    break ;
            cosx = cos( x ) ;
            multi = cosx*ymult ;
            ay = multi ;
            ax = newx + x*xmult ;
            setcolor( random( MAXCOLORS+1 ) ) ;
            moveto( ox , midy-oy ) ;
            lineto( ax , midy-ay ) ;
            x = x+0.01 ;
            ox = ax ;
            oy = ay ;
        }

        newx = ax ;
        x = 0 ;
```

```
        while( 1 )
        {
           if( x > 3.1420 )
                  break ;
           cosx = cos( x ) ;
           multi = cosx*ymult ;
           ay = multi ;
           ax = newx+x*xmult ;
           setcolor( random( MAXCOLORS+1 ) ) ;
           moveto( ox , midy+oy ) ;
           lineto( ax , midy+ay ) ;
           x = x+0.01 ;
           ox = ax ;
           oy = ay ;
        }
        newx = ax ;
        x = 0 ;
     }
}

void tanwave(int xmult , int ymult )
{
   x = 0 ;
   newx = 0 ;
   ox = oy = 0 ;
   maxx = getmaxx( ) ;
   midy = getmaxy( )/2 ;

   setlinestyle( SOLID_LINE , 0 , NORM_WIDTH ) ;

   while( newx < maxx )
   {
      while(1)
      {
         if( x > 3.142000 )
                break ;
         tanx = tan( x ) ;
         multi = tanx*ymult ;
         ay = multi ;
         ax = newx + x*xmult ;
         setcolor( random( MAXCOLORS+1 ) ) ;
         moveto( ox , midy+oy ) ;
         lineto( ax , midy+ay ) ;
```

```
      x = x+0.01 ;
      ox = ax ;
      oy = ay ;
   }

   newx = ax ;
   x = 0 ;

   while( 1 )
   {
      if( x > 3.142 )
          break ;
      tanx = tan( x ) ;
      multi = tanx*ymult ;
      ay = multi ;
      ax = newx+x*xmult ;
      setcolor( random( MAXCOLORS+1 ) ) ;
      moveto( ox , midy+oy ) ;
      lineto( ax , midy+ay ) ;
      x = x+0.01 ;
      ox = ax ;
      oy = ay ;
   }
   newx = ax ;
   x = 0 ;
  }
}
```

The functions *sinewave( )* , *cosinewave( )* and *tanwave( )* are called to generate sine, cos and tan waves respectively. Each requires two parameters: the x multiple and the y multiple. In the main program we pass 3 parameters: the x multiple, the y multiple and the type of wave required, i.e. sine, cos or tan.

The x and y multiples relate to the frequency and amplitude, respectively. The product of the x multiple and the angle, which is given in radians, is inversely proportional to the frequency. The product of the y multiple and the sine of the same angle is directly proportional to the amplitude of the wave.

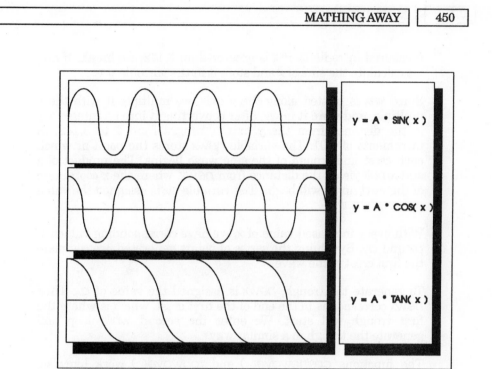

DIAGRAM 10.1

Next, we calculate the maximum value along the x and y coordinates by calling *getmaxx( )* and *getmaxy( )* . We also calculate the midpoint of the y axis. These three values are stored in three global variables. Now we draw the x and y axes. The x axis passes through the center of the screen.

A set of case statements follows, where the third parameter, which corresponds to the type of wave desired, is specified. If the flag is set at 1, the type is sine, and the x multiple and y multiple are given. Similarly, 2 corresponds to cos, and 3 to tan.

When the flag is set at 1, we call the function *sinewave( )* . Then we enter a *while* loop and check the value of *newx*. If *newx* is less than *maxx*, we enter the second *while* loop. The angles are measured in radians; if *x* is greater than 3.142, we break. If not, we calculate the sine of *x* and store it in the variable *sinx*.

Since *sinx* is plotted along the y axis, we multiply it with the y multiple, and store it in *ay*, after converting it into an integer. *ay* is the distance from the y axis. *x* ranges from 0 to 3.142, in increments of 0.01. The variable *newx* stores the point at which each crest and trough of the sine wave begins. The product of *x* and *xmult* yields the distance from *newx*, where the x coordinate of the next angle will begin. The variable *ax* is assigned the value *newx+x*xmult*.

With every increased value of *x*, we have corresponding values of *ax* and *ay*. By joining the series of points generated, we complete the first crest of the wave.

To generate the trough, *newx* is assigned the value of *ax*. Thus *newx* corresponds to the end of the first crest, which is where the first trough will start. We enter the second *while* loop and generate the trough in a similar way.

The functions *cosinewave( )* and *tanwave( )* work likewise, except that they call the functions *cos( )* and *tan( )*, respectively, instead of *sin( )*.

Plotting Curves : The Parabola And The Circle.

Now let's move from waves to curves.

PROGRAM 287

```
#include <graphics.h>
#include <math.h>
#define OFFSET 50

main( )
{
    int gm , gd=DETECT ;
    double y=0 , x=0 ;
```

```
int ax=0 , ay=0 , ox=0 , oy=0 ;
int maxx , maxy , midy ;

initgraph( &gd , &gm , "" ) ;

maxx = getmaxx( ) ;
maxy = getmaxy( ) ;
midy = maxy/2 ;

setlinestyle( SOLID_LINE , 0 , THICK_WIDTH ) ;
setcolor( LIGHTRED ) ;
rectangle( 0 , 0 , maxx , maxy ) ;
setcolor( YELLOW ) ;
line( 1 , 0 , 1 , maxy ) ;
line( 1 , midy , maxx , midy ) ;

setcolor( LIGHTCYAN ) ;
while( 1 )
{
    if( x == maxx-20 ) break ;
    y = sqrt( 4*16*x ) ;
    ax = (int) x ;
    ay = (int) y ;
    x = x + 1 ;
    moveto( ox+OFFSET , midy-oy ) ;
    lineto( ax+OFFSET , midy-ay) ;
    ox = ax ;
    oy = ay ;
}

x = 0 ;
y = 0 ;
ox = oy = 0 ;

while( 1 )
{
    if( x == maxx-20 ) break ;
    y = sqrt( 4*16*x ) ;
    ax = (int) x ;
    ay = (int) y ;
    x = x + 1 ;
    moveto( ox+OFFSET , midy+oy ) ;
    lineto( ax+OFFSET , midy+ay) ;
```

```
ox = ax ;
oy = ay ;
}

outtextxy( maxx/2 , midy-50 , "P A R A B O L A" ) ;
getch( ) ;
closegraph( );

}
```

In the previous program, we drew the waves in two parts, the crest and the trough. Similarly, when drawing a parabola, we do so in two stages -- above and below the x axis. The equation for a parabola is:

$$y^2 = 4 * a * x$$

DIAGRAM 10.2

Thus y is the square root of $4*a*x$ a is given the value of 16, x increases in increments of 1. ax is the x coordinate, ay is the distance from the y axis.

We enter a *while* loop and check the value of x. Note that x increases in increments of 1. When $x=maxx-20$ we break out of the loop. y is calculated for each value of x. The corresponding values are assigned to ax and ay. And the points then plotted.

After plotting each point, the values of ax and ay are assigned to ox and oy.

The second *while* loop goes through the same motions to generate the lower part of the parabola.

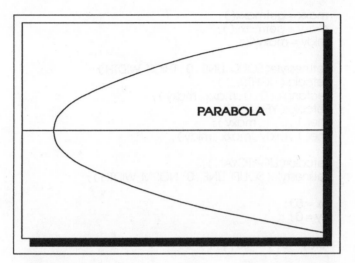

PARABOLA

DIAGRAM 10.3

You will have noticed that in this and the previous program, we had two *while* loops, one after the other. This is in order to account for the two values (positive and negative) yielded by the square root operation. In Turbo C, the function *sqrt( )* yields only the positive value. To overcome this limitation and account for the negative value, as well, we introduce the second *while* loop.

PROGRAM 288

```
#include <graphics.h>
#include <math.h>

main( )
{
    int gm , gd=DETECT ;
    double y=0 , x=0 ;
    int ax=0 , ay=0 , ox=0 , oy=0 ;
    int maxx , maxy , midy ;
    int p ;

    initgraph( &gd , &gm , "" ) ;
```

```
maxx = getmaxx( ) ;
maxy = getmaxy( ) ;
midy = maxy/2 ;

setlinestyle( SOLID_LINE , 0 , THICK_WIDTH ) ;
setcolor( LIGHTRED ) ;
rectangle( 0 , 0 , maxx , maxy ) ;
setcolor( YELLOW ) ;
line( 1 , 0 , 1 , maxy ) ;
line( 1 , midy , maxx , midy ) ;

setcolor( LIGHTCYAN ) ;
setlinestyle( SOLID_LINE , 0 , NORM_WIDTH ) ;

ox = 50 ;
oy = 0 ;

for( y = 0 ; y <=50 ; y++ )
{
    x = sqrt( 2500 - y*y ) ;
    ax = (int)x ;
    ay = (int) y ;
    moveto( ox+maxx/2 , midy - oy ) ;
    lineto(ax+maxx/2 , midy - ay ) ;
    ox = ax ;
    oy = ay ;
}

for( y = 50 ; y >= 0 ; y– )
{
    x = sqrt( 2500 - y*y );
    ax = (int)x ;
    ay = (int) y ;
    moveto( maxx/2-ox , midy - oy ) ;
    lineto( maxx/2-ax , midy - ay ) ;
    ox = ax ;
    oy = ay ;
}

ox = 50 ;
oy = 0 ;
```

```
for( y = 0 ; y <=50 ; y++ )
{
    x = sqrt( 2500 - y*y );
    ax = (int)x ;
    ay = (int) y ;

    moveto( ox+maxx/2 , midy +oy ) ;
    lineto(ax+maxx/2 , midy +ay ) ;

    ox = ax ;
    oy = ay ;
}

for( y = 50 ; y >= 0 ; y- )
{
    x = sqrt( 2500 - y*y ) ;
    ax = (int)x ;
    ay = (int) y ;

    moveto( maxx/2-ox , midy +oy ) ;
    lineto( maxx/2-ax , midy +ay ) ;

    ox = ax ;
    oy = ay ;
}

outtextxy( 10 , 10 , "I Don't Know What This Can Be Called" ) ;
outtextxy( 10 , 20 , "On an EGA its an Ellipse , on a VGA , "
                     "a Circle : ASPECTRATIO !!!!!" ) ;

getch( ) ;
closegraph( );
}
```

We have four *for* loops in this program, one for each quarter of the circle. The first quarter lies in the first quadrant, the second quarter in the second quadrant, the third quarter in the fourth quadrant, and the fourth quarter in the third quadrant. The coordinate axes pass through the center of the screen.

Generating a circle merely involves using the equation

$$x^2 + y^2 = a^2$$

DIAGRAM 10.4

where a is the radius.

Note that the same equation will generate an ellipse on an EGA monitor, and a circle on a VGA monitor. This, as we know by now, is because of the aspect ratio. Recall that in the EGA monitor, the pixels are a third taller than they are wide, whereas in the VGA monitor, the pixels are square. This accounts for the difference in output.

I Came , I Saw , I Saved It On Disk !!

After creating graphic images on the screen, we may want to restore them. For this purpose, we have developed a program which saves the screen and restores it. Although this is not a very space-efficient program, it is simple, and serves our purpose .

We know that each pixel on the screen has a color, which we can get by calling *getpixel( )*. What we do is as follows: we scan the entire screen from top to bottom and from left to right. Then we call *getpixel( )* for each pixel. This gets the color, and then stores it on disk. To restore the image, the contents of what we have stored on disk are retrieved byte by byte. Lastly, we call *putpixel( )* in the same order to restore the screen.

PROGRAM 289

```
/* saveimage( ) : used to store entire screen on disk */

#include <graphics.h>
#include <stdio.h>
#include <stdlib.h>
```

```
void saveimage( char *filename , int startx , int starty ,
                int endx , int endy )
{
    int i , j ;
    unsigned ch ;
    FILE *fp ;

    fp = fopen( filename , "wb" ) ;

    for( i = startx ; i <= endx ; i++ )
    {
        for( j = starty ; j <= endy ; j++ )
        {
            ch = getpixel( i , j ) ;
            fputc( ch , fp ) ;
        }
    }
    fclose( fp ) ;
}

main( )
{
    char name[100] ;
    int gm ;
    int gd = DETECT ;
    int maxx , maxy ;
    int i ;

    printf("FILE NAME : " ) ;
    gets( name ) ;

    initgraph( &gd , &gm , "" ) ;

    maxx = getmaxx( ) ;
    maxy = getmaxy( ) ;

    for( i = 0 ; i < 150 ; i++ )
    {
        setcolor( random( MAXCOLORS+1 ) ) ;
        setfillstyle(SOLID_FILL ,random(MAXCOLORS+1)) ;
        pieslice( random(maxx), random(maxy), 0 , 360 , random(50) );
```

```
    }

    getch();

    saveimage( name , 0 , 0 , maxx , maxy );

    getch();
    closegraph();
}
```

The function *saveimage( )* is passed five parameters: the name of the file, the x coordinate of the starting point, the y coordinate of the starting point, the x coordinate of the ending point and the y coordinate of the ending point.

Within the function, we open the file in 'write binary' mode. In the outer *for* loop, the variable *i* starts at *startx* and ends at *endx*. In the inner *for* loop, the variable *j* starts at *starty* and ends at *endy*. Within the inner *for* loop, we call *getpixel( )*, which gets the color from the point *(i,j)*. Then we store this color in a file. We do this for the entire screen and then close the file.

In the main program, we call the function *saveimage( )* and pass it the relevant parameters. Then we get the name of the file and generate an image on the screen. We have chosen pie slices. We then save this image on the file specified.

On the EGA monitor, the file will be 640*350=224000 bytes large. On the VGA monitor, the file will be 640*480=307200 bytes large. As you can see, the results are not space-efficient, but our purpose is served.

I Came , I Did Not See , So I Restored It !!!

The next program is designed to restore the screen, and follows a parallel rationale. The file is picked up bytewise, and restored on the screen in the same order.

PROGRAM 290

/* to restore the image stored by saveimage( ) using restore( ) */

```
#include <graphics.h>
#include <stdio.h>

restore( char *filename , int startx , int starty , int endx , int endy )
{
    unsigned int ch ;
    FILE *fp ;
    int i , j ;

    fp = fopen( filename , "rb" ) ;
    for( i = startx ; i <= endx ; i++ )
    {
        for( j = starty ; j <= endy ; j++ )
        {
            ch = fgetc( fp ) ;
            putpixel( i , j , ch ) ;
        }
    }
    fclose( fp ) ;
}

main( )
{
    char name[100] ;
    int gm ;
    int gd = DETECT ;
    int maxx , maxy ;

    printf("FILE NAME : ") ;
    gets( name ) ;

    initgraph( &gd , &gm , "" ) ;

    maxx = getmaxx( ) ;
    maxy = getmaxy( ) ;

    restore( name , 0 , 0 , maxx , maxy ) ;

    getch( ) ;
    closegraph( ) ;
}
```

In this case, the file is opened in 'read binary' mode. The *for* loops are identical to those in the previous program. Here, a character is obtained and we call *putpixel( )* to position this character at *(i,j)* using the color specified in the variable *ch*.

Hello Fractals...

Fractals open up a wide new world of perception. The concept is the brainchild of Benoit B. Mandelbrot and seeks to explain how what is measured depends on how it is measured.

For example, if the length of an entity is measured with a yardstick of 10 kilometers, a certain result will be obtained. If the measurement is made with a 1 kilometer yardstick, the result will be fractionally larger than the first. A third measurement, using 100 meter yardstick, will yield a result correspondingly larger than the second. Thus, with every decrease in the size of the unit of measure, ever-smaller irregularities are accounted for, and every subsequent measurement exceeds the previous one.

This concept, which seems to defy all norms of reason and rationality, is in fact very real. In fact, it underlies many everyday occurrences. The structure of snowflakes, the configuration of a protein molecule, crystal morphology, the intricate pattern of a fern and even some physiological structures are all governed by the same equations.

Take a line and bisect it. Bend it at the midpoint. Now bisect the two halves and then bend these at their midpoints. Continue this process till the segments can't be divided further. With each subsequent division, decrease the amount of bend. We are left with a set of points.

Fractal equations serve to position these points so as to simulate reality most faithfully. For example, the configuration of a mountain would be much rougher than that of a seashore. Thus, the equation of the former would have a decay factor smaller than that of the latter. The decay factor controls the roughness or smoothness of a line.

The algorithm to divide a line is a recursive function since we repeat it till further subdivision is not possible. To avoid complexity, we standardise the smallest line element at 20 pixels.

The amount of the bend can be specified. We take a random number ranging from 0 to 5. Imagine a vertical scale ranging from 0 to 5. We specify a series of values, eg. 3, 4, 2, 3, 1, 5. The line generated would join these points, much like how a child would generate a figure by joining numbered dots.

Yonder , Across The Horizon , They Fly Away....

PROGRAM 291

```c
#include <graphics.h>
#include <stdlib.h>
#include <conio.h>
#include <dos.h>

void plane( int x , int y )
{
    setcolor( LIGHTRED );

    line( x , y , x+10 , y-3 );
    line( x+10 , y-3 , x+25 , y-2 );
    line( x+25 , y-2 , x+29 , y-7 );
    line( x+29 , y-7 , x+27 , y );
    line( x+27 , y , x , y );
    line( x+11 , y-1 , x+15 , y-1 );
}

void fract( int newx , int x , int oy )
{
    static int y , rnd = 5 ;

    setcolor( LIGHTBLUE ) ;
    moveto( x , oy+y ) ;
    y = random( rnd ) ;
    lineto( newx , oy+y ) ;
}

void main( )
{
    int gm , gd = DETECT ;
    int maxx ;
```

```
int newx ;
int x = 0 ;
int x1=0 , newx1 ;
int x2 , newx2 ;
int px , py ;

initgraph( &gd , &gm , "" ) ;

maxx = getmaxx( ) ;
x2 = maxx-280 ;
newx=newx1=newx2 = 0 ;

px = maxx ;
py = 40 ;

while( !kbhit( ) )
{
   delay( 300 ) ;
   cleardevice( ) ;
   setcolor( YELLOW ) ;
   circle( maxx-50 , 40 , 20 ) ;
   px -= 15 ;
   if( px+30 < 0 )
      px = maxx ;
   plane( px , py ) ;
   plane( px+10 , py+10 ) ;

   while( newx < maxx )
   {
      newx = x+50 ;
      fract( newx , x , 100 ) ;
      x = newx ;
   }

   while( newx1 < maxx/2 )
   {
      newx1 = x1+50 ;

      fract( newx1 , x1 , 200 ) ;

      x1 = newx1 ;
   }
```

```
while( newx2 < maxx )
{
    newx2 = x2+50 ;

    fract( newx2 , x2 , 300 ) ;

    x2 = newx2 ;
}

x = newx = 0 ;
x1 = newx1 = 0 ;
x2 = newx2 = maxx-280 ;
}

getch( ) ;
closegraph( ) ;
}
```

fract( ) is passed 3 parameters: the x coordinate of the starting point (*x*), the x coordinate of the end point (*newx*) and a constant y coordinate (*oy*). The static variable *y* does a twofold job: it stores the previous y offset and determines the offset. The *fract( )* function joins the starting point to the ending point, taking into account the offset. Thus a segment which deviates from the horizontal as specified by the offset is generated. For the next segment, the starting point is now the endpoint of the previous segment. The segment is similarly generated with the specified offset.

We have created a wave in our landscape. We create three similar waves at different positions by specifying different values for all the coordinates in the main program. Now we have to get the waves to move. To do this, we'll have to clear the screen and draw the three waves again with different sequences of random numbers. This process continues till a key is pressed. The illusion of the waves moving is created by successively clearing the screen and displaying a different set of waves with the changed sequence of random numbers.

The aircraft and the sun are purely ornamental.

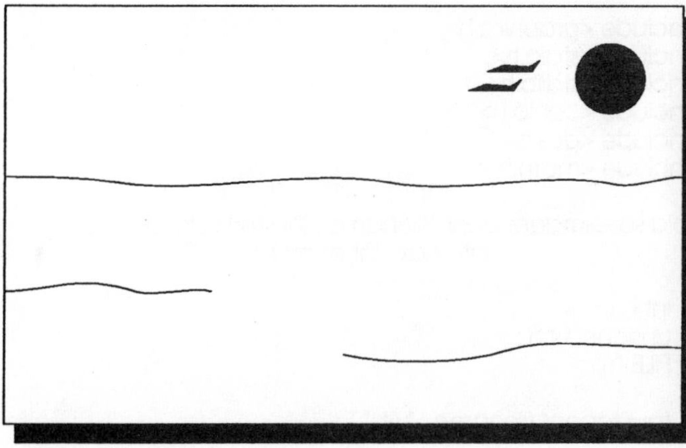

DIAGRAM 11.1

A purist may not consider the above application an example of fractal graphics since it doesn't incorporate intricate mathematical processes. However, it serves our purpose of an introduction to fractal graphics. The mathematics is beyond the scope of this publication.

In fact, that is the reason why we have not discussed algorithms that draw circles and ellipses. Our motive has been to take you to a point where you can take on the complexities with confidence and ease.

A Landscape

In the next program, we create another landscape. We are already familiar with the function *sinewave( )*, which will here be used to generate mountains; the function *fract( )*, which creates the sea; and the function *floodfill( )*, which renders everything colorful. We're sorry, but it is meant for the EGA only.

PROGRAM 292

```c
#include <graphics.h>
#include <stdio.h>
#include <stdlib.h>
#include <conio.h>
#include <dos.h>
#include <math.h>

void saveimage( char *filename , int startx , int starty ,
                int endx , int endy )
{
    int i , j ;
    unsigned ch ;
    FILE *fp ;

    fp = fopen( filename , "wb" ) ;

    for( i = startx ; i <= endx ; i++ )
    {
        for( j = starty ; j <= endy ; j++ )
        {
            ch = getpixel( i , j ) ;
            fputc( ch , fp ) ;
        }
    }
    fclose( fp ) ;
}

void fract( int newx , int x , int oy , int color )
{
    static int y , rnd = 5 ;
    setcolor( color ) ;
    moveto( x , oy+y ) ;
    y = random( rnd ) ;
    lineto( newx , oy+y ) ;
}

sinewave(int xmult , int ymult , int startx , int starty)
{
    double x=0 , sinx , cosx , tanx ;
    double multi ;
    int ay , ax , newx=0 , ox , oy ;
    int maxx , maxy , midy ;
```

```
    x = 0 ;
    newx = startx ;
    ox = startx ;
    oy = 0 ;
    midy = starty ;

    setcolor( WHITE ) ;
    setlinestyle( SOLID_LINE , 0 , NORM_WIDTH ) ;
    while(1)
    {
        if( x > 3.142000 ) break ;
        sinx = sin( x ) ;
        multi = sinx*ymult ;
        ay = multi ;
        ax = newx + x*xmult ;
        moveto( ox , midy-oy ) ;
        lineto( ax , midy-ay ) ;
        x = x+0.01 ;
        ox = ax ;
        oy = ay ;
    }
}

makemountain( )
{
    int newx = 0 , x = 0 , maxx = getmaxx( ) ;

    setfillstyle( SOLID_FILL , LIGHTBLUE ) ;
    floodfill( 10 , 0 , WHITE ) ;

    while( newx < maxx )
    {
        newx = x+50 ;
        fract( newx , x , 180 , WHITE ) ;
        x = newx ;
    }

    setfillstyle( SOLID_FILL , YELLOW ) ;
    setcolor( YELLOW ) ;
    pieslice( 500 , 50 , 0 , 360 , 40 ) ;

    floodfill( 0 , 185 , WHITE ) ;
```

```
    setcolor( WHITE ) ;
    sinewave( 150 , 100 , 0 , getmaxy( )/2 ) ;
    sinewave( 95 , 60 , getmaxx( )/2 + 73 , getmaxy( )/2 - 50 ) ;

    setfillstyle( SOLID_FILL , BROWN ) ;
    floodfill( 10 , getmaxy( )/2 + 5 , WHITE ) ;
}

makesea( )
{
    int maxx ;
    int newx ;
    int x = 0 ;
    int x1=0 , newx1 ;
    int x2 , newx2 ;
    int x3 , newx3 ;

    maxx = getmaxx( ) ;
    x2 = maxx-280 ;
    x3 = 50 ;
    newx=newx1=newx2=newx3= 0 ;

    cleardevice( ) ;

    while( newx < maxx )
    {
        newx = x+50 ;
        fract( newx , x , 200 , WHITE ) ;
        x = newx ;
    }

    setfillstyle( SOLID_FILL , LIGHTCYAN ) ;
    floodfill( getmaxx( ) , getmaxy( ) , WHITE ) ;

    while( newx1 < maxx/2 )
    {
        newx1 = x1+50 ;
        fract( newx1 , x1 , 250 , LIGHTBLUE ) ;
        x1 = newx1 ;
    }

    while( newx2 < maxx )
```

```
    {
        newx2 = x2+50 ;
        fract( newx2 , x2 , 300 , LIGHTBLUE ) ;
        x2 = newx2 ;
    }

    while( newx3 < maxx-200 )
    {
        newx3 = x3+50 ;
        fract( newx3 , x3 , 320 , LIGHTBLUE ) ;
        x3 = newx3 ;
    }
}

main( )
{
    int gm , gd = DETECT ;
    int maxx ;
    int maxy ;

    initgraph( &gd , &gm , "" ) ;

    maxx = getmaxx( ) ;
    maxy = getmaxy( ) ;

    makesea( ) ;
    makemountain( ) ;

    getch( ) ;

    saveimage( "SCENE.RCT" , 0 , 0 , maxx , maxy ) ;

    getch( ) ;
    closegraph( ) ;
}
```

We have two functions: *makesea( )* and *makemountain( )*.
Makes you feel a bit like God, doesn't it?

The function *makesea( )* uses *fract( )* to generate the sea.
floodfill( ) is called to fill it in light cyan. *makemountain( )* calls
floodfill( ) , which fills the top half of the screen with blue,

creating the sky. The *fract( )* function is called to draw the beach, which is colored yellow by *floodfill( )* . Next, *pieslice( )* renders a yellow sun. Finally, *makemountain( )* calls *sinewave( )* to create the mountains, and *floodfill( )* colors them brown. The overlapping effect is engendered by the order in which the images are drawn. And so, we're left with a composite landscape of our making.

We said let there be *makemountain( )*, and there were mountains. We said let there be *makesea( )*, and there were seas. We gazed upon all that we had made and found it good. So we saved it!

Fractals : The Real Thing..

The Malthusian Curve, which incorporates fractals, is a denizen of the land of fascinating mathematical concepts. It is a recursive function which purports to measure the growth of a population through successive generations, and is expressed as follows:

$$P_{n+1} = R * P_n * (1 - P_n)$$

DIAGRAM 11.2

where R is the rate of growth for successive generations of the population.

The Malthusian Curve has some fractal properties. As R changes within a specified range (2.3 to 3.8), a series of curves is produced with each value of R creating a curve approximately every 7 generations.

The Malthusian Curve is best understood if it is observed in the process of its generation, i.e. while it is being formed, rather than when it is complete.

The next two programs deal with this mathematical concept.

PROGRAM 293
/* MALTHUSIAN FLUX - POPULATION EQUATION */

```c
#include <graphics.h>
#include <conio.h>
#include <stdio.h>
#include <stdlib.h>
#include <stdarg.h>

int gd , gm , mcol , maxx , maxy , maxgen = 0x00ff , err ;

void init( )
{
   gd = DETECT ;
   initgraph( &gd , &gm , "" ) ;
   maxx = getmaxx( ) ;
   maxy = getmaxy( ) ;
}

void strange( )
{
   int i , j , k , l , color , cnt , x , y ;
   double popold , popnew , rate ;

   popnew = 0.0 ;
   rate = 2.3 ;
   color = BLACK ;
   for( j = 0 ; j < 152 ; j++ )
   {
      color++ ;
      if( color >= WHITE )
         color = BLUE ;
      cnt = 0 ;
      rate += 0.01 ;
      popold = 0.01 ;
      for( i = 0 ; i <= maxgen ; i++ )
      {
         popnew = rate*(popold*(1-popold)) ;
         x = popold*maxx ;
         y = maxy- (popnew*maxy) ;
         putpixel( x, y , color );
```

```c
            if( popold == popnew )
            {
               cnt++ ;
            }
            else
            {
               cnt = 0 ;
            }
            if( cnt > 10 )
            {
               i = maxgen ;
            }
            popold = popnew ;
         }
   }
   outtextxy( 10 ,10 ,"MALTHUSIAN FLUX" ) ;
}

void pause( )
{
   while( kbhit( )) getch( ) ;
   getch( ) ;
}

void saveimage( char *filename , int startx , int starty ,
                int endx , int endy )
{
   int i , j ;
   unsigned ch ;
   FILE *fp ;

   fp = fopen( filename , "wb" ) ;

   for( i = startx ; i <= endx ; i++ )
   {
      for( j = starty ; j <= endy ; j++ )
      {
         ch = getpixel( i ,j ) ;
         fputc( ch , fp ) ;
      }
   }
   fclose( fp ) ;
}
```

```
void main( )
{
    init( ) ;
    cleardevice( ) ;
    strange( ) ;
    pause( ) ;
    saveimage( "MALTHUS.IAN" , 0, 0 , maxx , maxy ) ;
    closegraph( ) ;
}
```

The two graphs represent populations at different rates of growth. The discontinuities become even more accentuated and further discontinuities become apparent as the scale is increased.

The next program also incorporates the principle of the Malthusian Curve.

PROGRAM 294

/* MALTHUSAN FLUX - RINGS OF SATURN */

```
#include <graphics.h>
#include <conio.h>
#include <stdio.h>
#include <stdlib.h>
#include <stdarg.h>

int gd , gm , mcol , maxx , maxy , maxgen = 0x00ff , err ;

void saveimage( char *filename , int startx , int starty ,
                int endx , int endy )
{
    int i , j ;
    unsigned ch ;
    FILE *fp ;

    fp = fopen( filename , "wb" ) ;

    for( i = startx ; i <= endx ; i++ )
    {
        for( j = starty ; j <= endy ; j++ )
        {
```

```
            ch = getpixel( i , j ) ;
            fputc( ch , fp ) ;
        }
    }
    fclose( fp ) ;
}

void init( )
{
    gd = DETECT ;
    initgraph( &gd , &gm , "" ) ;
    maxx = getmaxx( ) ;
    maxy = getmaxy( ) ;
}

void strange2( )
{
    int i , j , k , l , color , count ;
    double popold , popnew , x , y , rate ;

    popold = popnew = 0.0;
    rate = 2.3 ;
    y = 0 ;
    color=0 ;
    for ( j = 1 ; j <= 15 ; j++ )
    {
        color++ ;
        if( color > WHITE ) color = BLUE ;
        for( k = 1 ; k <= 10 ; k++ )
        {
            count = 0 ;
            rate = rate + 0.01 ;
            popold = 0.01 ;
            for( i = 1 ; i <= 1000 ; i++ )
            {
                popnew = rate * ( popold * ( 1 - popold ) ) ;
                x = popnew - popold ;
                putpixel( ( x*maxx/2) + maxx/2 ,
                        ( maxy/2) - (y*maxy/2) , color ) ;
                if( popold == popnew ) count++ ;
                else
                count = 0 ;
                if(count > 100) i = 10000 ;
```

```
            popold = popnew ;
            y = x ;
        }
    }
}
outtextxy( 10 , 10 , "MALTHUSIAN FLUX" ) ;
}

void pause( )
{
    while( kbhit( )) getch( ) ;
    getch( ) ;
}

void main( )
{
    init( ) ;
    cleardevice( ) ;
    strange2( ) ;
    pause( ) ;
    saveimage( "MALTHUS1.IAN" , 0 , 0 , maxx , maxy ) ;
    closegraph( ) ;
}
```

The discontinuities seen here are apparent even in areas of wide continuity. The Rings of Saturn exhibit similar discontinuities.

We'll now look at the Mandelbrot Set. Of all fractal landscapes, this is probably the most famous. It is named after Benoit Mandelbrot, who coined the term 'fractal'.

The Mandelbrot Set is an equation lying between -2.0 and +0.5 longitude and -1.25 and +1.25 latitude. It appears as a fractal sea with bays, tributaries and inlets.

The concept of imaginary numbers is a prerequisite. Imaginary numbers, when squared, produce negative results. Longitude is measured in real numbers, while latitude is measured in imaginary numbers. Thus, all latitudinal values are denoted by i, which represents the square root of -1. This will be an imaginary number.

Thus, each time the latitudinal value is squared, it will yield a negative value, which will no longer be imaginary.

PROGRAM 295
/* mandelbrot */

```c
#include <graphics.h>
#include <conio.h>
#include <stdio.h>
#include <stdlib.h>
#include <stdarg.h>
#include <math.h>

int gd , gm , err ;

void saveImage( char *filename , int startx , int starty ,
                int endx , int endy )
{
    int i , j ;
    unsigned ch ;
    FILE *fp ;

    fp = fopen( filename , "wb" ) ;

    for( i = startx ; i <= endx ; i++ )
    {
        for( j = starty ; j <= endy ; j++ )
        {
            ch = getpixel( i , j ) ;
            fputc( ch , fp ) ;
        }
    }
    fclose( fp ) ;
}

void init( )
{
    gd = DETECT ;
    initgraph( &gd , &gm , "D:\\TC3\\BGI" ) ;
    err = graphresult( ) ;
    if( err != grOk )
    {
```

```
                printf("ERROR: %s\n" , grapherrormsg( err ) ) ;
                exit(1) ;
            }
        }

        void pause( )
        {
            while( kbhit( )) getch( ) ;
            getch( ) ;
        }

        int xsize , ysize , limit , i , j , steps , done ;
        double xstep , ystep , xpos , ypos , xorg , yorg ,
                xmax , ymax , xiter , yiter , xtemp ;
        int maxx , maxy ;

        void main( )
        {
            init( ) ;
            xsize = getmaxx( ) ;
            ysize = getmaxy( ) ;
            maxx = xsize ;
            maxy = ysize ;
            limit = 100 ;

            xorg = -2.0 ;
            yorg = -1.25 ;
            xmax = 0.5 ;
            ymax = 1.25 ;

            xstep = (xmax - xorg)/xsize ;
            ystep = (ymax - yorg)/ysize ;
            for( i = 0 ; i <= xsize ; i ++ )
            {
                for( j = 0 ; j <= ysize ; j++ )
                {
                    xpos = xorg+i*xstep ;
                    ypos = yorg+j*ystep ;
                    xiter = 0.0 ;
                    yiter = 0.0 ;
                    done = steps = 0 ;
                    while( !done )
                    {
```

```
                    xtemp = (xiter*xiter)- (yiter*yiter) + xpos ;
                    yiter = 2* (xiter * yiter) + ypos ;
                    xiter = xtemp ;
                    steps++ ;
                    if(hypot(fabs(xiter),fabs(yiter)) >= 2.0 )
                        done ++ ;
                    if( steps >= limit )
                        done ++ ;
                    if( kbhit( ) )
                    {
                        i = xsize ;
                        j = ysize ;
                        done++ ;
                    }
                }
            if( steps < limit )
                putpixel( i , j , steps ) ;
        }
    }
    pause( ) ;
    saveimage( "MANDEL.PIX" , 0 , 0 , maxx , maxy ) ;
    closegraph( ) ;
}
```

To say that this program takes a long while to be generated would be an understatement. This is due to the number of points calculated. A co-processor would speed things up considerably.

All these programs are a matter of one-time generation. This is largely due to two functions: *saveimage( )*, which saves the entire screen, and *restore( )* , which returns the image to the screen for ready reference.

Consider the long-winded equations cited above for fractals, Malthusian Curves and the Mandelbrot Set. Compare them with their graphical avatars.

Need we say more?

The Beginning

In the course of our journey into the wide cosmos of graphics, it has become apparent that this realm is no longer limited to the domain of mere entertainment. Graphics, per se, has mushroomed far beyond being relegated to children's games and the like. What we have covered so far is just the beginning.

Several apparently daunting interfaces are rendered accessible and user-friendly by utilising graphical user interfaces, or GUIs. For example, products like Microsoft Windows, Presentation Manager for OS/2, X-Window System and Quarterdeck's DESQView are all powerful products which facilitate our job.

To the sceptics, who still maintain that this genre of computer science is, and will always be, a diversion, an antidote to the more weighty matters at hand, we'll do more than merely shrug our shoulders and shake our heads.

We'll cite the examples of diverse fields that are contingent on graphics -- ranging from the mundane to the esoteric. Graphic arts, scientific applications, robotics, computer typesetting, computer aided design, business applications, fractal mathematics, experimental chemistry, advertizing, special effects and a host of other subjects. All these use graphics.

Graphics are here, and by all accounts, here to stay. And, yes. You can also have fun with them. Bye for now....

Index

A

J

K

L

M

N

O

Other COMPUTER TITLES From
TECH PUBLICATIONS

AUTOCAD
ENCYCLOPEDIA AUTOCAD (REL 11)
INSIDE AUTOCAD (REL 10)
MASTERING AUTOCAD 3RD ED. (REL 11)
ABC'S OF AUTOCAD (REL. 11)
TEACH YOURSELF AUTOCAD (RLS 11)
AUTO CAD 11 INSTANT REF

ASSEMBLY LANGUAGE
USING ASSEMBLY LANGUAGE

AUTOLISP
THE ABC'S OF AUTOLISP (VER. 10)
ILLUSTRATED AUTOLISP

BASIC
LEARNING IBM BASIC FOR THE PC
MORE THAN 32 BASIC PROG, FOR THE IBM PER/COM
THE BASIC HANDBOOK 3RD ED.
THE IBM BASIC HANDBOOK 2ND ED

C
ENCYCLOPEDIA C
TEACH YOURSELF C
DOS – THE CHARTED WATERS
ADVANCED DOS – THE UNCHARTED WATERS
UNIX – THE OPEN-BOUNDLESS C
NETWORKS AND RDBMS – NEW WORLDS TO CONQUER
C++ AND GRAPHICS – THE FUTURE OF C
WINDOWS – THE BRAVE NEW WORLD

CLIPPER
ILLUSTRATED CLIPPER 5.0
CLIPPER PROGRAMMING GUIDE 3RD ED. VERSION 5.01
THE UNOFFICIAL CLIPPER 5.0 MANUAL
UP & RUNNING WITH CLIPPER 5.01

COMPUTER VIRUS
THE COMPUTER VIRUS PROTECTION HDB (WITH DISK)

CROSSTALK XVI
MASTERING CROSSTALK XV

COREL DRAW
MASTERING COREL DRAW 2

DAC EASY
MASTERING DACEASY ACCOUNTING (VER. 3.1/4.1)
MASTERING DACEASY ACCOUNTING (VER. 4.0/3.0)
ILLUSTRATED DACEASY ACCT.

DATA BASE
SALVAGING DAMAGED DBASE FILES
THE DATABASE DICTIONARY

DBASE III PLUS
DBASE III PLUS APPLICATIONS LIBRARY
DBASE III PLUS PROGRAMMER'S REF. GUIDE
UNDERSTANDING DBASE III PLUS

DBASE IV
THE DBASE LANGUAGE HANDBOOK (INCL. DBASE IV)
UNDERSTANDING DBASE IV (VER. 1.1)
ILLUSTRATED DBASE IV (1.1)
DBASE IV (1.1) USERS' INSTANT REF.
THE ABCS' OF DBASE IV (VER 1.1)
MASTERING DBASE IV 1.1 PROGRAMMING
DBASE IV (1.1) PROGRAMMERS INSTANT REF.
DBASE IV 1.1 DESKTOP REFERENCE

COMPUTER DICTIONARY
THE COMPUTER DICTIONARY

DOS
MS DOS-PC DOS QUICK REF. (VER. 5.0)
TEACH YOURSELF DOS VER. 3.3 & 4.0
MASTERING DOS (VER. 3.3 & 4.0)
THE ABC'S OF DOS 5
MASTERING DOS 5
UP AND RUNNING WITH DOS 5
DOS 5 USER'S HANDBOOK
DOS 5 INSTANT REF

EXCEL
MASTERING EXCEL 3 FOR WINDOWS
UP & RUNNING EXCEL 3 FOR WINDOWS

FOX PRO
MASTERING FOX PRO 2

HARVARD GRAPHICS
UP & RUNNING WITH HARVARD GRAPHICS (VER. 2.3)
HARVARD GRAPHICS INSTANT REF. (VER 2.3)
MASTERING HARVARD GRAPHICS (VER. 2.3) WITH DISK
MASTERING HARVARD GRAPHICS 3 (WITH DISK)
HARVARD GRAPHICS 3 INSTANT REFERENCE

HARD DISK
HARD DISK INSTANT REFERENCE
HARD DISK MANAGEMENT 2ND ED.
MANAGING YOUR HARD DISK
UNDERSTANDING HARD DISK MANAGEMENT ON THE PC
UP & RUNNING WITH YOUR HARD DISK
HARD DISK SURVIVAL GUIDE (WITH DISK)

HARDWARE
THE ABC'S OF UPGRADING YOUR PC
TROUBLESHOOTING & REPAIRING/PERSONAL COMPUTERS
UPGRADING AND REPAIRING PCs
MICROPROCESSOR DATA HANDBOOK
FROM CHIPS TO SYSTEMS AN INTRODUCTION TO MICROPROCESSORS
THE COMPLETE PC UPGRADE & MAINTENANCE GUIDE

IBM PC/XT/AT/PS-2/386/486 & CLONES
86 COMPUTER HANDBOOK

ABSOLUTELY ESSENTIAL UTILITIES FOR THE IBM PC.
IBM AT CLONE HANDBOOK
IBM PC & PS/2 GRAPHICS HANDBOOK
IBM PS/2 HANDBOOK
IBM XT CLONE HANDBOOK
THE ABC'S OF THE IBM PC AND COMPATIBLE 2ND ED.
HAND ME DOWN PC HANDBOOK
THE 386/486 PC A POWER USER'S GUIDE

LASER PRINTERS
LASERJET UNLIMITED 2ND ED
PROGRAMMING LASER PRINTERS HP & COMPATIBLES

LOTUS 1-2-3
ILLUSTRATED LOTUS 1-2-3 REL. (2.2)
LOTUS 1-2-3 TIPS & TRICKS (REL. 2.2)
TEACH YOURSELF LOTUS 1-2-3 (RLS. 2.2)
THE ABC'S OF 1-2-3 RLS 3.0
THE ABC'S OF 1-2-3 RLS 2.2
THE COMPLETE LOTUS 1-2-3 RLS 2.2 HANDBOOK
UP & RUNNING WITH LOTUS 1-2-3 (2.2)
UP & RUNNING WITH LOTUS 1-2-3 (REL 3.1)
UP & RUNNING LOTUS 1-2-3 (REL 2.3)
LOTUS 1-2-3 (REL 2.3) INSTANT REF
THE ABC OF 1-2-3 (REL 2.3)
UNDERSTANDING 1-2-3 (RLS 2.3)
UP & RUNNING WITH LOTUS 1-2-3 FOR WINDOWS

MULTIMATE
MASTERING MULTIMATE ADVANTAGE II

NETWORKING
NETWORKING IBM PCs (2ND EDITION)

NORTON UTILITIES
MASTERING NORTON UTILITIES 5.0
THE BEST OF THE PETER NORTON CHRONICLES
NORTON UTILITIES 5 INSTANT REFERENCE
UP & RUNNING WITH NORTON DESKTOP FOR WINDOWS
UNDERSTANDING THE NORTON UTILITIES 6

NOVELL NETWARE
MASTERING NOVELL NETWARE
ILLUSTRATED NOVELL NETWARE 2.15

POSTSCRIPT
INSIDE POSTSCRIPT

PAGEMAKER
UP & RUNNING WITH PAGEMAKER 4 ON THE PC
MASTERING PAGEMAKER 4 ON THE IBM PC

PC TOOLS DELUXE 6/7
MASTERING PC TOOLS DELUXE 6
UP & RUNNING WITH PC TOOLS DELUXE 6
UNDERSTANDING PC TOOLS 7

PFS
UNDERSTANDING PFS: FIRST CHOICE (VER. 3.0)

PROCOMM PLUS
MASTERING PROCOMM PLUS

QUATTRO PRO. 3
MASTERING QUATTRO PRO 3

QUICK C
MASTERING QUICK C VER. 2.0
QUICK C
THE ABC'S OF QUICK C VER. 2.0

RS-232
THE RS-232 SOLUTION

SQL
UNDERSTANDING SQL

TURBO PASCAL
MASTERING TUBRO PASCAL 6

UNIX/SCO UNIX
TEACH YOURSELF UNIX
UNDERSTANDING UNIX (2ND ED.)
UNIX POWER UTILITIES
THE ABC'S OF SCO UNIX

VENTURA
VENTURA INSTANT REFERENCE (VER. 2)
VENTURA POWER TOOLS (VER. 2)
VENTURA TIPS AND TECHNIQUES (VER. 2.0)
MASTERING VENTURA FOR WINDOWS VER 3.0
MASTERING VENTURA 3.0 GEM EDITION

WORD
MASTERING MICROSOFT WORD (VER. 4.0)
USING MICROSOFT WORD (2ND ED.) VER. 4.0
MASTERING MICROSOFT WORD FOR WINDOWS 3.0

WORD PERFECT
MASTERING WORDPERFECT 5.1
TEACH YOURSELF WORDPERFECT 5.1
THE ABC'S OF WORDPERFECT 5.1
WORDPERFECT 5.1 INSTANT REF
WORDPERFECT 5.1 TIPS & TRICKS
UP & RUNNING WITH WORDPERFECT 5.1
WORDPERFECT 5 DESKTOP COMPANION
WORDPERFECT 5 MACRO HANDBOOK

WORDSTAR
UNDERSTANDING WORDSTAR 2000 (REL. 3.0)
ILLUSTRATED WORDSTAR 6.0

WINDOWS/X WINDOWS
MASTERING WINDOWS 3.0
THE ABC OF WINDOWS 3.0
WINDOWS 3.0 INSTANT REF.
X WINDOWS APPLICATIONS PROGRAMMING (AS)

AVAILABLE FROM ALL GOOD BOOKSELLERS AND COMPUTER STORES.
In case of difficulty please contact:
TECH PUBLICATIONS PTE. LTD.
10, JALAN BESAR, #B1-39 SIM LIM TOWER,
SINGAPORE O820. TEL: 2914595 FAX: 7449835